SELLING
TO VITO

THE VERY IMPORTANT TOP OFFICER

Anthony Parinello

Second edition

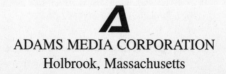

ADAMS MEDIA CORPORATION
Holbrook, Massachusetts

To my beloved mother, Josephine Rose Parinello, for her unshakable love, guidance, support, and confidence in me—and for teaching me right from wrong.

And to my greatest mentor, my brother Al, who left this world too soon. I will continually strive to make them both proud of me.

Published by Adams Media Corporation
260 Center Street, Holbrook, MA 02343

ISBN: 1-58062-224-0

Printed in the United States of America

J I H G F E D C B

Library of Congress Cataloging-in-Publication Data
Parinello, Anthony.
Selling to VITO: the very important top officer / by Anthony Parinello.—[2nd ed.]
p.   cm.
Includes Index.
ISBN 1-58062-224-0
1. Sales personnel—Training of. 2. Selling—Personnel management.
3. Executives. I. Title.
HF5439.8.P37   1999
658.85—dc21   99-15771
CIP

This publication is designed to provide accurate and authoritative information with regard to the subject matter covered. It is sold with the understanding that the publisher is not engaged in rendering legal, accounting, or other professional advice. If legal advice or other expert assistance is required, the services of a competent professional person should be sought.
—From a *Declaration of Principles* jointly adopted by a Committee of the American Bar Association and a Committee of Publishers and Associations

Cover design: Marshall Henrichs.

This book is available at quantity discounts for bulk purchases.
For information, call 1-800-872-5627.

Visit our home page at http://www.businesstown.com

Contents

The purchase of this book includes career-long tele-mentoring

*"My coach is the nation's leading expert.
That's why I am 184% of quota!"*
David Wilson, Charleston, NC

Anthony Parinello, personal success coach to over one million professionals, will guide you step-by-step on the journey to your own success! This one-of-a-kind commitment is without equal. No other author has devoted more personal time, energy, and passion to the success of others.

*"Tony is FOR REAL! Real experience, real ideas,
and real commitment to his student's success."*
Vinnie Deschamps, San Jose, CA

Each month you'll have an opportunity to join Anthony Parinello's tele-conference calls. Ask the critical question to make the sale, or listen to other people's challenges as they make their way to VITO's office and total success!

*"In the last seven months, my team has generated
$18 million in new sales. We couldn't have done it
without Tony's tele-mentoring!"*
Mike Adami, San Ramon, CA

Don't miss one day of tele-mentoring!
Mail or FAX your registration form as soon as you purchase this book!

*"This is real-world, real-time material that can make
a difference between success and failure!"*
Mark Thatcher, Suwanee, GA

"Real-world concepts that can be taken with you and used the very next day."
Ron Gadek, Oakbrook, IL

"This is how we need to sell in the remainder of the '90s and beyond."
Don Stout, West Chester, PA

"Tony is a salesperson's sales trainer!"
Thomas Smith, Chicago, IL

"Implementing these ideas may be the only way for salespeople to survive in telecommunications today."
Dan Liljeberg, Paramus, NJ

"Absolutely mandatory for my company— but not for my competitors."
Joe Emmert, Washington, D.C.

"The best single sales course I've seen in the last fifteen years."
Ed O'Reilly, Camden, NJ

"Will take you to the next income level if you invest the time and energy. Fantastic!"
Tim Gargain, Memphis, TN

"Differentiates you from every other salesman who calls."
Mark Reese, St. Louis, MO

Foreword

TONY PARINELLO IS AMAZING.

He is one of the most imaginative and determined people I've ever met. That imagination is apparent the minute you pick up his book or audiotape album and see the name VITO describing the top person in an organization— the Very Important Top Officer with the ultimate "veto" power. Seldom have I known a name or word to take hold so quickly—to become such an integral part of the sales culture. "VITO" is an overnight addition to the lexicon!

Walk into the sales department of any company that has participated in one of Tony's programs and you'll hear managers asking their salespeople, "Have you talked to VITO yet?" You'll hear salespeople saying, "I have a meeting with VITO scheduled for next Tuesday," or "I met VITO—she gave me the go-ahead to do a corporate-wide study!"

Tony's not afraid of challenges or changes. From getting his first job in sales after a tour in the Navy as an airman, to starting his own sales training company, Tony has always stretched beyond his own comfort zone. He sets the bar high, higher than he's ever had it before, and then goes for it.

He's not a perfectionist (that takes too much time), but he always strives for excellence in whatever he does. When he falls short, he picks himself up and tries again. When I asked Tony where he got his determination, he said, "From growing up in the inner city. Hoboken, New Jersey, was a rough town. I learned a lot about risks and taking chances, and how to size up challenges on the spot. Watching my dad in the ring—he was a Golden Gloves fighter— was invaluable. I learned that you can't stay down for long if you want to win."

Tony shows that kind of courage and determination in the field he chose to speak and write about. He has taken the most unpopular topic in sales training—prospecting and selling to hard-to-reach top decision makers—and given it new life, spirit, and excitement. Tony challenges and exhilarates even the most experienced salespeople. He doesn't just preach about how important prospecting is, or tell you that it's "all a numbers game." He's developed a comprehensive, logical, and innovative sequence of steps that will *get you to the top decision maker.*

His is a process that is based on twenty-three years of award-winning sales performance—in other words, Tony's own trial and error, with his own feet in the street. In that period of time, Tony made over sixteen thousand prospecting calls to top decision makers and conducted hundreds of interviews with receptionists and executive secretaries all across the nation. He listened to these people carefully. He knows what they want, what they expect, what makes them see red. And he knows how to get their attention. As a behavioral scientist, I can easily see and understand why his unique methods for building trust and rapport with decision makers work so well—and result in appointments.

Tony redefines many of the most outdated beliefs about selling; my favorite example of this has to do with the idea of "closing the sale." Tony never "closes" a sale. He "opens" business relationships, mutually beneficial partnerships that last for many, many years.

Keep in mind that Tony is a tactician—a salesperson's sales trainer. He uses the methods in this book every day; he never suggests an idea that he hasn't already found to be effective in his own sales work. He takes full responsibility for his ideas, a trait that is essential for any professional. Simply stated, he walks his talk.

In my audiotape album, *Time to Win,* I address the idea that success depends on choice, not chance. Your decisions are what cause your rewards and the consequences you face. Let's think, for example, about the decision of who to call on first in a new prospect company. Clearly, that's a choice you have to make just about every day of your sales career. Tony makes clear that it's also a choice that will have a greater impact on your level of success than virtually any other. In my tape, I also talk about the Statue of Responsibility, a counterpart to the Statue of Liberty that serves as a reminder of lost freedoms and opportunities arising as a result of irresponsible choices and actions. Tony argues persuasively that one of those lost opportunities is neglecting to call at the top. (And he points out that if you don't do it, your competition will!)

Calling at the highest level first is certainly not the easiest, safest, or most comfortable route. But risk—and even a certain amount of discomfort—can be a healthy part of growing, of seeking out opportunities, of learning. And it's been my personal experience that the road less traveled is the one that often pays the biggest dividends in the long run.

When you're talking about getting appointments with VITOs, the dividends will take the form of time saved, opportunity coverage, and customer loyalty—not to mention increased commissions for you, if only because you won't be wasting as much time as before. My guess is that, on some level, you probably already know about the potential advantages of calling high—and the perils of calling too low—in a prospect organization. So let's move on to the real challenge, making the initial contact with VITO.

That's where Tony's *Selling to VITO* program comes in—and where you will come to benefit from his imagination and his street-smart instincts. His innovative ideas and proven tactics *will* separate you from your competition. Try them and see.

If you were to compare the process of selling to top decision makers to a competitive sports event, you'd have to liken it to a marathon. Like a marathon, half of the job of selling to VITO is preparing yourself, and the other half is employing the proper psychological and tactical edge. If you prepare properly, then use all the advantages at your disposal, you will know, without any doubt, that you can attain your goal. And then you will go out and do just that.

With Tony as your coach and *Selling to VITO* as your training guide, you'll not only finish the marathon—you'll become unstoppable. You'll develop unshakable confidence. You'll set your next goal higher, higher perhaps than you've ever set it before. And you'll make success your own.

— Dr. Denis Waitley

Acknowledgments

In 1994 when I wrote my very first book, (the first edition of *Selling to VITO*) I was amazed at the number of steps, individuals, and the amount of work it took to create and publish an intellectual work! Well, guess what? The reality of it is, the second edition of *Selling to VITO* has taken even more hands, time, energy, and work to create. I can liken this experience to a major "remodel" versus "new construction" of a house! If you've ever been through a remodel and lived to tell about it, you'll know what I mean! In many respects changing something that already exists takes a lot more thoughtful planning and careful consideration and finesse than starting anew. In the case of *Selling to VITO* it meant taking something that was already popular, working and selling, and making it even better!

Perhaps, you may never meet the people who helped bring this second edition to the bookshelves. Then again, you may know at least one individual quite well.

First and foremost, my sincere thanks to each alumni from my live seminars. Without their interest there would be no demand. They kept me reaching and searching for newer, even more creative (not to mention) faster ways to get to VITO. It is their intense field use and constant questioning of my original ideas that over the years have helped make each and every tactic totally bullet proof!

Additionally, a huge thank-you must go to my many wonderful corporate clients. They gave me the greatest gift of all, the gift of opportunity. They trusted me with one of their greatest assets, their sales force!

There are many other silent soldiers that played an enormous and important part in bringing to you the book that you are holding in your hands: Bob Adams and Jere Calmes for their insights and knowledge of the industry, Mike Adami for his assistance with the appendix on creating greater Equal Business Statute with VITO, Elin Woodger for her editing, Marshall Henrichs for taking a good cover design and making it fantastic! Catherine Jones and Diane Durbin whose long hours, dedication and belief play a major role in my continued success and finally, to you, the person who will take the contents of this book, add personal experience and individual style and put it to work! As you turn to the first chapter please know from my heart it's an honor to be at your side.

Introduction

Think for a moment . . . if you were given an opportunity to make one and only one sales presentation, who would you want to make your presentation to?

Think for a moment . . . if you could ask someone for advice, sponsorship, mentoring, or a golden referral, who would that someone be?

"It's time to turn *Thinking* into *Action*"

Dream of a time in the future when you are making all the money you want to make . . .

Dream of a time in the future when you are named "Salesperson of the Year" for the tenth year in a row . . .

"It's time to turn *Dreaming* into *Living*"

Are these guarantees that I am making? Yes they are, and here is why: To date I have personally taught and mentored over one million sales professionals to use the tactics contained in this book. I receive numerous cards, letters, e-mails and telephone calls telling me of accomplishments, new sales records being set, greater income and personal satisfaction.

Are these salespeople more fortunate? More intelligent? Do they have a better territory? Greater products to sell? Not likely. The difference is that they decided to change. To do things differently than ever before. They decided to sell to VITO. If you are not ready to change or challenge your "conventional" sales wisdom, or to engage in a process that is totally different from any other you've ever read in any other sales book, then simply place this book back on the shelf. From this point on, you must have a wide-open mind. Because your greater success is exactly what's at stake.

Even if what I suggest isn't that you're used to doing, isn't what other people in your office are doing, or sounds flat-out crazy, do it anyway. Take the advice of over one million people who do what you do for a living. Believe me, you'll like what happens.

Anthony Parinello, your new success coach

Anthony's Tactics Work:

The following are excerpts from professionals who like you were looking for a different way of getting to the top of their sales game. They were holding Tony's first edition of *Selling to VITO* in their hands trying to decide whether to invest their money and their time. Now, they're glad they did.

"Tony has shown me how to take action and make things happen—rather than wait for things to happen. As a result of implementing his ideas, I won my company's Rookie of the Year award, became the third-ranked salesperson in a company of 1,000 salespeople, and emerged as the #1 sales rep in the West. Now, it's time for you to take action—and read this book!"

—Peter T. D'Errico, Sales Representative

"There is nothing Tony suggests in this book or on his telementoring sessions that he doesn't do himself every day. That's the reason he earns the respect of so many salespeople. To me, he's more than a top-level author, more than a compelling speaker, more than a mentor. He's a friend and colleague who does the same thing I do for a living."

—Chad Robertson, Sales Representative

"People need confidence to succeed. Tony's techniques have helped boost my confidence both personally and professionally. I've learned to look in the right places instead of in the usual places, for my sales opportunities. When Tony's kind of sales preparation becomes second nature, every sales call is taken to the next level—and productivity soars. That's unshakable confidence!"

—Kathy Pierce, Sales Representative

"For several years I'd focused my telephone prospecting efforts on people in lower and middle management levels. Then Tony took me to the top! Now, I'm meeting with presidents, CEOs, and senior management levels and I'm expediting the sales process. Now, Tony's at your side too!"

—Dave Irish, Sales Manager

"Tony's selling techniques are different than anything I've ever used before. It would be impossible to ever get "into a rut" by implementing these ideas. And they work! If you don't have fun selling using Tony's tactics, then you will probably never enjoy selling."

—Doug Gelatti, Sales Representative

"Tony's approach to selling will immediately enhance your position within your accounts, you'll gain tremendous confidence and determination, but more importantly, you'll have a blast. The ideas in this book have tremendous upside potential for your career growth. Take advantage of them."

—Steve S. Hirano, Sales Representative

"Using Tony's methodology, I'm able to position myself as a partner and consultant. I'm able to listen 'between the lines'—and that differentiates me from the competition!"

—Linda Murphy, Sales Representative

"The first telementoring session we had with Tony sparked one of my sales representatives to win a $200,000 account that had been stalled for over three months."

—Mike Adami, Vice President

PART 1

Meeting and Becoming VITO's Business Partner

*"Now I understand why professional salespeople
have the right to call on VITO."*
—Lou DeGiulio

When you mastered this section you will have the ability to:

1. *Add value to VITO's day*
2. *Get into the "VITO Zone"*
3. *Understand VITO's personality style and the results
    they look for*
4. *Avoid wasting time with low-level influencers*

═══ Key Thought ═══

Whenever you approach VITO, you're on a job interview. Because
if a VITO would hire you as a salesperson, VITO will do business
with you as a business partner.

Chapter 1

The Time Is Right

WELCOME TO THE NEW ECONOMY. WELCOME TO THE NEW MILLENNIUM. IF you're a salesperson, you have your work cut out for you.

It's more difficult than ever to sell for a living, and every salesperson who's likely to still have a job twelve months from today knows it. The competition is tough, and finding new customers (not to mention keeping the old ones) can be brutal. Prices are down, the cost of sales is up, overhead is up, margins are down. More than ever, companies are looking for strategic alliances and business partnerships today, not quick fixes. And how about the latest trend in the sales world—the moves by companies to tie the commissions of their salespeople to the profitability of the company (or the sale recorded by the rep)? This can mean that if a salesperson spends too much time in an account trying to get an order, then that time and the associated cost of sales is going to be reflected in that salesperson's paycheck. Companies today are also tying customer service responses to the compensation their salespeople receive. And, in yet another twist, there are new payment schemes whereby salespeople are penalized if a company bails out, say, three or four months after signing on. Those "short-term" sales, the ones that relied on low price or a less-than-perfect match with the customer's needs, are being noticed. And, more and more, they're costing salespeople money.

Things just aren't the way they used to be. Today's difficult, surrealistically fast-paced business climate is probably one of the main reasons you bought this book in the first place.

You probably know about all this. And while you may consider this state of affairs to be pretty desperate, I have a surprise for you. It's *because* you know about how difficult things can be these days that you have a remarkable opportunity with today's most important businesspeople. Top decision makers—whom I call VITOs, short for Very Important Top Officers—know all about the often intense market pressures you face. They deal with those pressures every moment of every working day. VITOs, of course, come in both genders. They are presidents, CEOs, executive vice presidents, and the like. Actually, the titles aren't as important as the function. VITOs have the ultimate veto power in an organization. They have power, control, and authority. They're the people who can say "yes" and have it stick when everyone else is saying "no." They're the people who are most concerned with gaining market share, increasing revenues, controlling expenses, decreasing expenses, reducing time to market, and dealing with the changes in our unpredictable economy. They're the people who have to focus on solutions—and, in that, they have something in common with you.

Perhaps you've tried selling to top decision makers before—and perhaps you found the experience intimidating. Perhaps a VITO gave you the impression that he or she considered all salespeople to be timewasters who are simply never worth bothering with. (Actually, VITOs consider only *bad* salespeople to be timewasters, and they're right.) You may even have come away from your encounter with a VITO convinced that he or she was speaking a completely different language than the one used by most of your contacts. However, most VITOs have sold for a living at one time or another—or, at the very least, appreciate the value of good salespeople.

It's true, VITOs do tend to see the world in terms that are a little different than most of the other people you sell to. While other low-level contacts may worry about protecting their turf, or impressing others in the organization, or even holding onto a position they consider shaky, VITOs' interests are usually much more straightforward. VITO wants to *improve the company's bottom line* by raising revenues, improving efficiency, or lowering expenses. Not surprisingly, the language VITO speaks when it comes to dealing with the rest of the business world is a little more direct, a little less patient than that of your average contact. But don't worry. You can reach and do business with VITOs, no matter what your past experiences in dealing with them may have been. If you follow my advice, you'll understand that there's a food chain in every sale. VITO is at the top; the other people in the organization are lower. As a general rule, salespeople make their biggest mistake when they initiate contact at a comparatively low point on the chain!

One of the purposes of this book is to teach you VITO's language—and show you how to use it to your (and VITO's) benefit. The techniques you'll be learning about have worked for over one million salespeople in businesses throughout the country. They can work for you.

Once you finish reading this book, you will no longer be a distraction for VITO. You will no longer be something that stands in the way of VITO's attempt to deal with today's value-sensitive, ultra-competitive market conditions. You will be *someone,* not something—and an extremely important someone at that. You will be someone who understands what VITO is up against and knows how to offer what VITO wants most to find: *solutions.*

You will be VITO's business partner.

Once you've done that, you won't have to worry about most of the things salespeople keep complaining about. You won't have to worry about getting shunted off to a lower level. You won't have to ask yourself who really has the decision-making authority. You won't be left without any recourse if some low-level influencer within the company decides he or she doesn't like what you have to offer.

You won't have to worry about any of that because you'll be working, not with just anyone within the organization, but with VITO. And I can tell you working with VITO makes sense because it's what turned my own career around.

Selling to VITO affects the entire sales cycle. Unlike many other sales training programs, where you might approach qualifying, questioning, and closing as separate components, the program you're about to learn is about ideas, tactics, and methods that will move the sales in such a way that you save time, avoid grief, and *compress* the standard sales cycle, so that it runs according to a new and accelerated time frame: VITO's time frame. This makes selling more enjoyable and rewarding, and that's no small feat.

Who Is This Guy?

Let me tell you a little bit about myself. In addition to being an author and a radio talk-show host, I'm a salesperson—and I'm also a sales trainer.

As you read this book, you're going to come across a lot of suggestions about ways to do things differently. I know that's sometimes hard to do once you've built up a routine in your sales work. But you should know that I will never, under any circumstances, offer you any advice or outline any technique that is not something I myself have tried and found successful—and continue to use daily.

The ideas in this book are practical, down-to-earth, and, most important of all, proven to work in today's business environment. Try them and see. These are not the theoretical constructs of some business-school whiz. I'm a salesperson, like you, and I think my revenue and commissions over the years indicate that I'm a pretty darned good one.

Right now I'm going to give you a little bit of background to demonstrate that to you. But remember, what I've done isn't the issue here. It's what *you* can do. I'm bringing up my own career because I think talking about it here will make you want to listen to what I have to say on the topic of selling to VITO. And that was what made all the difference for me.

When you get right down to it, though, it would be a little misleading to say that I actually *wanted* to sell to VITO in the early days. The truth was, I was in such a horrible situation that I had no other choice.

I started out as a sales rep for Hewlett-Packard. You had to have a college degree even to interview with HP. They didn't call their reps salespeople back then, they called them "sales engineers." You can imagine how popular an ambitious young kid with no college degree must have been with some of the people there! But they liked what they saw, and I liked the company. (The way I figured it, any company bright enough to bend the rules to take me on had to have *something* going for it.)

I worked hard and had three stellar years at HP. Then I got cocky and let up a little bit. Guess what happened then. The fourth year rolled around, and I had a very, *very* bad first half.

When I say "bad half," I don't mean that I was a little under quota. I mean I had a *horrendous* half. I was at 19 percent of quota. I was placed on probation and given a formal memo that was placed in my personnel file. That memo informed me that I had to get my act together within the next six months or I would be fired.

Looking back now, I can see where I went wrong. Slowly but surely, I had stopped prospecting for new business. It happens to a lot of successful salespeople. I was sticking with the old reliables—my existing customer base—and knocking on all the familiar, safe doors. At the rate I was going, there was no way I could support the quota I'd been assigned. I had gradually convinced myself that I could get by with taking shortcuts, and as a result I had nothing, absolutely nothing in the pipeline.

I had six short months to sell enough new computer systems to meet my quota, or I'd be gone.

I finished that year at 103 percent of quota—and got to keep my job for another year.

At the awards banquet, my regional manager came over to shake my hand, which was quite satisfying considering all the pressure I'd been under. He said, "Tony, I have two questions to ask you. The first one is, are these new accounts you sold going to back out after the first of the year?"

I said, "Absolutely not." (And I was right.)

He said, "Okay. The second question is, how the hell did you do it?"

The answer to this question was that I used tactics that I rely on to this very day. I became less of a salesperson, and more of a businessperson. I began to focus on selling to VITO. I didn't realize it, but my recovery from being put on probation would be the genesis of the book you are holding in your hands.

Think about it. I was in what certainly seemed to be an impossible position. I had to sell maybe half a dozen big new computer systems—not today's PCs, mind you, but high-end, high-priced systems—in *six months.* If you're at all familiar with the computer industry, or any industry that relies on big-ticket sales, you'll realize how tough it is to get large company bureaucracies to requisition a box of blank disks over that period of time, much less approve the purchase of a $250,000 to $500,000 computer system. I *couldn't* go through the standard channels. I had to reach real, live decision makers, people who could say yes or no *instantly* to the ideas I had—and who could actually make things happen within the organization once they realized the potential benefits of my solutions.

I *had* to reach VITO. And I did.

Now, a lot of time has passed since the day I received that awful memo. But you know what? The pressures I faced during that extremely challenging year were not unlike the pressures today's salespeople—and that includes me—face day in and day out. I don't mean to suggest that everyone in sales is failing to meet quota, of course, but I do think it's fair to say that today's salespeople have to produce more, faster, and find more new business than the salespeople of ten or twenty years ago. In effect, today's salespeople are often on an unofficial "permanent probation." They're being told, "Keep us ahead of the competition."

My biggest surprise from that experience with probation was that, after a while, I realized that it was actually *fun* to contact VITOs! All of a sudden I wasn't getting kicked around by data processing managers. I was having good conversations with the people at or near the very top of their organization. I was using my time more effectively than ever before. I was finding out who in the company was the right person to get things done in the time frame I was working under. I was *learning* more about each of the organizations I was contacting than I had ever dreamed possible. And the information was coming from sources I could trust!

And, yes, wonder of wonders, these tactics I developed actually worked. Let me give you an idea of how well they worked. One week, I went so far as to sell a $400,000 computer system by making unannounced visits on VITO! You read that right. I was selling computer systems worth nearly half a million dollars using new and creative door-to-door cold calling selling tactics.

Now, in answer to the question you're probably asking yourself right now: No, this book is not about sneaking up on decision makers in person when they're not expecting you. And no, door-to-door techniques were not the only way I made it through that year. But the point is, I did make it through—by challenging some cherished assumptions that a lot of salespeople have when it comes to dealing with VITOs. How many do you have?

I know one thing. If I'd stopped to ask my colleagues what they thought about the idea of trying to cold-call on a VITO, I probably never would have made that sale. Fortunately, I was focused enough not to ask. And fortunately,

I was focused enough not to listen to my own little voice, which would have told me exactly the same thing!

Tony, you can't walk right in to see VITOs and ask if they want to buy a computer system!

Really?

We're all taught to listen to that little voice. You know what? Sometimes the little voice is right. But most of the time it's self-limiting.

We salespeople spend a lot of time worrying about how to get our foot in the door. And usually we're pretty good at it. But sometimes we need to stop and ask ourselves whether or not the doorway we're sticking our foot into is the right one!

It Worked!

I saved my job! You can't imagine how happy I was about that. (Okay, if you've ever been in a similar situation, maybe you can imagine how happy I was.)

So here's the first pop quiz of the book. What do you think I did after I met the quota that my sales manager, all my colleagues, and even simple common sense said I could never meet? (Okay—*after* I went to Disneyland.) I kept using my new tactics. After the results I had gotten, what else was I going to do? Go back to calling the people at the bottom of the totem pole?

I developed the system, sharpened it, identified what it was that made it work, and turned it into a series of very specific steps and a process for contacting VITOs. That system, which has, of course, evolved over the years, is the subject of this book. And the reason you need to find out about it is that *what I faced that year is now what most of us face every day.* Unless you're selling in a different economy than the one I'm working in, the odds are you simply don't have time to sell the old way any more.

So don't!

Three Groups

The VITOs you'll be dealing with fall into three main categories.

Category one: brand new accounts. More than one sales manager would argue that these accounts are why salespeople exist in the first place. A large part of your job is to get new market share. By selling to VITO, you'll get new business more quickly than ever before—because your focus will be on getting to the most important person in the organization first. You'll start your sales cycle where it would have ended anyway. And you'll do it a whole lot quicker than you used to, which means your company is going to save money. You'll spend more time with the right accounts, and less time with people and organizations that end up wasting your time.

Category two: in-process opportunities. These are accounts where you've already started your sales work. You've made some progress in the sales cycle. Typically, you're trying to forecast your likelihood of success with this company for your sales manager by assigning a percentage figure to reflect the likelihood that you'll get an order. Even if you call it a 50% account, however, the process seems to drag on for months no matter what you do. Often, you have no idea what's really holding things up. But the sad fact is, you've never met the person ultimately responsible for the decision to award the business. By following this program, you'll be able to cover all the bases. You will break the gridlock without burning the bridge. The prospect will finally either become a customer or move off your list.

Category three: existing customers. This is where you'll be using the program to solidify loyalty and build a genuine business partnership at a very high level. You won't have to worry anymore about "your" people in the organization being overruled by higher-ups. The highest-up person in the place will be your person! And once you earn loyalty at the highest level, the chance of a sudden, unexpected "disconnect" is remote indeed, and instead of having just a "thin slice" of their business, you'll get all of the precious add-on sales that you deserve.

In the final phase of my career at HP, I was named Most Valuable Player in my region. Talk about satisfaction! A couple of years back I had been called on the carpet and formally told my job was in jeopardy because I was such a lousy salesperson. Now I found myself walking onstage at our year-end meeting and accepting a huge trophy commemorating an unbelievable year.

I was able to perform at that level because I perfected my system of reaching top decision makers. I applied it religiously and shared it with other salespeople. You can perform at top levels too, if you consistently apply the same system. That's my promise to you.

Read what follows. *Implement* what follows. Make it yours. Customize it to your environment and your personality.

And keep doing it and always remember:

> *What goes up does not necessarily have to come down.*

Have I piqued your interest in this system? I hope so. Keep reading; in the next chapter you'll find out the first and most important thing you must be prepared to do if you want to do business with a VITO.

Chapter 2

Adding Value to VITO's Day

THIS PART OF THE BOOK WON'T TAKE LONG TO READ, BUT IT'S VITALLY IMPORTANT. It starts with a simple, powerful idea that is the foundation for everything that follows in this book. Here it comes. Ready?

VITO pays attention to things that *add value to VITO's day*. And not a heck of a lot else.

If you want VITO to pay attention to you, it follows that you will have to find some way to convey the important message that *you can add value*. The problem is, VITO knows from bitter experience that talking with salespeople who don't speak his or her language is a great way to a) hear a lot of empty promises and b) waste time that could be spent doing something more productive. (The sad truth is that we salespeople usually have only ourselves to blame for this state of affairs.) So VITO has learned to spot bad salespeople, and has come to assume that very few of them are reliable or even vaguely results-oriented when it comes to VITO's interests. As a general rule, VITO is right about this.

Therefore . . .

You must look absolutely, utterly different from any other salesperson VITO has ever encountered. And I'm not talking about wardrobe. I'm talking about personal commitment. When we call on VITO, we're on a job interview. We're proving to VITO that we—not someone else—can offer the best possible solutions. So we must act the part and do anything and everything necessary to build this all-important alliance.

When you get right down to it, *people who are committed to making things happen for VITO* are the ones who earn a spot in his or her day. You may or may not have something distinctly different from the competition to offer VITO with your product or service, but I can guarantee you that you can come off a heck of a lot more committed to helping VITO run a business successfully than your competitors. You can do this by showing VITO from the very first instant that you are not the average salesperson.

In the end, *you* will make the difference. And you will do it by . . .

Changing Your Focus

The most important thing you will ever do when it comes to earning a spot in VITO's busy schedule is stop being a salesperson.

That's right. This is a book about sales, I run sales seminars all over the country, you're trying to increase your sales performance, and the advice I'm giving you is to stop thinking like a salesperson—and start thinking like a businessperson. A problem-solver. Someone willing to focus on the issues that affect VITO's top, middle and bottom line. You must, repeat, *must* make that transition if you want VITO to take you seriously.

We are talking about changing our style, changing our approach, and changing our attitude. We are talking about changing the way we are perceived. The aim is to be perceived by VITO as more of a businessperson—and less of a salesperson. That means changing vocabulary, changing the way we look at ourselves and our products, services, and solutions, and, perhaps most important, getting out of our world and into VITO's. Remember, VITO has a tough job! Getting a company to meet its goals is no mean feat. We are going to begin focusing on how we can help in this effort. Once we make that transition, the doors to VITO's suite will open.

If you get shunted to a lower level after you have finished reading this book, rest assured that it will be because you have started thinking like a salesperson again. As long as you change your outlook and approach VITO in such a way as to demonstrate that you are a *business ally,* not someone who just wants to "sell VITO something," you will succeed.

At this point in my seminars, someone usually raises a hand and says something like, "Wait a minute, Tony. This all sounds great in theory, but if I put it into practice I'll end up ticking people off! After all, VITO already *has* business allies—the people in the organization, the people I've been calling on! Why on earth would I want to alienate those contacts by going straight to the top?"

What I am going to show you in the chapters that follow is not about going over people's heads or jeopardizing existing contacts. You know and I know that that doesn't work. This system is about professionalism, inclusion, and mutual success for everyone in VITO's organization.

Shareholder Value

Another piece of precious information is that VITOs have a responsibility to their stockholders to personally investigate every single idea, suggestion, notion, or inclination that may lead to an increase in shareholder value. Look at it this way: shareholder value is increased by:

- a sustained increase in revenues
- consistent increases in efficiencies and effectiveness
- ongoing lowering of operational expenses
- any other combination of positive effects on the top, middle, or bottom line

The key words here are: "sustained," "consistent," and "ongoing." You must think of it as an annuity, a result that grows and continues to pay dividends long after VITO's initial investment. We'll discuss this in much greater detail in a later chapter, but for now let's not forget that VITOs are always on the look-out for measurable, memorable, sustainable results. Our job is to be able to present our products, services, and solutions in such a way that VITO can understand and immediately see the connection to shareholder value.

Stick by VITO's Side When Times Are Rough

Like friendships, careers, and just about everything else in life, VITOs and their organizations also have ups and downs. You'll find that if you continue to call on VITO even when the chips are down and no sales have the possibility of being made, you'll be making an investment in future sales. If lay-offs, right-sizing and economic downturns have VITO's organization in a tail-spin, don't push this relationship to the back burner! That's the time to become a part of a possible solution! Look for ways to add value that don't necessarily include you or your solutions. When things ease up for VITO, they'll go out of their way to give you the business.

New Accounts, In-Process Accounts, and Current Customers

Whether the focus is on brand new accounts, in-process accounts at which you've already started the sales cycle, or your current customers, in this book we'll look at the best ways to bring VITO into the picture to your (and everyone's) benefit.

My belief is that, in dealing with *any* brand new account, you're much better off going straight to VITO before you talk to anyone else. (It's better to start too high than too low!) I'll be going into the details of how to deal with existing contacts who aren't VITOs later on in the book. For now, though, let me tell you how you're going to win points with people at lower levels when you talk to VITO. You're going to turn them into heroes in VITO's eyes! And you'll assume all of the risk for them, too.

Of course, getting to that point is going to take some work on your part. Before you can make anyone *else* look good to VITO, you have to be able to make *yourself* look good to VITO. And I'm not going to kid you. You're going to have to make a serious, sustained effort to make this system work, and along the way, you're going to have to become a much better, more competitive businessperson than you've ever been. But you know what? Your career is worth it.

Don't Sell Futures to a VITO!

One more thing—some salespeople love to talk about what's coming out next quarter or worse yet, next year—the newest, latest, and greatest technological advancement that will knock down the competition and win the loyalty of their most important customers. Beware! Why? Because it's a sure-fire way to eliminate today's sale! VITOs are great visionaries, and therefore would most likely pick up the phone right then and there as soon as you tell them about the new idea, wonderful result, unstoppable gain in market place dominance and call a low-level influencer say; "Johnson? V here. Apex has a great new solution. I want you to follow it closely." End of sentence, end of sale. Products will always change; new technology will always be developed. The message is pure and simple when it comes to selling to VITO: sell what's on your price sheet (that you can deliver) and nothing else.

Let's get specific. There are five keys to working with VITO that you will have to master in order to make this book work for you. You can read about them in the next chapter.

Chapter Three

The Five Keys to Working with VITO

As PROMISED, HERE IS A SUMMARY OF THE FIVE KEY QUALITIES YOU WILL NEED TO have or develop further if you want to build a businessperson-to-businessperson relationship with VITO.

To Work with VITO You Will Need Unshakable Confidence

That's unshakable confidence not only in your product, service, or solution, but in yourself as well. How do you develop this? Well, VITOs are pretty similar in their most important qualities. If you learn to deal with one, it's a pretty good bet you'll soon be able to deal with more than one. So . . .

Join Toastmasters. It's a great organization, one that will get you feeling comfortable in front of a whole auditorium full of formerly intimidating decision makers. (And VITOs are birds of a feather, so you're likely to expand your prospect list by attending the meetings.) Toastmasters will be one of the best investments of time you will ever make when it comes to building the confidence necessary to deal with VITOs. So do it.

Go out of your way to deal with the VITOs within your own organization—presidents, executive vice presidents, and the like. When your organization's VITO gives a speech, be sure to attend—and at the end, when he or she asks if there are any questions, *ask a question.* But don't ask just *any* question. Ask a question you've researched for a week and a half, a question that has undeniable relevance to the company's well-being, a question you've practiced in front of the mirror for half an hour or so. And—here's an important technique for dealing with VITOs—*frame the question in terms of VITO's interests and opinions.* ("VITO, what's important to you personally about our plan for capturing the Atlantic market with our widgets?") If your office is far-flung, or there is some other obstacle preventing you from meeting with your own organization's VITOs, search out a group that can offer you exposure to VITOs who will not necessarily be sales prospects. The

14

point is not to score points within your own firm (although that's certainly nice), but to become comfortable interacting with VITOs, discussing key points with them, and eliciting their opinions.

Join at least one nonprofit organization. Not only will you be adding your efforts to a good cause, you'll meet VITOs! They usually have a strong desire to give something back to the community. (Of course, they also know when something is deductible.) This setting can give you an excellent opportunity to interact with VITOs in a neutral, low-pressure setting. Take advantage of it.

Next, make a point of meeting the VITOs in every one of your current accounts once you've read the later parts of this book on setting up appointments. You may feel that doing this will be easier in some accounts than in others. Fine. Start with the easy ones. You may be nervous about going "over the heads" of your existing contacts. Don't be. You only help your business when you set these appointments up properly—and a little later, we'll be covering exactly how you can arrange things in a way that keeps everyone happy. My bet is that you'll be pleasantly surprised. And, of course, we'll be talking later about referrals to other VITOs; VITOs tend to recommend good companies to other VITOs. How many of your existing accounts should you visit asking to meet with VITO? Only the ones you want to keep. The ones you don't visit will vanish all by themselves.

Buy yourself a beautiful leather journal. Carry it during your VITO meetings and take lots of notes. As a matter of fact, whenever VITO talks, make sure you are writing! This is a great way to make sure that VITO knows you are listening intently.

I am often asked during my seminars, "Tony, how much do I have to know about VITO's company before I talk to VITO?" I shock people when I respond with: "Not much!" The fact is that no one—and I do mean *no one*— knows more about VITO's organization than VITO. Period. Sure, I've read annual reports, financial reports, and mission statements in preparation for my VITO calls, but just about every time I make an attempt to "tag into" my new-found knowledge about VITO's organization (i.e., "VITO, your annual report stated that compressing the time factor of all critical processes is one of your top three goals for this year, which is great news because the solution we offer—," etc.), I all too often hear from VITO: "We've already completed that initiative. We're working on our financial reporting system now." Darn! I hate it when that happens.

It didn't take me too long to figure out that I needed to become an expert in VITO's *industry,* not VITO's organization. Here's how you can do it: When you're with VITO, you'll be asking very specific questions (I'll get to that later on), and you'll be writing the answers to those questions in your VITO journal. Guess what? You won't have to meet many VITOs at all before you pick up on a pattern! The truth is that VITOS in similar industries have similar problems and challenges. Once you fully understand exactly how you're able to help with your solutions, you'll be able to target these specific areas of opportunities with all VITOs. Now, that's unshakable confidence!

To Work with VITO You Must Be Willing to Develop Synergy Within Your Organization

That means doing whatever it takes to build a teamwork-first orientation. VITOs know the importance of teamwork these days. We must show VITO that we appreciate the importance of the team, and must demonstrate the effectiveness of our own team. Specifically, you should be willing to:

Give awards or see that your company does. Not just for top salesperson—that award's going to be yours, after all, and you want to spread the wealth around—but for all aspects of contribution to your company's success. Talk to your manager about this if necessary. Trophies and awards have a powerful galvanizing effect on team members. (And by the way, when it's your turn to receive an award, why not take the unforgettable step of engraving the names of other team members who helped you? Don't put the trophy on *your* desk—circulate it to the other team members. Move it around once a month. That's a great way to show those who helped you that you care, and that their efforts are recognized.)

Acknowledge the contributions of others in a public way. At company meetings, mention the help you received from people in production, customer service, or any other applicable area. Give honest and frequent thanks to those who helped to make your success possible. I once received a sales award at a huge company banquet and, as my acceptance speech, simply listed the names of all the people who had helped me to perform at the level I had attained that year. As I mentioned each of their names, I motioned for them to come up onstage with me to take a well-deserved bow. How long do you imagine that gesture was remembered?

To Work with VITO You Must Be Able to Build Business Rapport

Rapport is one of those overused words in our profession. Rapport means "having a reciprocal relation" or "to be in close communications with." That's why words like model, mirror, and pace are touted by the gurus as surefire ways to build rapport. If you remember the process and follow their advice, you will have a much better chance at building rapport with other individuals. But beware! For those of us who want and need to build unshakable confidence when dealing with the VITOs of the world, there must be an understanding of the many differences between "personal" rapport and "business" rapport. The differences are profound. If you can build effective business rapport, then your career, financial horizons, and overall success in business will be as good as guaranteed. If you master the art of building personal rapport, then you'll widen your social circle of influence and interpersonal network, and you'll find greater opportunities, resources, and personal fulfillment in just about every corner of your life. Let's take a closer look at this.

Business Rapport: When you build effective business rapport with VITO, you're building skyscrapers where two story buildings once existed. You're tapping into VITO's greater influence and authority and you're multiplying your results accordingly. One of the key operative words here is "effective," which should not be confused with the word "efficient." Being *efficient* is having the ability to do whatever needs to be done as fast as possible. Being *effective* is making sure that whatever needs to be done is being done the best it can be. This difference is vitally important in a business relationship. For instance, if you try to build business rapport too quickly, it will not have the critical ingredients of loyalty and strength needed to withstand the many ups and downs that business relationships typically face. Inadequate rapport built in haste simply will not last.

Personal Rapport: Good, solid personal rapport is built on a basis of mutual understanding and appreciation for another person's point of view, culture, feelings, and whatever else that person stands for or happens to be headed to. A great deal has been written on the topic of personal rapport; it's almost impossible not to find this topic covered in books about success in sales and personal fulfillment. Many (if not all) of these books suggest that you attempt to be "like" the person with whom you're trying to build personal rapport—that is, model your behavior on theirs and mirror what they do. This is based upon the likelihood that if you are "like" someone they will, in turn "like" you. Of course, this makes for a rather interesting scenario if both individuals model each other's voice intonation, body posture, and breathing. I'd love to be there to see it—the perfect set-up for an identity crisis if I've ever heard of one!

As professionals, we must effectively separate business and personal rapport, and since what we're trying to do is become a responsible business partner to VITO, we must focus our attention on building business rapport. If it happens that our efforts lead to a strong personal rapport, that's great! But the sequence should always be business rapport first, personal rapport second (unless, of course, you happen to be lifelong friends with a VITO whom you are now approaching with a business opportunity).

Let's take a look at the behaviors you would want to *avoid* when building business rapport:

1. Ice breaking. This is a technique that suggests using "small talk" when meeting someone for the first time as a way of reducing tension, relaxing the atmosphere, and getting things off to a smooth start. But take it from me, this tactic has more risk and potential pitfalls associated with it than any positive results! In twenty-six years of professional selling, I've heard enough horror stories that tell me it's far better to shy totally away from ice breaking—and I have a few of my own. Here's one:

I once had a *ten-minute* appointment scheduled with a VITO at a top manufacturing firm. I'm not kidding—my appointment was for between 1:00 and 1:10 P.M. The office door opened at 1:00 precisely, and Harry Wall led me into his office and sat at a massive mahogany desk. Behind him was a magnificent framed photo of a long, elegant racing sloop, and emblazoned on its sail were the words "WALL STREET." Putting two and two together, I realized I was looking at a photo of this man's personal racing boat. So after we exchanged pleasantries, I decided I'd do the textbook "ice breaker" maneuver. "That's a very impressive racing sloop," I said. "Tell me, Mr. Wall, does it have running or fixed back stays?" He launched into a ten-minute discussion about the boat—how it was constructed, how many races he'd won, where he'd competed. Then, at the end of his discourse, he glanced at his watch, looked at me, and said, "Sorry, Tony. We're out of time. I have to run." He walked out of the office and left me sitting in front of his desk. I had just blown the ten most important minutes of the sales cycle listening to VITO talk about his yacht—and I never did get another appointment with him, or the sale. Ouch!

No matter what any other book may tell you about this, don't try to "break the ice" with VITOs. Get right down to business and talk about your record and your solutions. When you're done talking business, and you're on your way out, that's the time to make chitchat and end on a positive personal note.

2. Overstating and under-delivering of anything. It's okay to openly and honestly fail at something. But it's not okay to knowingly set a false expectation by making inflated or exaggerated statements. Your business rapport with

VITO will rely heavily on your honesty, integrity, and ability to deliver on your promises as well as exceed the expectations you have set.

3. Criticizing anything or anyone's efforts. We had just wrapped up the site tour and were waiting in the outer lobby for the Vice President of Operations to bring us some additional information. This VP was a key decision maker, and I had built some good business rapport with him during the course of the four-hour tour. As he handed me some documents, he asked, "Can I answer any other questions?" "Just one," I said casually. "How long have you had that disorganized and somewhat confusing maze of cabling in your data center?" His reply came so quickly, it stunned me: "Since my son designed and installed it five years ago."

4. Telling a trade secret or sharing "confidential" or "company private" information. When asked what two traits executives look for when they hire someone, they consistently say: Honesty and Integrity. If you show or say anything to someone that you don't have the authority to show or say, you won't gain any points or earn trust. The question will always become: What's stopping you from betraying their confidence and trust in you to someone else?

5. Assuming that business rapport will carry over to personal rapport. Personal rapport takes certain liberties that may not be acceptable or reasonable in a business relationship, in the initial phases. Some individuals lead very private personal lives well outside the business world, and do not want their two worlds to intertwine. Right or wrong, if that's the way it is, then you must honor it.

6. Showing up late for anything. There just isn't any good reason for not being punctual. We've all been late for something and more often than not, there was no reason, just excuses. Being late sends a clear message that you place two values on the other person's time: little and none.

7. Procrastination of any kind. Similar to being late, procrastination tells the other party that you have let some other activity (or no activity at all) take precedence over the business relationship. Your credibility takes a severe blow whenever you procrastinate.

8. Negative talk about anyone or anything. Gossip or making a negative statement will not do anything favorable for business rapport or for the person being discussed. Sometimes winds can shift and change direction. So can loyalty.

People who were once "enemies" can become overnight "allies" due to mergers, re-engineering and reorganization. It's best to follow the advice my dear Mother gave to me at an early age:

"If you can't say anything nice about someone, don't say it at all."
(Thanks Mom. You're an angel!)

9. Saying you know someone or something when you don't. Salespeople who stretch the truth by saying they know this person or have been to that place when they haven't are taking an awfully big risk of being found out. After all, it's getting to be a smaller and smaller world all the time. Your credibility will be severely damaged if you get caught in a lie or exaggeration.

10. Asking for a favor before you've earned the right to that favor. This is greed at its finest (or worst) hour. When it comes to business rapport, it's always best to have the other person offer a favor rather than to prematurely ask for one.

Here is what you must *always do* if you want to build effective business rapport:

1. Make the best first impression possible. We've heard it said often, and it's very true: "You only get one chance to make a first impression." But what "they" haven't told us, and what we've learned the hard way at times, is that there are actually two parts of a first impression:

What VITO hears, sees, and/or feels during the first few seconds of your interaction with him or her.

What VITO hears, sees and or feels during the last few seconds of your interaction with him or her.

Your best bet is to be as prepared as possible. What topics will you be discussing? What questions should you be asking? What outcomes do both parties expect? To help you end your first impression on a high note, try to find out something about VITO's world, such as recent accomplishments or other assignments or positions they've had. With this information in hand, you'll be able to say: "When we get together next, I'd love for you to tell me what your greatest challenges were when you . . ."

2. Consistently exceed expectations. Credibility is a cornerstone of strong, lasting business rapport. The fastest way to build credibility is to simply do what you say you'll do and be willing to go the extra mile beyond that. When you exceed VITO's expectations, sooner or later VITO (and, yes, you) will get the message that there is only one way to operate:

In order to succeed with VITO, you must exceed for VITO.

3. Make yourself an appreciating asset. Like any other great investment, you must increase in value over time without the need to have VITO make a greater investment in you. You must continue to bring new ideas, greater information, and enhanced services to the table—and whatever you bring, "it" and "you" must increase in perceived and real value. The key words are *perceived and real value.* Get in the habit of focusing on how to do this. Make sure that whatever you come up with is sincere and appropriate for this VITO. We'll be discussing some very specific ways to do this in later chapters.

4. Position yourself as someone who is indispensable. This goes hand in hand with becoming an appreciating asset. You need to be someone who can't be replaced by your competition. Others may have more knowledge or skill or expertise, but you and only you will be called upon time and time again if you have unique offerings.

5. Make your self-improvement apparent. Never let yourself become intellectually, emotionally, or physically stagnant. Why have VITOs risen to positions of importance and influence? Because they are on a constant self-improvement journey. Progress and growth are what make businesses and people increase in value. You, too, must constantly seek ways to increase your personal and business value. I suggest you read the sorts of industry and trade-specific books and periodicals that VITOs read and find other ways to expand your knowledge and demonstrate that you, too, are upwardly mobile.

6. Always, always, always be upbeat. Everyone appreciates a winning attitude and VITO is no exception. Of course, life is not always as good or as happy as you would like it to be, but if you maintain an uplifting mood, attitude, and opinions, then VITO will see and appreciate that you are the kind of person who knows how make the best of every situation. Enthusiasm and a positive outlook will take you a long way!

7. Dress for success. Personal image is an important part of building business rapport. Every successful person likes to look the part. Success has an aura all its own, and you can take on that aura with the tasteful way you dress. Have you ever put on an outfit that made you feel like a million bucks? If you have, then you need to own that outfit! But beware:

> *Don't use dressing for success as an obstacle*
> *or something to hide behind.*
> *Don't be an empty suit!*

8. Speak with an appropriate vocabulary. The proper use and understanding of words can provide us with the tools we need to make the best possible first impression and build excellent business rapport. We must therefore constantly expand our use and understanding of words to make our verbal communication as epic as possible. The easiest way to do this is to have a small pocket or electronic dictionary at your side whenever you read a business book or journal. When you spot a word that's unfamiliar to you, take the time to look it up and learn its meaning at that moment. Repeat it several times, use it in a sentence, and then as soon as possible make it a part of your own conversations.

9. Become a useful team player. Every one of VITO's teams has room for another player, and the player they will want the most is a "giver." "Takers" are considered to be liabilities who are avoided or, once discovered, eliminated from the team. You must be looked upon as an asset, not a liability. When VITO sees you coming or hears that you're on the phone, your presence must elicit a response like: "Oh! It's Tony" not: "Oh, it's Tony." Of course, the difference between these two phrases is the intonation and excitement placed upon the word "oh." Business rapport is established and grows on the basis that a contribution is being made without the other person asking for that contribution. That's what team work is all about.

10. Listen intently. That means listening with undivided attention, focus, and understanding. It means listening with rapt attention. Let me tell you how I first learned about the importance of this. After a tour in the Navy, I began to lose my hearing. Over the years, my hearing got progressively worse. I actually taught myself how to read lips! You know, reading lips is interesting: you really have to concentrate. Your eyes have to be glued to the lips of the person you're talking to, and your mind has to be very focused. You can't daydream. You have to watch every single movement.

Now, back when I was selling large computer systems, I had an interesting experience. I had a number of very important sales meetings with the president of a good-sized company, and I was always right out on the edge of my chair, watching him like a hawk. I'd get as close as I could without getting into the president's personal space. If a distraction took place—if the secretary walked into the office, for instance—I couldn't let the secretary take my attention away. I couldn't afford to miss a single word of what the president had to say.

Throughout those meetings, my eyes and my full attention *belonged* to the president of that company. And I got that sale. I sold his company a fairly large computer system. And you can bet I felt good about it. In part as a reward, I got myself two powerful new hearing aids, almost invisible. As it happened, that president was the very first business contact I met with after I got my hearing aids.

It was great! I could hear everything! I didn't have to lean forward in my chair anymore! I asked the president, "VITO, how's the installation going?" And as VITO started to tell me, guess what happened? I didn't have to look at VITO's lips anymore! Why, I could look around the room! When there was a noise, I could turn to see what it was! When the secretary walked in, I could smile and nod hello!

All of a sudden, the president stopped right in the middle of his sentence. I turned and looked at him. He looked me right in the eye and said, "Tony, please take your hearing aids out."

I said, "Why on earth would I want to do that?" And he said, "Tony, I feel you're not listening to me. I felt really special before you had those hearing aids. You used to watch every move I made. Please take them out." And I did.

Right then and there I learned one of the most important lessons in my sales career: When you're with a prospect, you listen to them as if you're hard of hearing! Listen to them as though you must read their lips. Give them your undivided attention. Show them you are interested in understanding how they feel. Listen with empathy.

Whenever a VITO makes a complaint, they are really saying they want the business relationship to work. This gives you the opportunity to:

- Show how good you and your company really are
- Learn how to perform even better, thereby lessening any future complaints
- Gain ideas on how to make your future solutions fit the precise needs of your marketplace
- Make your existing business relationships stronger and more loyal

11. Forget about closing. Now if this isn't a departure from standard sales advice, nothing is! You read right. I want you to commit yourself to *never meeting with VITO with the intention of closing a deal.* News flash: VITOs don't like "being closed." Think about it. You probably don't like it either. You are not *closing* doors, but *opening* them. You are working to develop an ongoing business relationship for which you will always be willing to take ultimate responsibility. Remove the word "closing" from your vocabulary.

Just go out and open relationships and business opportunities. When you get VITO's first order, it's the beginning, not the end.

When you come right down to it, most of all of this seems like good, common "people" sense doesn't it? Let me then leave you with this one thought:

> *Building rapport is not about manipulating or controlling people.*
> *It's about controlling the effect you have on people.*

To Work with VITO You Must Have an Unlimited Desire to Succeed

And you know what? I can't give you this. I can, however, share some of my own feelings on the subject and give you some idea of the degree of commitment to personal success required if you want to deal with VITO.

Remember that the first time is hard—but follow-through takes guts, too. Let me give you a perfect illustration of this. I was conducting a seminar in the Northeast once. There was a young man named Scott who sat right up in front, took copious notes, and paid rapt attention throughout. I later learned that, very early on the Monday morning following this seminar, this rep went into his office, picked up the phone, and started calling VITOs in his territory. The director of sales happened to notice him making the calls.

Later on that day, the director walked into his little cubicle. Now you have to picture this: he was sitting down, and the director of sales, who's rather a big man, was standing up. The director of sales said, "I noticed you in here early this morning making calls. Are you doing that stuff that you learned at Tony's seminar last week?" Scott looked up and said, "Yeah, I'm giving it a try." The director of sales said, "Well? How's it going? Are you getting through to any VITOs?"

"Yeah," he answered. "I just got through to the president of a big company." The director of sales grinned broadly. "So?" he asked. "How did the call turn out?"

Scott looked at the floor and said, "I got so nervous I hung up on him."

Can you imagine that? Now, I'll grant you, it's not always going to be easy. But if you follow the program and follow through as I suggest, you will become more familiar with it in time—and your confidence will increase.

By the way, there's a happy ending to the story. When this incident took place, that rep was in serious trouble—just a little over halfway to his first-quarter quota, not a good place to be in early spring. He kept at it. He wasn't satisfied with the result he got the first time out, so he summoned up the mental energy to come back, change the approach a little bit, and try again. Scott closed the year at 240 percent of quota!

Do you think he would have posted those results if he'd given up after the very first try? Of course not!

Look at everything as a result. If you're not happy with a result, you take the right steps to change it. If, when you try to change it, you find that it gets a little bit worse, don't panic! You know now not to try to change it in that direction. Keep at it.

Hate the word failure. I do, and I simply refuse to admit it into my day. I have setbacks, disguised opportunities, and new selling environments. But I do not have failures until I give up the idea of learning from my experiences, and I never, ever do that. Ditto for the words *no, rejection, slump,* or anything else that removes selling power and authority from you and places it somewhere else.

To Work with VITO You Must Have Unlimited Energy

And that's not just physical energy, but mental energy as well. I'm talking about determination on top of determination. Streetfighters know that the most formidable opponents are not always the biggest ones, but the ones who leap right back up fiercer than ever after you've knocked them down. *That's* trouble. Without for a minute losing sight of the fact that our relationship with VITO is based on mutual benefit and mutual victory in a business setting, we also have to remember that getting over the barriers and into VITO's office takes staying power. Fortunately, VITOs, above all other businesspeople, know the value of persistence—and appreciate it. If all else fails . . .

Remember the space shuttle. Did you know that 50 percent of the fuel stored in those huge tanks strapped onto the bottom of the space shuttle is expended just to get one thousand yards off the launch pad? It's true. And that's just the way it is with VITO. Half of your energy is going to be expended initiating the relationship. Once you get over that hump, you and VITO will be riding to the stars and back again.

When you partially accomplish a goal, reward yourself with a little of the reward you've got planned for attaining the entire goal. Let's say you hit your targets for each month of a quarter—and you've just been named Salesperson of the Quarter by your manager. Treat yourself, in some small way, as if you had achieved your yearly quota! As long as you are on target to achieve your yearly goal, do something special as a reward to yourself—something you would normally associate with the reward you will receive for attaining your yearly goal. If you planned a ski vacation, for instance, you might decide to take a long weekend to visit the slopes. If you do something like this throughout the course of the year, you will feel as though you've *already* made your goals for the year. In most cases, this will instill you with a sense of confidence—not complacency. Visualization is good, but actually *experiencing* a partial reward you associate with your yearly goal can work wonders, too.

For my part, I'm always chasing a goal. A few years back I promised myself that if I made my yearly revenue goals, I'd buy myself a new Jaguar. Halfway through the year, I was on target—so rather than wait until the end of the year, I took the opportunity to reward myself for my good work by *renting* a Jaguar for a week. I loved it! In fact, I so hated giving it up at the end of the week that I was *supremely* motivated to hit my targets for the remaining two quarters. And I did!

(By the way, my Jaguar convertible is French vanilla with a blue cloth top. It does 140 miles per hour. Or so I'm told.)

So much for the profile of the businessperson who can get through to VITO. What about VITO's profile? It's time to take a close look at the person you'll be building this new business relationship with.

Chapter 4

A Portrait of VITO

W<small>HO IS</small> VITO?

VITO is the person who can make your sale happen (or take your sale away from you), regardless of what anyone else has to say about it.

Simple, isn't it? VITO is the person with the ultimate power, influence, and authority to make things happen in an organization, even if everyone else in that organization disagrees with a particular decision. As we pointed out earlier, VITO has the ultimate veto power. VITO can stop something from happening even if everyone else in the organization says "yes"; VITO can make something happen even though everyone else in the organization says "no."

VITOs are CEOs, presidents, chairpersons of the board. Sometimes VITOs have what appear to be less-than-all-encompassing titles (executive vice president, for instance), but still fit the definition because *even people technically above them on the organization chart do not proceed with a course of action if they perceive that VITO objects to it.* We are concerned with the real world here, not with fabricated hierarchies. If the president of a company has difficulty making decisions, runs every meaningful decision past the vice president of operations for "input," and always follows that vice president's recommendations, then the VP, not the president, is your real VITO.

As a general rule, there is one VITO per organization or division. They fly alone. Just as flocks of eagles are pretty rare sights, you don't often see a flock of VITOs.

As demanding and intimidating as they can sometimes appear to be, VITOs are people too. They are still subject to essentially the same factors that govern just about every other human being on the planet. They want to maximize pleasures, rewards, and satisfactions; they want to minimize errors, waste, and other setbacks. They want to do the best they can by their companies, their shareholders, their customers, their employees, and their families. They also have a great many responsibilities, of course, and they've learned a lot and developed the ability to make shrewd judgments over the years.

They're often quite tough to convince. But if they can find a way to do things better, more effectively—without committing what their experience tells them is likely to be a mistake or taking an unnecessary uncalculated risk—they will do so.

Now, a good many salespeople have learned over the years exactly what it takes to talk a good game. And a good many salespeople are so removed from what customers actually experience with their products and services that they develop, knowingly or unknowingly, a severe credibility gap with top decision makers in general—and VITOs in particular.

So if your aim is to keep sounding like a standard salesperson, or to leave the actual execution of your promises to someone else in your organization whose work you don't have to worry about—guess what? VITOs will simply have no patience for you. They may have resigned themselves to the fact that their organization will have to do business with those kinds of salespeople from time to time, but they *will not* take calls from them if they can possibly avoid doing so, and they certainly won't agree to any appointments.

On the other hand, VITOs *enjoy* getting calls from other businesspeople who have new ideas—and will decide to meet with them and do business with them if they feel it is in their best interest to do so. You have your doubts about this? Don't. I promise you, this principle has been borne out time and time again—by me and by thousands upon thousands of others. The general rule of thumb seems to be that if you have just one new valid, workable idea, VITO will agree to meet with you. Believe it. But the key is, VITO must perceive that the idea is coming from someone of *Equal Business Stature.*

That's a terribly important point, so important that I'm going to ask you to forgive me for repeating it. VITO must perceive that the ideas you are proposing are coming from someone of *Equal Business Stature.* No, that doesn't mean you must have an equal business *title.* If that were the case, only a company president could talk to another company president, and you have my word that nothing could be further from the truth than that. What I mean is that when you call VITO, you have to communicate as one professional businessperson to another.

If what you have to say and the way you say it sounds like it's coming from the basic, run-of-the-mill, get-the-signature-and-don't-worry-about-any-follow-up sales rep, forget it. VITO will hang up—fast. But if VITO senses that the person on the other end of the line is a businessperson who is responsible for actually making things happen and delivering results, you will be able to find an opening.

I want you to have Equal Business Stature with VITO. Now, you don't have an equal business *title* with VITO, but that's okay. You don't need it.

What do I mean by Equal Business Stature? I mean that you should have an *understanding of some of VITO's problems* and a new idea for some possible solutions to those problems. If you can show VITO in a way that he or she can understand, you will have Equal Business Stature. And when you have that, VITO will spend time with you.

Let me underscore the importance of building Equal Business Stature—and, in so doing, making the effort to understand what VITOs face every day. Once you commit to this, you will have effectively moved out of that "salesperson" category and into the "businessperson" category. And that's what this program is all about!

If you take only one idea away from this chapter, it should be what we have just reviewed: VITO prefers to talk to people of Equal Business Stature, and by that I mean people who understand problems and have ideas for solving them. I mean people who are committed to delivering results and are willing to be held accountable for them. (As a matter of fact, it's a good bet that, on any given day, VITO will talk *only* to people who fall into this category.)

At this stage of the training I give, many salespeople feel a greater gap than ever opening up between themselves and the VITOs they know they will have to try to contact. Don't panic yet! Let's look in a little more detail at some of VITO's typical characteristics. I'm willing to bet you'll be pleasantly surprised.

VITO in a Nutshell

VITO's titles include:
- Chief Executive Officer
- President
- Owner
- Partner
- Board Member
- Executive Vice President

VITO's key characteristics are:
- Leadership
- Credibility
- Passion
- Vision
- Understanding of the "big picture"
- Strong ego
- Emphasis on power, control, and authority
- Decisiveness
- Creativity

- Openness to new ideas
- Willingness to take calculated risks

VITO's agenda and favorite business discussion topics are:
- Leading-edge success for the company and VITO
- The company's image and what it stands for
- How to define the company's mission statement
- The team and the product
- Keeping ahead of competitors
- Measurable, tangible results on the top, middle, and bottom line

VITO wants to see results like:
- Increased revenues, stock prices, market share, and shareholder value
- Increased efficiencies and effectiveness for revenue-generating employees, mission-critical employees and mission-critical processes
- Protection of existing market share
- Securing all of the add-on business from that existing market share
- Reduction of fixed and variable expenses

For VITO, victory means:
- A winning organization admired by all
- Being recognized as a leader by both industry and community
- Gaining greater power and control

Now, What about Your VITO?

What you just saw was my summary of the VITOs I've come in contact with. That's good for you to know, but it's not as important as the characteristics of the VITOs *you're* likely to run into. On a separate piece of paper, jot down the important facts about a VITO you know. Although it's best to profile a VITO from an organization you have either sold to or plan to sell to, you don't have to do that. If you want, you can write about the head of your own organization.

Your profile should include:

- VITO'S name and title
- VITO's key characteristics
- VITO's agenda and favorite business discussion topics
- VITO's desired results
- VITO's definition of victory

Do you notice anything interesting about the profiles of VITO we've been examining in this chapter?

VITO has many of the qualities of a successful salesperson! If you were to list your own personality traits, my bet is that you would find that you share some very important characteristics with the people who head up companies. After all, according to industry research 85 percent of the VITOs running companies today *began their careers in sales.* In other words, they know good (and bad) sales work when they see it.

So you must show VITOs the good work. Make it obvious that you are willing to share new ideas and stand behind them.

At the end of the day, you're likely to find that you have a lot more in common with VITO than you'd first imagined.

Results

I can't emphasize enough that VITOs are big on making things happen. Another way to phrase this is that they have a strong *results orientation.* Tangible results that VITOs like to see—and quantify—might include:

- Raising revenues
- Increasing efficiency
- Attracting new customers
- Increasing market share
- Increasing repeat customer rates
- Getting higher dividends
- Keeping shareholders happy
- Getting products to market quicker than the competition does
- Decreasing the downtime of revenue-producing employees
- Lowering the cost of sales
- Lowering expenses

There are intangibles, too. For instance:

- Less risk, worry
- Greater peace of mind
- Being the supreme leader
- Having a good personal image
- Having a good company image
- Retaining happy employees who stay late and come in early

And so on. But the key for VITOs is results; these people are big on specific, demonstrable progress and measurable results.

Please reread that list of results I just outlined. Now ask yourself: Does your product or service do any of those things? Of course—otherwise you wouldn't be in business! And remember:

> *Leaders were once followers who paid very close*
> *attention to where they were being led!*

VITOs Always Tell the Truth

Have you ever noticed that lower-level prospects use excuses to put off decisions? These excuses can really run the gamut: "We don't have the time." "It's not a priority now." "We'll need to collect more data." "We're going through a reorganization." "I'm in no rush . . . let me think about it." "Let me talk everything over with the members of my committee, and we'll get back to you later." Just to mention a few! The excuse list is a long one—but short in comparison to the sales cycle it creates!

Many times these lower-level prospects are not really interested and/or perhaps never had a real need for what we have to offer to begin with, so they use these excuses as a convenient way of getting themselves off the hook and letting you down easy. But unlike you, they have probably never had to explain to a sales manager why "the hottest deal" on a forecast disappeared!

On the other hand, VITOs will never waste time—theirs, yours, or anyone else's, especially people within their organization. If you ever want to know what your chances are of getting that sale, just ask VITO this: "VITO, if you didn't have a committee researching all the possibilities and you had to make your decision today, which solution would *you* choose?" A real VITO will always answer that question. And when you get the answer, don't ignore it, under any circumstances! If VITO indicates a strong preference for your solution, then move quickly to open the business relationship. If VITO has concern and hesitations, then use the four-letter word that you know best: SELL!

So. That's VITO. Now, then, who else will you be dealing with?

Chapter 5

Other Players in the Drama—and the Influence and Authority Network

IN ADDITION TO VITO, OF COURSE, THERE ARE A NUMBER OF OTHER PEOPLE WHO populate the offices and hallways of the typical business or organization. For our purposes, there are three more categories; we'll be looking at them in this chapter. One in particular is likely to be pretty familiar to you.

Every company you call on has a four-step network of people with surprisingly different levels of influence and authority regarding purchasing decisions. No surprise: VITO is at the top. But you should also be able to categorize others in the organization according to the breakdown we'll be examining in a moment, which I call the *Influence and Authority Network*.

You may be asking yourself what I mean by influence and authority—and how they affect the way an organization works.

As I use the term in this book, influence means "having the ability to change the minds of others, especially those in high places." And authority means "having the power to make decisions and the control to spend money." VITOs, of course, outrank everyone else on the chart in these two categories. But there is a distinct hierarchy beneath the top level that you should be aware of, as well.

Managers and Directors

These people are one step below VITO. They're the ones who take the vision VITO has defined and turn it into workable policy objectives. They translate the mission statement into a series of instructions and initiatives for others in the organization to follow. In short, they're the people who march the troops toward the goals defined by VITO.

Let's keep in mind here that their titles may not be manager or director at all, but rather their *job* is to "direct" the work force. Managers and directors have fairly high levels of influence and authority—but not, of course, as much as VITO.

Intellects (or "Seymours")

One step below the managers and directors you will find the intellects, the all-important advisors to managers and directors. I also call them "Seymours" because they always, *always* want to "see more" data, demonstrations, presentations, flip-charts, and full-color regression analyses. My guess is that, if you've been in sales for more than a month or so, you have spent more than your share of time with various Seymours (who, like VITOs, come in both genders). Seymours poke holes in proposals. Seymours want you to provide lots and lots of charts and samples and spreadsheets and full-color animated scenarios before they will consider agreeing to anything. Very often, they will refuse to agree to anything even after you have supplied them with enough truckloads of information and samples to alter the earth's gravitational balance.

Seymours look at solutions in terms of technical capabilities to fit their *real or perceived* needs. Often, of course, for all their expertise, Seymours have a skewed perspective that derails proposals that can be of real benefit to the organization.

Seymours have lots of influence (which, given their distaste for decision making, is another way of saying that they spend a great deal of time shooting things down); however, they typically have very limited authority; they are not movers and shakers within the organization.

Consumers

No, these are not the *organization's* customers; these are the people who will actually use what you are selling, the ones who carry out the policies of the managers as per the specifications of the Seymours. These are the worker bees; they have little or no authority and very limited influence—unless, of course, they are related to VITO!

Before you dismiss this group altogether, however (as many salespeople do), you should remind yourself that these people know a lot about the organization they work for—and knowledge is power, especially when it comes to dealing with VITOs. And getting information from a consumer carries the not-insignificant advantage that doing so does not run the risk of stalling your attempt to reach VITO! So your relationship with the word processing worker or warehouse person may be a good deal more important than you think.

The Influence and Authority Network

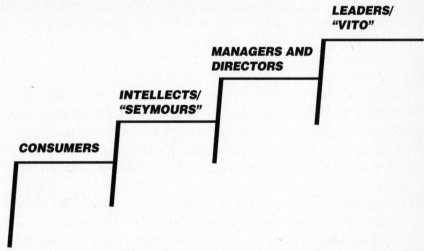

**LEADERS/
"VITO"**

**MANAGERS AND
DIRECTORS**

**INTELLECTS/
"SEYMOURS"**

CONSUMERS

At this point in my seminar, someone usually points out that a good many VITOs pride themselves on seeing things from the point of view of their employees, and may actually be so brazen as to make a habit of fielding calls on the 800 line customers use to call in and file complaints.

So—can a VITO also be a consumer?

The answer is Yes, if you are selling something VITO will be using—but that doesn't really change the landscape that much. Managers and Seymours may decide to become members of the group or groups *below* them—but never above. In other words, VITO may be a consumer, but a consumer can't be VITO.

As a matter of fact, VITO can be in any of the other three categories, or all four at once! But the key thing to keep in mind is that, while VITO may decide to wear every hat, *no one else in the organization can do this!*

Another question salespeople often have at this stage has to do with that hard-to-categorize title, vice president. Does the VP automatically fall into the manager category? There is no definitive answer, because the most important factor is not what the VP is *called,* but what he or she *does.* If the VP drives the company's sales and marketing efforts and can veto the decisions of others in that area, it's a pretty good bet that she's a VITO. (Remember, though, that there is usually one and only one supreme mover and shaker in an organization or division.)

Usually, when referring to VITO, I use the term "president" because it's easiest that way. However, the president of an organization may well be a figurehead, someone whose main function in life is to shake the hands of shareholders and employees. You're interested in identifying the person with *ultimate influence and authority*. In a municipality, that might be the treasurer. In a law firm, that might be the senior partner. Focus on functions, responsibility, power, and authority—not titles.

VITO Power

So let's review what we know. VITO has the ultimate "Yes" power, and the power to veto the decisions of others in the Influence and Authority Network. Regardless of what you know about the organization, and regardless of any efforts on your part, you can rest assured that VITO will become *very* involved in the decision to buy your solution *if* any of the following conditions exist.

1. Your solution is likely to have an impact on the way VITO's organization interacts with its customers, and VITO knows it.
2. The economy in general or VITO's industry in particular is in a state of flux, and VITO knows that what you are offering will make a transition period easier.
3. Your solution crosses departmental or divisional lines.
4. Your solution will definitely have a significant impact on company revenues or expenses, and VITO knows it.
5. Your product, service, or solution represents a change in source of supply, *and* one or more of the other four situations I have just outlined exists.

Of course, sometimes it's not so apparent to us that VITO is involved with our sales. But you can bank on the general principles I've just outlined.

Why not take a moment now to write down, on a separate piece of paper, the instances in which VITOs in your accounts have become involved with your sales. Do they parallel the reasons I have set out above?

> *Looking for a place to sell that's not crowded with competitors?*
> *Sell at the top!*

Of course, VITO will be more *directly* involved in the decision to buy from you when you call on VITO first. Doing that empowers you and allows you to shorten your sales cycle—because VITO sees the big picture! (That's part of VITO's job, remember?) VITO will, repeat, *will* understand the importance of the solution you are offering—if you only take the time and trouble to communicate what you have to offer in such a way that it addresses the items on VITO's agenda.

Chapter 6

The Seymour Problem

CONSUMERS AND MANAGERS ARE IMPORTANT PLAYERS WITHIN THE ORGANIZATION, and we may even have some experience in dealing with them. For most of us, however, the sales cycle begins—and, all too often, drags on and on before coming to an inglorious end—with Seymour, the intellect.

Sometimes I'm accused of being a little too hard on Seymours—or intellects, as I sometimes call them—and I imagine there's probably some truth to that accusation. But I must admit, intellects play a tremendously important role in just about any organization you care to name. The problem is that we as salespeople tend not to realize exactly how they fit into the Network of Influence and Authority. Accordingly, we're often frustrated when we try to work with them. But the problem is usually ours, not theirs.

I've found, from personal experience, that good salespeople tend to work better with VITOs than they do with Seymours. That doesn't mean that Seymours aren't likable, hard-working professionals. It just means that, for our purposes, we're better off contacting VITO first. You see, there is a food chain: VITO is at the top and Seymour is at the bottom. After you read, understand, and put into practice what you'll learn between these two covers you'll be calling on VITO *first* and Seymour *second*. I'll repeat: VITO first and Seymour second. The only time Seymour comes before VITO is in Webster's Dictionary!!!

What's in a Name?

This is important. Sometimes Seymour goes by a fancy name like "Manager of Data Processing" or "Senior Executive Human Resource Development Coordinator." Again, you should not be fooled by titles. If a contact is an advisor, a tester, a look-around-corners first and foremost, that contact is a Seymour.

Mistaking a Seymour for a manager or director is a common mistake that will stall your sales cycle, your progress toward your quota, and your career!

Seymour in a Nutshell

Seymour's titles typically include:
- Analyst
- Systems Manager
- MIS Manager
- Engineering Manager
- Consultant
  (Consultants are usually, but not always, prime Seymour candidates. Accordingly, they are usually, but not always, loathed by salespeople. By the way, have you ever noticed how consultants get in the door by promising to be objective, then simply recommend the products of the company they used to work for? Could there be a connection there?)
- Telecommunications Manager
- Accounting Supervisor
- Buyer
- Purchasing Agent
- Plant Manager
- Office Manager
- Head Accountant

Seymour's key characteristics are:
- Technical background; almost always formally educated, and often serves as "backbone" of company on complex technical issues
- Loves to find problems and solve them
- Is focused on job at hand
- Is security-minded
- Is loyal to current source of supply
- Doesn't like to make decisions or take risks
- Always wants to see more data

Seymour's agenda and favorite business discussion topics are:
- Techno-facts: features, functions, figures, and future products
- How your technical solutions fit Seymour's real or perceived needs
- How your solution actually works and what will happen if it doesn't

Seymour wants to see results like:
- Accumulation of knowledge as power
- The most correct, perfect, zero-defect solution possible

For Seymour, victory means:
- Getting the best performance for the price

- An ever-increasing skill and knowledge base
- Recognition as the ultimate problem-solver
- Continuous job security
- Knowing more about products and technology than a salesperson (sound familiar?)

Now, What about *Your* Seymour?

If you've been selling for any period of time, you've probably run into more Seymours than you care to remember. Nevertheless, I want you to take a moment now to profile a Seymour who seems to you to be most typical of the kind you run into. Again, it's not *my* observations on Seymour that will make the difference for you, but your own knowledge base of how Seymours act in the industry you're selling to.

Think of a Seymour you know. Now, on a separate sheet of paper, list:

- Seymour's name and title
- Seymour's key characteristics
- Seymour's agenda and favorite business discussion topics
- Seymour's desired results
- Seymour's definition of victory

Some Further Observations on Seymours

Let's review what we have.

For one thing, Seymours don't like making decisions.

This is a defining characteristic of Seymours the world over, and the trait that most frequently drives to distraction the salespeople who come their way.

Seymours are analytical; they don't like taking risks; and they love to gather information. It's not surprising then that they feel there is a right or wrong answer for any situation. (A side note: It's been estimated that college graduates take over 2,600 tests by time they get their degree! Most of them look for right and wrong answers when confronted with something new. Seymours are usually quite well educated and *nearly always* look at things in an on-off, right-wrong way. If you don't have the right answer for a Seymour, you'd better be able to explain why.)

Seymours have tunnel vision—they usually attack one job at a time. They are loyal (often fiercely so). They are sometimes impressed by increased efficiency as long as it does not decrease the size of their project, department, or empire. They have little or no tolerance for change; they are security-minded and zealously guard their interests against perceived threats.

Seymours love technology—especially if they're the only ones who can get a particular piece of it to do something. In general, though, we have to remember that Seymours are *risk-averse*. They'd like to be the first (and, per-haps, only) person on the block to get the new model Z—but not if doing so will expose them to what they perceive as unjustifiable gambles.

This brings us to an interesting dynamic. Typically, your aim is to high-light ways *the prospect's company* can increase its efficiency. Often, though, these ways will infringe on Seymour's monopoly on an existing, and ineffi-cient, technology! Less equipment? How will Seymour fill the day? This phe-nomenon—technology as a symbol of empire, rather than as a means of attaining a company objective—represents yet another reason you must be willing to present your solutions initially to VITO!

Seymours are the ones who never seem to take a vacation. They're afraid something might change when they're gone.

Seymours are often thin-skinned. They don't take criticism well.

Seymours may be tinkerers. "Can we take the top panel off this thing and look inside?" (Engineers are often the most influential Seymours in an orga-nization.) They will talk facts, features, and functions (the "F words" beloved by Seymours the world over) all day long if you let them.

Who Does This Sound Like?

Well, it sounds like any number of contacts you've encountered over the course of your career. But the salient point is, the person we've just described *doesn't* sound like he or she could do what you do for a living. How many things do you as a salesperson have in common with Seymour? My bet is that, if you have been earning your living as a salesperson for more than a month or so, there are very few.

Just take a moment and think of some people in your company or depart-ment who didn't work out as salespeople. I'm talking about people who had to leave due to income problems, or who were fired, or who simply decided they weren't cut out for your line of work. Didn't one or two of them remind you of Seymour? Many of these characteristics (intolerance for change, inability to take criticism, and tunnel vision, to name only a few) are ones that would spell certain doom for anyone pursuing a career in sales.

And yet Seymours are our most common contact in an organization, aren't they?

Picture this. Seymour is at home one evening reading *Scientific American* and, at the same time, watching the Discovery Channel. Seymour's kid walks in the room and says, "I know what I want to be when I grow up!" Seymour puts down the magazine and presses the mute button on the remote, looks at the kid, and says, "Oh? What?" And the kid says, "I want to be a salesperson."

Can't you just picture Seymour bolting out of that easy chair, looking to the heavens, and asking, "God, please tell me—where did I go wrong?"

We have very little if anything in common with Seymour. We have all sorts of things in common with VITO. (And note that, while we may think of *closing* sales with Seymours, we always *open* relationships with VITOs.)

The Seymour Trap in a Nutshell

We recognize the portrait of Seymour in an instant, and there's a reason. Seymour's personality quirks and professional foibles are almost universally accepted as part of the territory the average salesperson must master. If you doubt it, think of the sales managers you've worked with. Most sales managers spend the majority of their time talking their salespeople through problems with various Seymours.

Seymour is the one (or so we tell ourselves) whom we must somehow convince to come down on our side despite all of those analytical digressions; the one we have to cajole into issuing a recommendation in our favor by providing more colorful charts, more detailed reports, more exhaustive surveys; the one we must bury with an avalanche of information so thorough and so detailed that not a single one of those finely honed problems, questions, and skepticisms will be left standing. We assume that if we can only give Seymour what he or she wants and then some, we will, we must, eventually get a decision.

Without exploring the validity of these assumptions, let's look for a moment at a separate issue. Isn't it interesting that we salespeople spend so much of our time talking to Seymours, who have, as we have seen, so little in common with us?

Why do you suppose we do that?

Well, one major reason is that Seymours, unlike VITOs, are usually relatively easy to get to. In fact, most of them *love* meeting with salespeople. But do you know why that is? They want us to do their work for them! All too often, Seymours schedule appointments with us because they know we are willing to give them a free education!

We set up all the meetings: all the graphs, all the charts, all the tests, all the reviews. We summarize everything as neatly as a well-organized encyclopedia. And then we watch as Seymour takes the business somewhere else. If we win over two or two and a half Seymours out of ten in this way, maybe we call it a good quarter. But is it really?

Seymour is easy to reach. So we spend a huge portion of our typical day—of our year, of our *career*—in discussions with Seymour, who would never dream of being a salesperson, and with whom we have very little in common. VITO is hard to reach. So we spend little if any time with VITO, with whom we have almost *everything* in common.

What's wrong with this picture?

So Long, Seymour!

Seymours have their place in the world and in your prospect organization, but for your purposes Seymour should be regarded as *someone you will turn into a hero in VITO's eyes* and nothing more. If you haven't yet gotten religion and concluded that you *must* avoid Seymour at all costs in your initial contacts with a new organization, and *must* instead attempt to contact VITO, go back to square one and reread the preceding chapters of this book.

"But Seymour Is an Important Source of Information!"

So claim many (indeed, most) of the salespeople I have worked with. My response is a concise one requiring only one word, a rejoinder that can, for the purposes of this book, be euphemistically rendered as "baloney."

Of the four major players in the organization, Seymour is hands down the *worst* source of information you can appeal to. There are three reasons for this.

1. They don't mind misleading you. Seymours are the least likely people in the organization to be honest with you on matters of importance to your sale.
2. Seymours are often unaware of important new business initiatives in the organization, initiatives that managers, VITOs, and even informed consumers may know about. (Consumers, we must remember, often keep an ear out for gossip or have special contacts with key people in the organization.)
3. Seymours are the most likely people in the organization to use an "exchange" of information with you on a "confidential" basis as a means of obtaining facts that will then be relayed directly to your competition.

You may feel some skepticism on these points, and if you do, you're not alone. Many, many salespeople have, after years of developing a comfortable set of habits in dealing with Seymours, allowed themselves the luxury of a few myths regarding these "allies" within the organization. So let me address each of the points I've just made in a little more detail.

The most important reason not to make your first substantive contact in the organization with someone you know or suspect to be a Seymour is that *Seymour will mislead you about important issues.* You may feel perfectly comfortable, for instance, asking Seymour to tell you who is in charge of making the final decision to purchase a particular product or service your company offers. This is a serious error, and if you're really honest about your own contacts with Seymours you'll understand why. Seymour will *virtually always* tell you that he, Seymour, is the person totally responsible for making that purchasing decision, and this is rarely (if ever) the case!

Remember: Seymours jealously guard their territory within the organization. And they love to set aside an afternoon to pick the brains of salespeople. So why not tell you they're the ones who "handle that," or who must "approve" your proposals, or are "heading up a group" dealing with your product or service? Why not tell you that they will be making the final decision?

As a whole, Seymours are insular types who tend to focus on the project in front of them rather than the big picture. (If they were good at focusing on the big picture, they'd have graduated to the manager level!)

Finally, you should avoid contacting Seymours for information because they often "shoot the breeze" with you, take information you have provided on the (spoken or unspoken) hope that it is to be used only within that organization, and then drop key bits of information about *your firm's* plans, prices, or suppliers into a conversation with the sales rep who is the current supplier. If this has never happened to you, then you live in a different universe from the one in which I sell.

Now, it is true that this is a potential danger with persons who *aren't* Seymours. But it is much *less* of a danger with, say, managers, simply because of the sheer volume of contact Seymour has with salespeople in general and is likely to have with your competitors in particular. If *you're* calling Seymour, it's a good bet *they'll* be calling Seymour. (Of course, having read this chapter, you should now be more than willing to let them do so! After all, the primary virtue of a blind alley is that it exists for a rival to walk down.)

"So How *Do* I Make the First Contact?"

So much for why to avoid Seymour. If you're like most of the salespeople I've worked with, right about now you're asking yourself exactly how you're supposed to go about tracking down VITOs and getting meetings. What's the secret? Wash their car? Show up at their daughter's birthday party? Find out their favorite candy and burst into the office with an open box?

The actual technique is much simpler, and will not, I promise, require that you do anything absurd in public or private. All you have to do is write a letter, a letter unlike any you've ever seen or written. The first steps—the research steps—are outlined a little later in the book. In the next chapter, we'll look at your objectives during your first contact with each category of worker in VITO's organization.

I'll take this opportunity to remind you that the road to building a business relationship with VITO is not easy, not standard, and certainly not what you're used to when it comes to contacting decision makers. But the techniques we'll be looking at in the next few chapters (techniques that, I want to remind you, I personally use on a daily basis) *will* pay handsome dividends . . . and will help you initiate a genuine long-term alliance with the most important person in the organization.

> *Success is not determined by the lack of failure.*
> *Failure is not determined by the lack of success.*

PART 2

Contacting VITO

"I sent out 10 letters and ended up with
7 VITO appointments!"
—Robert Adam

When you mastered this section you will have the ability to:

1. *Understand how to make your products, services and solutions appeal to VITO*
2. *Ask the very best questions of everyone within VITOs organization, including VITO*
3. *Create the letter that VITO will read and remember*

Key Thought

VITO's think fast. They can size-up you and the situation very, very quickly. Forget words like typical, average and standard. Use words like exceed, creative, unexpected, extreme and success!

Chapter 7

Call Objectives

I'VE GOT A FRIEND NAMED DEAN WHO'S THE PRESIDENT OF A HUGE TRADING company. Going to his office is like taking a trip around the world. He's got artifacts from all over. One side of his office is taken up with a huge map of the world, with all the company's factories and processing plants and ships marked with color pictures. As the ships move across the ocean, Dean plots their progress.

I always get to Dean's office early when we have a lunch appointment, which is about once a month. One day, I was sitting outside in the reception area when Joyce, the secretary, said, "Go ahead and have a seat in Dean's office. He's on the phone, but he won't mind if you go in. Just be quiet—he's right in the middle of a big negotiation."

This guy has three phones on his desk. Each phone has four buttons. As I walk in, most of those twelve buttons seem to be flashing. Dean has a big legal pad in front of him; he's punching away at an adding machine; he's doing a lot of complicated calculations.

Dean picks up one line. "Harry! Thirty-three five? Okay. Hold." He punches a button, puts the phone on the hook, scribbles something, then punches a different button and picks up the receiver again. "Hey, George. Thirty-eight five? Okay. Hold."

He goes through this routine a couple of times, lights blinking and numbers crunching. He reaches a moment when he has to take a deep breath. I say, "Dean, what's going on?" Dean jumps out of his chair, walks over to the map on the wall, and points to a ship off the coast of Central America.

Dean says, "Tony, this ship is loaded with mesquite." (That's the kind of wood you use for barbecues.) "I'm looking for the highest price; I'm having a bidding conference on the phone. There are nine people bidding for that shipload."

"Dean," I say, "why don't you put all these people on one line? Put them all on your speakerbox. Then have an auction. You know how it is in an auction—the fever really gets going, and you'd probably get a better price."

"Can you do that right now?" Dean asks.

Well, I assure Dean that I can, and within thirty seconds I'm working with his assistant to set up the conference call. I show my little telephone credit card to Joyce and say, "Call this 800 number and tell the operator you want to have a teleconference with all these people." Eight minutes later, Dean is no longer sitting in front of a pad. He's standing up. He's walking around his office. He's got nine people on the phone, all of them bidding for that shipload of mesquite. The price keeps going higher and higher and finally closes at fifty. (To this day, I don't know if that's fifty Krugerrands, fifty thousand dollars, or fifty cents per metric ton.)

After everyone hangs up, there's one more light flashing on Dean's bank of phones. He picks up that line and says, "Arturo? Liverpool." He was talking to the captain of the ship!

Then I ask Dean, "What does it cost to have that ship waiting around for you to tell it where to go?" Dean answers, "Tony, you don't want to know. Hey, where can I get one of those cards?"

Just for the sake of argument, let's pretend that it was my job to sell long-distance phone service. What would I have just done?

Well, I created Equal Business Stature with Dean, for one thing. First, I showed him that I understood a problem he had. Then I presented a new idea for a solution in a way that he could easily and quickly understand. And I phrased it in the form of a benefit when I pointed out to Dean that he could get a better price for his goods by holding a real-live phone auction. When I showed Joyce how to use my card, I took on the role of the consumer by showing her how to use the service. If I had called on Seymour, I might have had to show him how many lines the service could accommodate in the event all twenty-one of Dean's lines had been blinking at the same time, explained the system's use of fiber-optic technology, and examined a dozen other techno-facts. And if I had called on one of Dean's managers, I would have had to describe how the long-distance service would have presented a unique advantage for that manager's department or the organization as a whole by describing the various service options and advantages.

Each player in VITO's organization speaks a different language. In your contacts with each, you must be able to speak the proper language.

Now, one of the ways you're going to enter VITO's world is by sending a letter. That may seem a little old-fashioned in today's email, fax, and phone-driven business environment, but it works. Surprise! The much-maligned Postal Service is going to be one of the ways you'll introduce yourself to the VITOs you identify.

But don't start tapping on your computer yet! You can't just send any old letter to VITO, and you can't stick it in any old envelope. As you know, an endless barrage of unexpected mail hits VITO's office daily. Your first goal is to *stand out from that traffic*. If you don't do that, all is lost. One way to do that is to pay close attention to the physical packaging of your message, and this is something we'll be addressing a little later in the book. Another way is to do a little research before you compose the letter. But the bottom-line, *best* way to stand out from those competing messages is to speak VITO's language. And before we can begin crafting that all-important letter, we'll have to look at the principle by which VITOs judge all attempts to communicate with them, written or otherwise.

As we've seen in the story I told about Dean, that principle is simple and can be summarized in two questions VITO will ask about what you have to say: *Does this benefit me? If so, how and just as importantly, when!*

Different Messages for Different People—and Pre-Letter Requests for Information
Let me underscore this vitally important point: Each of the types of workers in VITO's organization has a different objective in dealing with you. You will need to highlight different aspects of your product, service, or solution in your dealings with each of them.

- Consumers need to know about *functions*. They will be concerned with how to make your solution function properly, how you will help them do their jobs. Envision consumers as the end-users who must be able to work better as a result of your solution.
- Seymours need to know about *features*. That means what each component of your solution does, how all the parts and elements interact, what gives your solution its character. Seymours need to know why what you are proposing is needed. Think of Seymour looking "under the hood" to inspect all the component parts and characteristics of what you have to offer.
- Managers and directors need to know about *advantages*. They want to know what your solution will do for the department, whether what you have to offer provides a leading-edge advantage that helps the department achieve the company's mission statement.
- VITOs need to know about *benefits*. They want to know how your solution will help the company realize its fullest potential and what top, middle, and bottom-line results can be expected and when.

Depending on your own circumstances, you may decide that some kind of research call preceding the letter we're about to draft is necessary. In some cases you will need to make a trip to the library, surf the Web, visit their Web site, read an annual report, or gather information from a conversation with a consumer or manager within the organization.

Here's an important piece of advice. If you need information on a company, contact the company's sales rep! Your call will get right through or will be returned almost immediately. Nine times out of ten, you will get everything you want to know: VITO's name, the firm's competitors, any problems with the current service—it's really up to you. Don't quiz the receptionist, whose job it is to keep you from getting through and who is probably too busy to do much talking anyway.

Of course, you should be *prepared* to talk to anyone in the building. What follows, then, is a brief summary of the predilections of the people in the four major categories within your organization, as well as some ideas for topics you should find out more about in any dealings you may have with that person.

Consumers

These people focus on *functions*. If your company were introducing the world's first color photocopier, the Consumer would probably be most interested in *how* to use this new device. Would it need special paper, for instance, that would have to be kept in supply? The consumer wants you to save him or her time, make the job easier and more fun.

When dealing with a Consumer, DO: find out what is being used now; learn how it is being used; determine whether there have been any serious problems with the current product or service; find out who's who; try to obtain noncritical tactical information for this sale only (but see below).

This bears repeating. When dealing with a Consumer, DON'T: ask a receptionist for company information—instead, ask to speak to a sales rep and direct all fact-finding questions to him or her. (Yes, sales reps are considered Consumers, and, yes, you should identify yourself as a sales rep to this person.)

Seymours

Seymours tend to focus on *features.* The feature of your color photocopier might be that it copies thirty documents per second. As you know, I suggest you try to avoid Seymours on the first call, but when you do finally call on them after your meeting with VITO, here are some general guidelines to follow.

When dealing with a Seymour, DO: take everything he or she says with a grain of salt; try to find out the technical criteria of the product or service; focus on "how much/how big/how long" kinds of specifics; ask what else Seymour has been looking at and what Seymour likes about it; ask what the perfect solution to the problem in question would be if Seymour designed it. (You'd better get comfortable before you ask this; the answer may take some time.)

When dealing with a Seymour, DON'T: ask "What's next?" or "What's the procedure followed here in setting up this product (or service)?" (Instead, do *tell* Seymour what should happen next.) Also, *DON'T* ask Seymour whether the organization is happy with the current product or service. The answer you get is always yes, regardless of the facts of the situation.

Managers

These people focus on *advantages.* The advantage of your color copier will be tailored to many unique departmental needs. Managers must deliver winning performance by staying ahead of schedule and under budget.

When dealing with a Manager, DO: establish the person's perception of current departmental needs; ask about current and future projects and priorities; find out how long the organization has used the current source of supply, and whether that source is meeting the department's needs. (Note: Unlike Seymour, the Manager may be a good source of reliable information on the decision-making process within the company.)

When dealing with a Manager, DON'T: ask about likes and dislikes with regard to the current product or service. If this manager recommended the current source, you may well hear only about the likes. Instead, ask, "Is the current (product or service) still serving your needs?"

VITOs

VITOs focus on *benefits* and little, if anything, else! The *benefit* of that color copier could be that it will enable VITO's sales staff to assemble proposals that will attract more customers.

VITO wants to know how your solution will help the company realize its fullest potential, and, without anything even vaguely resembling hedging, what top, middle, and bottom-line results can be expected.

What follows is a *brief* summary of some of the most important factors to keep in mind during your first conversation with a VITO. (*Note:* The topic of your all-important first call to VITO is covered in much greater detail later in this book.)

When dealing with VITO, DO: ask about specific goals; ask about VITO's criteria for establishing a business relationship; confidently ask what it will take for VITO to do business with you. (And wouldn't VITOs love their own sales reps to ask that question of each and every prospect!)

When dealing with VITO, DON'T try to do "company research" by quizzing VITO about the organization's history of using your product or service or a competitor's product or service. VITO may not know!

To close this chapter, I want to refresh your memory with this revised outline of the Influence and Authority Network, which shows you where each of the four categories stands in relation to the other, and reviews some of the key questions you should be prepared to ask.

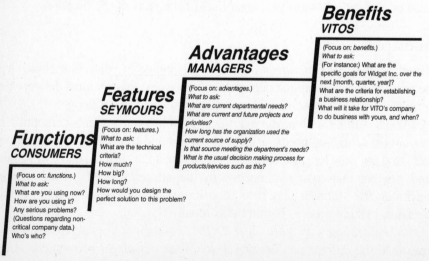

Benefits
VITOS

(Focus on: benefits.)
What to ask:
(For instance:) What are the specific goals for Widget Inc. over the next [month, quarter, year]?
What are the criteria for establishing a business relationship?
What will it take for VITO's company to do business with yours, and when?

Advantages
MANAGERS

(Focus on: advantages.)
What to ask:
What are current departmental needs?
What are current and future projects and priorities?
How long has the organization used the current source of supply?
Is that source meeting the department's needs?
What is the usual decision making process for products/services such as this?

Features
SEYMOURS

(Focus on: features.)
What to ask:
What are the technical criteria?
How much?
How big?
How long?
How would you design the perfect solution to this problem?

Functions
CONSUMERS

(Focus on: functions.)
What to ask:
What are you using now?
How are you using it?
Any serious problems?
(Questions regarding non-critical company data.)
Who's who?

Two Other Questions You Should Never Ask

You'll get in trouble (and quickly, I might add) if you were to ask our friend Seymour, "Who's who?" This would prompt an immediate response from Seymour that would sound something like this: "I am the person you'll be dealing with on this extensive evaluation process, so don't waste your time trying to contact anyone else!"

It's done. You've created an instant hole in the ground, jumped into it, and now you'll begin to play the part of a mushroom instead of a business person. Equally as dangerous is any attempt at asking VITO something like, "Who besides yourself will be involved in making the decision to choose a business partner?" Although, it may sound "VITO-ish," it's likely to get a response from some VITOs that may sound like this: "No one! I am the one who decides whom I'll be doing business with!" Ouch! Your attempt at establishing equal business stature just went down the drain.

A Little More on Benefits

The concept of the benefit is so important to understanding the world in which VITO lives that I want to review it very closely with you before we move ahead in the book. (Some of what follows was already discussed briefly at the end of Chapter 5, but it's important enough to look at once again.)

Parinello's Definition of a Generic "Benefit"

- A desired result
- A measurable improvement over existing conditions
- Added value (getting more than you paid for)
- A gain in a desired direction
- A return on investment that exceeds expectations
- Progress that leads to new opportunities.

Parinello's Translation of Tangible Benefits ("Hard Dollars") into VITO's Desired Results

Following are examples of *tangible results* VITO could realize from your solutions.

- Increased efficiency
- Measurable increase in revenues
- Increased sales
- Greater market share

- Substantial decrease in fixed or variable expenses
- Reduced time to market
- Reduced cost of sales

Parinello's Translation of Intangible Benefits ("Soft Dollars") into VITO's Desired Results

- Reduced risk and worry
- Greater convenience; ease in completing daily tasks
- Ability to set new trends
- Ability to be the first to recognize a new marketplace
- Recognition; praise; esteem by industry, peers, or community
- Increased customer loyalty
- Improved employee morale and motivation; improved labor relations
- An appreciating human or capital asset

So much for the call objectives and the importance of tangible and intangible benefits. In our next chapter, we'll look at some additional methods for getting information about VITO's organization.

Cold Calls to VITO Should Follow Every VITO Sale!

Your manager knows it, I know it, and you know it: The best time to make a "cold call" is whenever you make a sale. Now, I am not suggesting that you wait to do all of your cold prospecting calls until you make a sale! What I am suggesting is that you definitely make VITO cold calls during all the times when you're mentally and emotionally "up" and in the "zone." No, it's not superstition, it's fact. Our brain, as complex and amazing as it is, will take the easy way out and recall the last situation or task and associate it with the current situation or task. That's why when you're on a roll, keep your knees in the breeze, smile, and keep dialing for dollars!

Chapter 8

More Research You'll Need to Do Before Contacting VITO by Mail

AT SOME POINT BEFORE YOU MAKE YOUR FIRST CONTACT WITH VITO, YOU MAY decide it's appropriate to go beyond phone research on that new company. Such research may help you prepare yourself for your later letters and calls, and it may play a major role in the customized letter you'll be drafting in the next chapter.

By the same token, many salespeople (and I'm one of them) find that you really don't need a heck of a lot of company research to prospect VITOs effectively. What you really need to know about is the profile and industries of your *current* customer base—and then you need to know, in very broad terms, whether the VITO you're calling fits the same major categories. My experience is that, if I know that 85 percent of my current customers operate widget-processing firms employing between 50 and 100 people, with head-quarters within an hour of downtown Los Angeles, I can find out through calls to company sales reps whether or not I'm well advised to write a letter. If VITO's firm seems likely to fall into the target category, I write the letter. If it doesn't, I don't. I don't worry about whether VITO has worked with products like mine before, or under what conditions, or what the results were. A good portion of the time, *VITO* doesn't know about any of that stuff. (VITO tends to see things first in terms of his own organization—not in terms of the vendors that organization hires.) I figure that, if I know how I'm helping my current customers, and I know that VITO *could* fit their pro-file, I know enough.

You may decide that more research is in order, however, and in your cir-cumstances that may make perfect sense. So here are some other ideas for tracking down information about VITO's company.

Call and Ask Someone at the Front Desk or in Investor Relations to Send You a Brochure, Catalog, or Annual Report

Cheap, easy, and static-free—and infinitely preferable to trying to earn ten minutes of the receptionist's time with "a few quick questions." When combined with an upbeat call to one of the company's sales reps, this approach should get you a wealth of information.

Buy a Share of Stock in VITO's Company

I'm not kidding. If the firm is public, and if you're really gung-ho about tracking down good, solid company data, call up Investor Relations (or a broker), ante up the money, and take a look at the information the shareholders are getting. Obviously, this is a technique best employed when you have a little time. It may be perfect for that plum account you've had your eye on over the last year and a half, but can't quite crack.

Cruise the Information Superhighway

There are a number of efficient ways to use on-line information services to track down important information about companies. For my money, however, a trip to the library works just as well, but in the end it's your call and your time.

One of the metaphors I like to use in describing the way you must deal with VITO is this: *You are not trying to close a sale; you are applying for a job.* That job, partner to VITO, is a tough one to land.

Now, if you were preparing for a real-life job interview at a particularly highly ranked firm, one at which you knew many other top-notch applicants were also interviewing, you might well decide that it was worthwhile to boot up your computer—or make a few phone calls—and engage in a little electronic digging. For a particularly important spot, why not try to do a little on-line research if it will help you to shine at the interview?

If you decide that such an inquiry is in order in researching VITO's organization, you may want to use the article search features available on such services as CompuServe, Prodigy, or even the Info-Track service available at some of the larger libraries these days. Alternatively, you may wish to contact a service such as Nexis Express, which can search its immense databases for earning and finance reports, stock records, and much more—and get everything to you in short order. Check your telephone directory for contact information for these electronic resources.

All of these services require some sort of fee. If you're new to the idea of searching for data on-line, you may wish to recruit a friend who's well versed in the search methods of each service to track things down for you. Wandering aimlessly around cyberspace for four or five hours in search of the perfect bit of data can be an extremely expensive way to impress VITO!

Chapter 9

Benefits—and the Headline of Your Letter

FINALLY! YOU'RE READY TO START WORKING ON YOUR LETTER TO VITO. ITS first and most important component will be a headline statement.

Let me warn you once again that this is going to be a letter unlike any you have ever written. It will be only one page long, with the other side blank, but it will probably require more care, patience, and consistent effort than any other piece of business correspondence you've ever written. Since you'll be spending some time developing a couple of drafts of this letter, we'll deal with the actual content of the message first. Then we'll look at the physical form your letter must take. Note that this aspect, too, will be quite unlike your other written communications to prospects.

The letter we'll be crafting in this part of the book will work for both new prospects and existing accounts. Let me mention here that the alumni of my seminars and readers of the book you are reading right now have gotten some incredible results from these letters. Imagine, up to a 45 percent return! That's no typo, no that's not four-point-five . . . it's FORTY-FIVE percent! Now that I've got your rapt attention, let's move ahead.

How This All Started

Now, let me give you a little background on how I came up with the idea for the letter I use to reach VITO. A few years back, I started to look closely at the letters salespeople were writing to their prospects. I tracked down actual letters from actual salespeople, and I looked at the advice all the business-letter books were offering on how to compose correspondence to prospects. And by that I mean I went to the library and looked at every book on the topic, and went to the bookstore and *bought* every book on the topic that I hadn't seen. After looking at all that, I was horrified. The only saving grace I could find in the letters I looked at was that they were, in virtually all cases, going unread by their intended recipients.

One of the books that I read on how to write a good business letter was written in the year I was born—1947—and do you know what? The basic outlines of what that book suggested are still being parroted in today's books!

Do you think the average decision maker today has just as much time to read correspondence as the average decision maker had in 1947? Well, neither did I. The format you're about to see is a creative, original approach that I came up with after reviewing the needs and time pressures of *today's* reader.

The very first person I sent my new-format letter to was the president of a big high-tech firm. (I'd also been sending out a number of other letters to top people, letters that pretty much followed the standard formats.) Three days after I put it in the mailbox, my phone rang. I picked it up and said, "Hi, this is Tony. How can I help you?" A voice on the other end of the line said, "You sent my president a letter. He circled two words and gave it to me."

I said, "Oh? Which two words were those?"

The voice said, "The words were 'satisfaction guaranteed.' That's got to be a pretty big business risk for you, huh?"

"Actually," I replied, "it's one of the lowest business risks I've ever taken. Out of the twenty thousand people I've worked with, *nobody* has ever been dissatisfied. By the way, who is this?"

It was the executive vice president of sales and marketing of the largest computer manufacturer in Texas.

With that kind of result from a single letter, I had a feeling I was onto something. Experience has borne out that I was right. If you're half as excited now as I was after getting that first call, you'll be in a great position to take advantage of the letter we're about to review.

A word of advice before we begin: *Follow the instructions in this chapter to the letter.* By doing so and following up by phone as outlined later in the book, you will be taking advantage of a technique that has, for me, yielded an 85 percent contact rate with top decision makers. Yes, you read right: *85 percent!* Considering that the most common reason we hesitate to contact VITOs directly is their supposed inaccessibility, don't you think it's worthwhile to give this method an honest try, without altering it in any way?

The Headline Statement

Research shows that, on average, people decide within about eight seconds whether or not to continue reading an unexpected piece of mail. VITOs, of course, are not average, and some of them are likely to make that decision a little earlier. Therefore, you must earn VITO's attention within the first eight seconds, tops, and probably a few seconds earlier than that. You're going to need a compelling Headline Statement to do this job.

You'll place the statement at the top of the letter. When you read a newspaper, what's the first thing *you* look for? Headlines! VITOs, of course, read newspapers every day—so use the same principle here. Put your most compelling material at the top of the page. *Don't* include any superfluous, textbook, business-letter material—such as VITO's company name and address—in that all-important spot. VITOs already know where they go each morning and what the name of their company is. Make the Headline Statement the first thing that anyone seeing this letter would notice.

With this statement, you must win interest and avoid prejudging. In its most powerful form, your headline:

- is no more than thirty words long.
- has either numbers or percentages in it.
- balances the equation. Example: if you are able to increase revenues, you must explain that it's not at the risk of increasing expenses. Or, if you can lower expenses, it's not at the risk of reducing quality, reliability, or customer services.
- does not include any industry jargon, buzzwords, techno-babble, or any other words or phrases that VITO will not be totally familiar with.
- addresses this VITO's interests and is relevant to this VITO's industry.
- establishes your credibility.
- references a specific time frame.
- establishes your Equal Business Stature. (Remember, you are not approaching VITO as a salesperson, but as a businessperson.)
- is based on a *literal quotation*—or on verifiable *factual information*—from a credible source your VITO will recognize and respect. Typically, this source is either another VITO in the same or a similar industry or a recognized publication such as a trade magazine or industry newsletter. Another excellent source would be a quote from a VITO who sits on the board of directors of the company you're trying to do business with. Or, if your company is currently doing business with a retail firm, and if your product, service, or solution can also be used by a bank, you could make a very powerful appeal to the VITO who holds the top position at a bank by repeating the high praise for your company given to you by one of the bank's best customers! (How do you find out what bank your retail customer uses? Take a look at the next check they send you!)

Don't ever forget that your own VITO is a great source for headlines too! Later on in this chapter you'll see some examples of how you can take a headline and add credibility to it just by adding your own VITO's name to it. Of course, you'll always get approval BEFORE you put your VITO's name on it. Forgetting to do this is what I choose to call a career-limiting mistake.

- highlights or is based on the tangible benefits of doing business with your company.
- highlights or is based on the intangible benefits of doing business with your company. (Please take a moment now to review the tangible and intangible results VITO desires from his partners. You'll find the summary in Chapter 7.)

Your Headline Statement should sound the trumpet for actual events, not hypothetical situations. By this I mean that you should focus on measurable results that real, live customers have enjoyed from implementing your solutions—results that include percentages or other figures and *always* incorporate a specific time reference.

Words to the wise: VITOs hate generalities! They have learned from bitter experience *not* to trust phrases like "in the near future," "on or about," "approximately," or any similar language with built-in wiggle room. Far better to do a little research (believe me, your Headline Statement is worth it) and offer phrases like "in sixty days," "two weeks ahead of schedule," and "16 percent under budget."

Your Headline Statement *may* include your company name, as long as it comes *after* the name of a customer's company. (As you'll see a little later when we talk about stationery, the idea here is not to broadcast your company's name or logo, but to isolate solutions to VITO's problems.) Your Headline Statement *may* include words like *guarantee, discover, benefit, value, advantage, proven, results, quality, progress, growth, safe,* and *genuine*—but if you have a compelling third-party endorsement that omits these words, there's nothing wrong with going with that.

Wow!

That's a lot of requirements for a thirty-word statement! I'll be honest with you; it's quite possible that it will take you a good deal of time to find or craft just the right Headline Statement. But your letter is worth it.

Let's say you're selling laptop computers. Here's an example of how your Headline Statement might evolve:

High-resolution screen would be easy for your salespeople to read.

to:

Salespeople can file reports quickly and accurately.

to:

Salespeople can spend more time with customers.

to:

Our work with salespeople has shown that they are consistently able to spend more time with their customers.

to:

Our work with our customers indicates that salespeople can increase the time they spend in front of their customers by as much as 50 percent—within two months of using our laptops.

to:

Our work with our customers indicates that salespeople can increase the time they spend in front of their customers by as much as 50 percent—within two months of using our laptops—without increasing the cost of sales.

to:

We've increased the time XYZ Company's salespeople spend in front of their customers by 30-50 percent in just two months and lowered the cost of sales.

to:

XYZ's sales increased up to 10 percent in the past two months while they lowered the cost of each sale. Would you like to meet the team that made this possible?

When you put your VITO's name at the bottom of this quote you'll get the attention of whoever reads the headline!

Yes—you can, if you wish, completely eliminate any reference to your product or service. In fact, it may be an advantage for you to do so! Remember, your goal is to build interest and keep VITO reading.

Take a few minutes now, on a separate sheet of paper, to write a rough draft of a compelling Headline Statement. Try to come up with one that would stop VITOs in their tracks and keep them reading, even though they have fifteen other important things to do in the next hour.

Headline Statement

_____

_____

_____

_____

_____

_____

_____

_____

_____

_____

_____

_____

_____

_____

_____

_____

_____

_____

_____

_____

_____

_____

_____

_____

_____

_____

_____

Have you completed a draft of your letter's Headline Statement? If not, please stop here and do so.

If you have decided to use a direct quote from a respected source as your Headline Statement, but have not yet located the quote you want to use, you should *draft the quote* and submit it for approval. That's right—many times when I ask VITOs for a quote, they'll ask *me* to come up with wording for *them* to approve.

Here are some Headline Statements that work. How do yours compare?

(Audience: Mammoth Auto Company parts suppliers and engine suppliers.)

By January 2005, Mammoth Auto Company will reduce its suppliers by 50 percent without sacrificing one-time deliveries. Our proven solution will guarantee that you maintain your chosen position with Mammoth.

Twenty-eight words and notice how the equation is "balanced" comparing a lowering of suppliers without any sacrifice to its customers.

Note the inclusion of the Mammoth name as the very first element of the statement, a tactic guaranteed to win the interest of a VITO whose company sells to Mammoth. Also good here is the use of the term "revenues" rather than, say, "profits"—a term, by the way, you should *never* use in this letter or in any other communication with a VITO.

What if VITO's goal for the company this year is to lose one million dollars instead of twenty million, as it lost last year? What if, as is commonly the case, the Accounting Department takes its sweet time telling VITO whether or not there *are* any "profits"? Why remind VITO of that? (I'll tell you a secret—some VITOs have no idea how the company's "profits" are computed in the first place!) All raising this issue will do is get VITO mad in those first eight seconds, and you don't want anger. You want attention.

Of course, as powerful as that Headline Statement is, it would be even more so if you could incorporate a quote from Mammoth's annual report specifying the change in plans. Talk about credibility!

(Audience: the dean of Marywood College.)

We helped Armstrong College increased grade point averages while they lowered student registration costs by 30 percent all within six months.

Twenty words, balanced equation, and it also has the element of time.

Some nice things here, not the least of which is the specific record of delivering a measurable result (30 percent lower operating costs) within a definite period of time (six months). If you've made it this far in the book, however, you should already know that, if you have the slightest doubt about your company's record with regard to these results, *don't tell VITO you've done it!* VITO will very likely call up the president of Armstrong and ask how that student registration system is running. Tell the truth and be accountable.

Now, you're not promising (yet) that you can deliver the same results for VITO. You are reporting what, exactly, you've been able to deliver to other VITOs.

Note the use of "we" in the opening sentence of the last Headline Statement. That's a very strong formulation; it gets VITO wondering who's talking, and it's infinitely preferable to its two alternatives: your company name, or the word "I." The company name is to be avoided because it can encourage prejudgment on VITO's part. Use of "I" with a VITO is problematic if your objective is to build rapport. "I" is too self-centered; it takes the focus off VITO's favorite person (VITO) and puts it on someone about whom no information is available (you). VITO doesn't yet have any reason to care about you as an individual! You as a team member, however, may well have some solutions to offer. Stick with "we," "our" or, "together."

(Audience: president of a large California public television station.)

In the past year, KXET maintained its listeners' loyalty, reduced delays in scheduling while at the same time cut budgets by 34 percent!

Twenty-two words, to the point, and notice how I always place the results in the order of importance to VITO. (You'll recall from our previous discussion that VITO wants to increase revenue, efficiencies and effectiveness of revenue-generating employees, mission-critical employees and mission-critical processes; hold on to existing market share; get add-on business from that marketshare; and last on VITO's list of results is cutting expenses.)

That unprepossessing "while" is important; it means you're paying attention to both ends of the equation, just as VITO has to. Did you miss it? Look again. This Headline Statement tells VITO that you have been able to reduce delays *while* lowering operating costs.

Think about it. VITO hasn't gotten to the top spot by assuming that it's *impossible* to lower expenditures and increase quality or efficiency at the same time. Quite the contrary! VITO usually makes a habit of *assuming* there must be a better, cheaper, *and* faster way to do the same job his organization is doing now—if only his people would find that way!

Be one of those people. Find examples of how your company has helped your customers raise revenues *without increasing payroll expenses.* Tell VITO about the time you helped a customer get a product to market early *without compromising quality.* Locating such solutions is what real businesspeople in the real world have to do every day. Don't just promise to lower VITO's costs. VITO doesn't need your help for that—all that's necessary is a quick trip to personnel and an order to send a hundred pink slips out! Or nix an ad campaign! Or cancel a company party! On the other hand, increasing output while lowering VITO's costs—that's worth listening to.

Work both sides of the equation. When you do, you'll demonstrate to VITO that you can really tackle the tough problems. VITO's problems.

(Audience: the senior partner of a major law firm.)

We've increased client billable hours for one of the top five law firms in Dallas by up to 25 percent while reducing overhead cost as much as 10 percent.

Twenty-seven words and also take notice of how I use phrases like: "up to" and "by as much as." I do this for a reason and the reason is: if VITO "A" ever wants to talk to VITO "B", we need to make sure that we have not overstated any numbers or percentages. If results are off one month or quarter and they're only 14 percent instead of the stated 15 percent, I am ok because I used the words "by as much as 15 percent."

Look how much is gained by the use of that quote! VITO almost *has* to pay attention. But note that the person quoted is not a direct competitor of VITO's—or, at least, is not likely to be. You've quoted (with permission, of course) a senior partner from an out-of-state firm. (If your VITO worked in Texas, you'd find another headline.) Avoid directly quoting or citing competitors in your Headline Statement; it may be perceived as threatening. If you feel it's appropriate to cite your performance with someone who's competing with VITO, use the formulation that appears in this Headline Statement: "five of the top ten widget firms in Yourtown." That delivers important information but keeps things in the abstract. Of course, when asked by VITO to give details, you will.

(Audience: president of a large consumer goods corporation.)

"Jones and Company views XYZ as a strategic partner, crucial to the success of our business. XYZ will help keep us positioned as a leader in the retail clothing industry."

ANDREW JONES, PRESIDENT
JONES AND COMPANY
ANNUAL REPORT

Certainly nice if you can get it. Now, I grant you, your firm may not be the subject of glowing paragraphs in the annual reports of your customers—but are you sure there are no other forums in which the results you've delivered have been trumpeted to the skies? More to the point, have you ever *asked* your current customers to describe the work you've done for them? Let me repeat this. You may find that your customers are so happy with what they've been getting from you that they won't mind if you draft the endorsement yourself for their approval! If you find yourself in this enviable situation (and my guess is that, with very little effort, you can), take the time to find *exactly* what your company has delivered—then draft a hard-hitting Headline Statement *that you then take to VITO for approval.* It bears repeating: You must be a straight shooter here. Not only is it the best and only way to build the reputation you want, but to indulge in the alternative—composing and circulating quotes that your contacts haven't seen—is to limit your own career growth and court catastrophe for your company. VITO is just the type to call to check on these things, and it isn't going to do your cause any favors if the person you quote mumbles something about having met you once a few months ago and not remembering much else.

Don't cut corners. When developing endorsements, get all the proper authorizations. (Of course, that front-page *New York Times* article calling your company the single most dominant player in your industry can be quoted in your letter without further ado.)

The example given above doesn't cite specific figures. It works, but I'm going to encourage you to try to track down actual performance numbers from your customers anyway as part of the development of your Headline Statement.

Many salespeople, when asked to work with customers to develop specific figures and time references like those included in many of the previous Headline Statements, start to get cold feet. "Tony," they say, "I don't know the exact [employee turnover percentage, increase in billable hours, reduced time to market, or whatever] at this company, and neither does my contact. I can't get bogged down with this kind of stuff!" If this is your reaction, read the next few paragraphs very carefully, because we've just touched on something of paramount importance—something that will affect not only your Headline Statement, but your whole campaign to sell to VITO.

You cannot sell to VITO if you cannot produce documentable successes with either tangible or intangible results.

No ifs, no ands, no buts, no maybes. If you are unwilling to do the research necessary to find out exactly what kind of results your product or service has delivered for your customers, you should stop reading this book right now, because it's not going to do you any good. *VITO needs proven benefits,* and success stories preceding them. If you can't deliver same, don't bother trying to work with VITO.

Feeling unenthusiastic about tracking down the numbers? Well, get enthusiastic! Find out what you're actually delivering to your current customers. (And note that the much-maligned, analytical Seymour may be your most valuable ally in this effort.) What would happen if you got a call on Monday morning from the VITO at your prize account? "This is VITO—I want you to get your fanny in here and justify your existence. The budget ax has fallen, and we have to cut half of our vendors. Be in my office at two o'clock."

How's that for motivation? Well, guess what. That's the call you're lucky to get! The most common case is the one in which you simply fade away from your customer's list of preferred suppliers and partners. No comment, thanks. Goodbye.

> *It's always best to under promise and over deliver to VITO.*

Rationalizations for Not Doing the Research

Now, people come up with all kinds of reasons not to do this step. "The organization is too complex." "The products are too far removed from the end users." "Spreading these figures around—if we ever determined them—would be a breach of confidentiality because our competitors might hear about it." "Our customers buy so they can fill out their budgets at the end of the year." Then there's the most popular one: "My customers won't give it to me." My response: baloney! If you ask, they will give you the information.

You provide benefits to your customers—to VITO. If you want to be able to survive in today's marketplace, you must be able to show VITO exactly why and how and how much and how soon there will be a benefit to VITO's organization. Then—and this is more important than anything—you must keep VITO *conscious of the value of the relationship with you at all times.*

This is not to say that you must necessarily incorporate hard facts and figures into your Headline Statement. A compelling quote from a satisfied customer that doesn't discuss specific performance data can also work wonders.

(The quote from Jones and Company's annual report would be an example of this.) But you must *at some point* be willing to provide measurable details of the success stories you've made possible for your customers—and, just to be on the safe side, you should be able to recite chapter and verse on such success stories within, oh, say, a few seconds of encountering any VITO. Don't worry, we'll be covering this in full a little later in the book.

Now, then. This "I-can't-be-bothered-with-tracking-that-down" reaction that I get from salespeople sometimes arises from an (understandable) uneasiness at the idea of trying something new. That's human. We all tend to fear the unknown, and what I am telling you to do here is not common behavior for most salespeople. For the vast majority of us, the sale is either closed or pending; the customer is either happy or unhappy with what we're doing. The idea of *initiating* contact with a customer, and then trying to find out exactly *how* the product or service is performing, in terms that a VITO will understand and give credence to, is foreign. As foreign as it may seem, though, it's something you will have to give an honest try if you're going to see results from this part of my program.

Take the time right now and using the exercise below create a Value Inventory of one of your very best existing customers or prospects.

Value Inventory Exercise

Step #1. Select Your Best Existing Customer(s) or In Process Prospect(s):

- Make your list and sort it by industry/niche.
- Rank and place your best customers/prospects at the top of each industry/niche list.
- Place an asterisk next to customers/prospects that you've not met the VITO.
- From this list, select the one customer/prospect that you've delivered or have the potential of delivering the greatest hard and/or soft value to. Value has nothing to do with the amount of business *you've* received or have the potential of receiving.

Hard and Soft Value Defined:
Hard dollar value: A positive tangible, easy to observe and measure result. Dollars earned, dollars saved, time saved in critical processes or deadlines, etc. that your solution has had or has the possibility of having on VITO's top, middle, or bottom line. Hard dollar value can be expressed using numbers or percentages.

Soft dollar value: A positive but intangible, difficult to observe and measure result. Shifts in attitude, less risk, less stress/worries, guarantees, performance bonds, greater image/recognition, etc. that your solution has had or has the possibility of having on VITO's top, middle, or bottom line. Soft dollar value can be expressed using descriptive words and phrases.

Step #2. Interview and Establish Your Value Inventory:

Have a peer or your manager ask you the following questions.

IMPORTANT NOTE: Compile very detailed notes or record all answers on a cassette recorder.

- Q1: How long have you been servicing/working with this customer/prospect?
- Q2: What products, services, and solutions have you been providing or are you planning to provide?
- Q3: For each product, service, and solution answer the following:
- What positive impact* has your product, service, or solution had (or has the potential of having) on VITO's top (revenue-generating) line? What has been the gain? Hard dollar value? Soft dollar value?
- What positive impact* has your product, service, or solution had (or has the potential of having) on VITO's middle (expense) line? What has been the gain? Hard dollar value? Soft dollar value?
- What positive impact* has your product, service, or solution had (or has the potential of having) on VITO's bottom (gross or net margin or profit) line? What has been the gain? Hard dollar value? Soft dollar value?
- Has your product, service, or solution had (or could it have) an impact on this customer's/prospect's customers? Hard and/or soft dollar value?
- Has your customer/prospect experienced (or could they experience) any positive impact on the quality of their product, service, or solution or any part of their quality process?
- Has your customer/prospect experienced (or could they experience) any end product enhancements? Or, technical edge?
- Has your customer/prospect experienced (or could they experience) any competitive edge in pricing?
- Has your customer/prospect experienced (or could they experience) any competitive edge in their industry's position?

- What impact* has your product, service, or solution had (or could it have) on the customer's/prospect's critical processes? Are they better? More accurate? Being done with less cost/labor? Less expensive?
- What impact* has your product, service, or solution had (or is going to have) on any of this customer's/prospect's critical special or ongoing projects?

   REMEMBER: in all cases "impact" and "results" will be defined in terms of hard and/or soft dollar value.

Add any questions that are specific to your customer's/prospect's industry and the results that your product, service, and or solution provides or has the potential to provide.

IMPORTANT: With every answer, quantify the exact impact with numbers, percentages, and time frames, or by using descriptive words and phrases. Avoid the use of your unique terminology, product names and/or model numbers, industry jargon or technical facts, figures or other non-VITO lingo! Keep your answers focused in the area of *business impact,* not technology or systems impact.

Step #3. Transcribe:

Take your detailed notes or audiotape and create "bullets" which are a series of one or two sentences that describe each hard and soft value being delivered. It's best to keep these bullets as short, direct, and to the point as possible. Remember to avoid all techno-buzz, industry jargon, product mumbo-jumbo . . .

As we proceed through the following chapters, you'll be using all of the elements of your Value Inventories, plus it certainly won't do your career any harm to show these to your sales manager!

If your initial skepticism about what I'm suggesting is rooted in a feeling that you've simply never *done* anything like this before, congratulations. Assuming you've got happy customers somewhere, you've got it easy. All you need to do is work through the preconceptions you may have about "what a salesperson does." Ask for a meeting with a contact at your best account. Ask how what you've been working on has affected operations there. Ask for estimates of specific performance levels over specific periods of time. Ask for permission to incorporate these estimates into your sales materials, and provide all necessary confirming materials so your contact can approve what you'll be circulating.

Once you track down and quantify your product or service benefit, you will improve your rapport with your current customers, and you *will* see success from this program by incorporating the new information into your presentation to VITO. I've seen it happen too many times to think otherwise.

If, on the other hand, your hesitation comes from a well-founded suspicion that there may not *be* any success stories to speak of in your customer base, or a fear that if you were to call most of your current customers to go over the details of your product or service, they might act to cancel the account when reminded that they're doing business with you, then you've got big problems, which can easily be solved by updating your resume.

(Audience: CEO of a firm experiencing market share problems.)

"Excellent! I would highly recommend this seminar to all my colleagues—but not to my competition."

BILL WYERSON, SALES REP
ABC COMPANY
CORVALLIS, OREGON

This one demonstrates that a compelling Headline Statement can be considerably less than thirty words long—good news for VITO, because he doesn't have time, patience, or inclination to wade through a single extraneous word. (Please remember, too, that even a statement that is thirty words in length or shorter can be wordy, repetitive, and uninteresting.)

If you are inclined to work out an arrangement with one of your contacts to adapt this specific Headline Statement to your line of business, feel free to do so. That goes for anything in this book, of course, but I mention this quote now because it is concise, to the point, and extremely powerful. It's likely to serve salespeople in any number of industries quite well: "Excellent! I would highly recommend AAA Widgets to all my colleagues—but not to my competitors."

Just remember not to send a letter using this opening to any of your contact's competitors! Doing so would be a breach of trust, of course, but even if your contact for some reason didn't mind such use, it wouldn't earn you any points with the VITO reading the letter.

(Audience: Owner of a small chain of Arizona hotels.).

"Green Roof Inns has increased its revenue by 9 percent and improved customer service and satisfaction during the past year since implementing XYZ's guest communication services."

DAVID DAWSON, OWNER
GREEN ROOF INNS OF CONNECTICUT

Here's someone VITO can trust, someone VITO knows looks at the world as a businessperson. Here's a fellow VITO.

If you can secure a quote like this one, a quote from a *noncompetitive* fellow VITO who is familiar with or active in your VITO's identical line of work—or a similar line of work—use it. (A good bet: a quote from a VITO active in the same industry as your VITO, but in a different component of that industry. You might use a quote from a well-known literary agent, for instance, in a letter to a VITO who is the president of a publishing company.)

Words to Consider Using in Your Headline Statement

Good
Money
Easy
Guaranteed
Health
New
Proven
Results
Safe
Save
Own
Best
Complementary

Try Again

We've spent a lot of time reviewing the Headline Statement, and there's a reason for that. It's probably the most important part of your letter. If the Headline Statement works, you will have gained VITO's attention. (And, by the way, that's the only goal here—to win attention and draw VITO into your letter. You are *not* trying to convince VITO to purchase your product, service, or solution.) If your Headline Statement doesn't work, your letter goes into the circular file with all the other ignored messages of the day.

So: Now that you've had a chance to review a number of Headline Statements that work, why not take this opportunity to rewrite your own? Revising and reworking your efforts is a critical part of this process. If you have only completed one or two drafts of your statement, odds are very good that it is not yet ready to include in your letter.

Please take the time now to take one last look at the sample headlines that follow and then revise your Headline Statement. When you're done please proceed with the next chapter.

"One of the largest telecommunications companies in America has increased the efficiency and effectiveness of their employees while realizing an annual savings of over $XXX,XXX. How can my team serve you?"

"One of the world's largest electronic manufacturers reduced cycle time by XX days while eliminating $X.X million in inventory. They accomplished this within XXX days of using my team's ideas."

"This year one of the top three U.S. oil companies will increase their margins while reducing operating expenses by $XX,XXX per month as a direct result of my team's efforts."

"A major U.S. auto maker increased one division's revenue by XXX percent while saving $XXX,XXX annually."

"We created XX percent Time to Market savings for FDA submissions while reducing capital expenditures over $XXX,XXX in just XXX days of our business relationship for another CEO in *your* industry."

A word of caution: it's not a good idea to copy word-for-word the headlines you see in this book. Why? Because, your value must be unique to your product, service and solutions while at the same time serve the needs of the VITO you are sending your letter to.

Chapter 10

The Rest of the Letter to VITO

ASSUMING THAT YOU HAVE SUCCEEDED IN CRAFTING A POWERFUL HEADLINE Statement, it's now time to move on to another part of the letter. But it's probably not the part you're thinking of!

In a standard letter, after establishing the "grabber," the opening lines on the page, most of us would be inclined to move on to composing the body text. But we're going to focus on the elements of this letter in their order of importance—which means that we'll be looking at things in the same order that VITO does. (Actually, this is the order *anyone* in VITO's organization would read the letter, including VITO's secretary or assistant, who will probably be reading this first.)

Now, we know VITO is a very busy person, and we can make a guess, based on that, that this very busy person is not likely to read each line without satisfying a natural curiosity about who's making such dramatic and expressive claims. (Indeed, one of the main purposes of your Headline Statement is to instill curiosity in the reader.) So the next most important part of the letter will not be the body text, but the part of the message appearing at the *very bottom of the page*. In other words, we are going to take advantage of VITO's next move, which is going to be to leap from that headline statement down to the signature line to find out who on earth has sent this letter.

There, beneath your signature, VITO is going to find—and read—a very prominent Action P.S.

Unlike the Headline Statement, the Action P.S. follows a very definite form. It won't take you twelve drafts to develop. It may, however, require a little more telephone work—about which we'll talk in a moment.

The Action P.S. should look like this:

P.S. I'll call your office at 8:00 A.M. on Thursday, January 23. If you will not be in, or if I've chosen an inconvenient time, please have Tommie tell me when I should return the call.

Tommie, of course, is VITO's secretary or assistant. If you don't have VITO's secretary's name, you can't write the Action P.S. Believe me, replacing what appears above with "have *your secretary* tell me when I should return the call" will not work! So don't try that.

Remember, this is a customized letter. You must specify the secretary's name because *he or she is the person who will almost certainly be reading this letter first and deciding its fate!*

When Tommie opens the envelope and reads that P.S., what do you think is going to happen? Your letter survives, that's what happens! Tommie will be mightily impressed that there is someone out there who knows that he or she plays a vitally important role in making things happen for VITO. Tommie will probably check VITO's calendar and write in your calling date. Tommie will almost certainly be expecting your call. Tommie may even call *you* to say something like, "Ms. VITO will be out of town on the 23rd—but if you prefer, you can give her a call at 8:00 on the morning of the 24th." (Don't laugh—it's happened to me hundreds of times.)

But what if you don't know the name of VITO's secretary? That's easy. Presumably, you have already got VITO's name—otherwise there's really no point in drafting the letter. (You may want to review the ideas on finding company information that appeared earlier in the book. My first course of action is always to consult the business directories, such as the *Million Dollar Directory* or the *Corporate Yellow Pages,* at the local library, or you can surf the net and visit VITO's Web site.) To find out the name of VITO's secretary or personal assistant, call the company's reception desk and ask something along the lines of, "Does Ms. VITO Benefito spell her last name with one or two Fs?" You'll get an instant answer and no conflict whatsoever. Then say, "Thanks. By the way, what's her secretary's name?" You'll have exactly what you need.

Don't Skip That Call!

I should say here that the "how-do-you-spell-that" call technique I've just outlined is good to follow even if you happen to know the name of VITO's secretary. There are two reasons for this. First of all, it's a good idea to double check everything going out on paper to VITO, and the spelling of VITO's name is certainly no exception. Secondly, you should be dead-certain in your *pronunciation* of VITO's name as well as its spelling.

I once contacted a VITO whose company was located in Florida. The directory I consulted in the library told me that the president's name was Guy Rabat. I don't know how you'd pronounce such a name if you came across it in a directory, but to me it registered as "Guy Rabbit." "What an odd name," I thought to myself. I had to do my normal routine of checking the secretary's name—and checking, for that matter, that Mr. Rabat was still the president of this firm, and that I was spelling and pronouncing his name correctly. (I have learned from bitter experience never to give directories the last word on names and titles. They are, to some degree or another, out of date from the moment they hit the bookshelves. Often, they are flat-out wrong to begin with.)

So I called the receptionist and asked, "Could you tell me, please, does Mr. Guy Rabbit spell his name with one or two T's?" She laughed out loud and said, "It's not 'Guy Rabbit,' it's 'Guee Ruh-BAH.' There's only one T, and it's silent because he's French!"

Can you imagine what would have happened if I hadn't taken the time to call to make sure of the spelling and pronunciation of that name? If I'd written the letter without double checking, and followed up by calling and asking to speak to Mr. Rabbit, the president? If the receptionist had chuckled to herself and thought, "Here's a dumbbell who deserves whatever he gets," and put me through?

"Good morning, Mr. Rabbit. How are you today?"

That's what I call a "reload." You shoot yourself in the foot once, open the chamber, reload, and shoot yourself in the other foot. Don't do it. Check everything before you send out the letter.

Once again, *use the exact format I have described here for your Action P.S.* Don't play around with this. The wording here is important, and what I've provided really does work.

A note on scheduling the time of your calls to VITO is in order here. The approach that works for me and for the many salespeople I've trained is to set aside a whole day, schedule each call to a VITO every half hour, and focus on initial contacts for the entire day. I strongly suggest you follow this method.

Verticalize your letters. What do I mean by that? I mean you shouldn't pretend that the same letter that works for a senior partner at a law firm will work for the president of a manufacturing firm. Your letters must be industry-specific, heavy on experience and research, and compelling for the intended audience. That means you must address your letter to the concerns of a top person *in that industry,* and customize wherever you can. (To take the opposite, or horizontal, approach is to assume that all VITOs are concerned with the same issues, which is manifestly not the case.)

Warning!

Do not send VITO any letter with an Action P.S. attached unless you are *positive* you can follow up with a call at the time you indicate!

Actually, you should probably count on calling approximately two to three minutes *earlier* than you indicate in the letter. (Being early, by the way, is always what VITO means by "on time.") Woe unto you if you promise VITO that you will call Tuesday morning at 8:00 and the phone doesn't ring until 8:12! (And if you hold off until Wednesday, of course, you can simply forget about doing business with VITO.)

Remember—VITO lives in a world that cries out for tangible and intangible results. Your claim to be able to provide these will very likely be irreparably undermined if your first call to VITO is not a punctual and professional one.

Susan, a salesperson who took my seminar recently, had an unfortunate experience. She planned to send out a single letter as a test of the system. (Not a fair test, but never mind.) Her letter went out to the VITO at the largest health maintenance organization in the eleven Western states.

The next Friday afternoon, as Susan is closing out one week and getting ready for the next, the phone in her office rings. It's VITO's secretary. (That's a very common outcome, by the way, and a great start to your sales cycle.) The secretary says, "Susan, I see here that you're planning to call VITO at 9:00 on Monday morning. VITO's asked me to have you call him at 7:30 because he's got a staff meeting at 9:00. Here's his private number—use it so you can bypass the switchboard, which won't be taking calls until 8:30." Talk about a golden opportunity!

Unfortunately, Susan stayed out a little late on Sunday night with some friends who asked her whether or not she'd ever drunk tequila before. She hadn't, and to this day, I'll bet she wishes she could still say that. On Monday morning, she *woke up* at 7:30, scrambled for her notes, did her best to coax something resembling her normal voice out of her throat, and punched VITO's number. She was not ready for the call. And she blew it.

First of all, she ended up calling five minutes late, which is a near catastrophe when dealing with VITO. Worse, she was trying to speak to him from a blank spot within a yellow haze that hung like a puffy halo around her head. That's another example of a reload.

You can't do that with VITO.

Don't let it happen to you. Be ready to roll and in top form when dealing with VITO—and do whatever it takes to keep your promises. If you are faced with a sudden emergency, find someone to make the call for you.

Here's a Real Letter

The rest of the elements you'll be putting together for the letter will be easier to understand if you take a look at the genuine article first. Please bear in mind that the letter that follows is not something to *copy*—your experience, your industry, and your prospects will determine the actual text you use. But in terms of the structure of the letter, this will serve as a good model.

Important note: The format of your final letter should use an italicized larger font for the Headline Statement. The body of the letter should be set in a crisp, professional-looking font.

*"One of the top insurance companies in the United States
realized an unplanned XX percent increase in their profit margin.
Would you like to meet the team who made it possible?"*

Your VITO's name goes here

May 14, 1947

Ms. Importanta
President

Dear Ms. Importanta,

The above results are common achievements for our business partners.
As much as XX percent of revenues previously wasted on unintentional inefficiencies are now channeled directly into increased shareholder value, an
annuity stream that continues to provide ongoing benefits for everyone, except
the competition.

We are pleased to present the following areas of proven repeatable
achievements in the insurance industry, but more importantly: which one of
these areas are you personally convinced that there is room for improvement
between now and the end of this calendar year?

- *Increase the number of policyholders* serviced on a daily basis
  by as much as XXX percent. We agree it's amazing, but when
  contact rates go up so does revenue, renewal and expansion of
  existing policies.
- *Increased customer satisfaction* and reduced customer callbacks. Happier customers bring greater market share to your
  doorstep at lower levels of expense.
- *Increased efficiencies of knowledge workers:* Turnaround time
  of critical employee documents is decreased as much as XX percent. Now, they consistently have the *correct* information when
  they need it.

Ms. Importanta, with your direction we can quickly determine if we can
assist in providing equal or even greater results. Our personal promise to you
is that if we can't deliver, we will not ask for your business partnership.

To greater success,

Will Prosper
ABC Corp.
760-765-1321

*P.S. I will call your office on Thursday, April 16, at 10:00 A.M. If this is an
inconvenient time, please have Tommie inform me as to when I should place
the call.*

You probably recognized the Headline Statement and the Action P.S. at the top and bottom of the page. Now let's look in detail at the rest of the letter, the components that make up the body of the text.

The Tie-In Paragraph

This is what comes immediately after "Dear Ms. Importanta." Write a *brief* opening paragraph that follows the theme of your headline and will tie in to the benefits you're about to list. This part of the letter has to take the headline, follow the theme it has established, and bring the reader to the body of the letter. Although there are very few words here, this is a critical component of your letter.

Here are some examples of the kinds of tie-in paragraphs you should use.

The above results are common achievements for our business partners. As much as 15 percent of revenues previously wasted on unintentional inefficiencies are now channeled directly into increased shareholder value, an annuity stream that continues to provide ongoing benefits for everyone, except the competition.

During the past seven years, we have worked with thirty organizations in the advertising industry including ABC, XYZ and BBB. Collectively, we've been able to increase revenues and efficiencies while at the same time providing ways to increase shareholder value.

While you peruse this correspondence, ABC is enjoying a XXX percent cut in their expenses, XYZ is touting a 12 percent increase in customer service and BBB continues to compress their time to market.

Now, if you've written introductory letters to prospects before, this approach may come as something of a shock. But let me be plain: I want you to completely eliminate any opening pleasantries, any small talk, any mention of discussions with the receptionist at VITO's company—in short, anything and everything that doesn't relate to a benefit for VITO.

"But Tony! Shouldn't I follow standard business format, with VITO's address at the top of the page? The sales books I've read tell me that I should take a few sentences to develop rapport! My sales manager tells me to follow the examples in the sales books!" Now, I know full well that *most* sales letters open with a little chitchat. And I know that *most* sales letters follow the "rules" set down in sales books and other manuals. But most sales letters don't get results. Yours will. (Show your sales manager this part of the book if that helps your cause.)

How many letters do you imagine VITO receives that open with a text-book-perfect date, address, and salutation, and then continue with something like "I just wanted to introduce myself . . ." or "As a result of a discussion with Mike, your receptionist, I wanted to suggest that we might . . ." or "Ms. VITO, have you ever wondered how top performers . . ." or "Hi, my name is . . ." or anything else of the kind? How many? Dozens! Hundreds! Thousands, maybe! Honestly, now: What do you imagine happens to those letters?

Those openings (and their many companions) are guaranteed blind alleys with failure rates so high that salespeople have talked themselves into believing that a five-percent (or three-percent or two-percent) contact rate after sending them is somehow satisfactory. Well, it's not. As I mentioned earlier, you can do a heck of a lot better—specifically, you can reach VITO during your follow up call in the neighborhood of *85 percent of the time.* So stay away from the familiar, comfortable openings.

The Bullet Text: Nothing But Benefits

No features. Just benefits! That's the body of this letter. You must offer *only* short, meaningful, results-oriented statements that compel VITO to read every word. By that I mean a series of bullets (typically, three to five of them) that concisely state your best business benefits in order of importance.

Remember the order? Increase revenue; increase efficiencies and effectiveness of revenue-generating employees, mission-critical employees, and mission-critical operations; protect existing market share from the competition; get add-on business from that market share; and finally, reduce expenses.

You must identify credible, hard-hitting benefits of your solutions. Remember that benefits are both tangible and intangible.

The benefits you outline must relate to VITO's interests and be clearly connected to VITO's industry. They should not require explanation or elaborate technical language; in fact, technical terminology, industry buzzwords, product numbers and the like should be avoided entirely in this letter. The benefits you select must be customized to your business and to VITO's needs, and so I strongly advise you against trying to copy the examples that follow word-for-word. However, these benefit bullets will give you an idea of the style and form yours should follow.

Are any of the following achievements on your list of goals, plans or objectives for the balance of this calendar year? If so, the good news is that we have created a proven, repeatable process that we guarantee to deliver results such as:

- **Expansion of national account volume** by as much as XXX percent by adapting the precise sales and operations methodology these larger customers demand as a condition of doing business.
- **Reducing time to resolve unpaid invoices** from as long as X months to as short as five seconds! Imagine the impact to top, middle and bottom lines. Resolving these issues also improves customer retention by as much as XX percent—an unbeatable combination!
- **Expense reduction by as much as $XXX,XXX monthly** without compromising the level of services or associated assets.

We are pleased to present the following areas of proven repeatable achievements in the insurance industry, but more importantly: which one of these areas are you personally convinced that there is room for improvement between now and the end of this calendar year?

- **Increase the number of policyholders** serviced on a daily basis by as much as XXX percent. We agree it's amazing, but when contact rates go up so does revenue, renewal and expansion of existing policies.
- **Increased customer satisfaction** and reduced customer callbacks. Happier customers bring greater marketshare to your doorstep at lower levels of expense.
- **Increased efficiencies of knowledge workers:** Turnaround time of critical employee documents is decreased as much as XX percent. Now, they consistently have the *correct* information when they need it.

Here are three additional benefits we are providing our business partners:

- *Improved Time-to-Market* by as much as XX days. This single step generated $XX million in additional net working capital for one of our business partners while we consolidated expensive assets.
- *Streamlined global regulatory submission* process enabling reduced cycle time and substantially increased submission levels. This all equals greater team efficiency at lower costs.
- *Global strategic outsourcing confirmed* up to $X million in annual savings. Our other business partners chose to redirect these funds to R&D. Who would be your recipient of such savings?

The Body Copy: The Closing Paragraph

Next, we move to the closing paragraph. You may be tempted here to suggest a date and time for an in-person meeting. Or to suggest that VITO would be the perfect candidate to benefit from your product or service. Or to give VITO your 800 number to call for more information. Or to tell VITO that you look forward to doing business together. Don't do any of that.

Let me repeat: The material you develop for your letter, and specifically for your opening and closing statements, *is not intended to sell*. As a matter of fact, one of my favorite approaches in the closing paragraph is to express a measure of uncertainty or doubt on the question of whether or not the results I've been able to deliver to others will be able to be repeated at VITO's company. Can't you just see it? VITO reads that and starts stomping around the office, thinking, "Why *not*? Why *can't* you deliver these results to my company?"

After all, you're not like all those other salespeople who tell VITO how wonderful what they have to offer is before bothering to learn a thing about VITO's business. You're different. You're a businessperson who's eager to find mutual solutions, and you know that VITO hasn't had any input on what you have to offer yet. So you're going to stay detached, removed, and professional. You're going to focus on *VITO's* reactions, judgments, and opinions—not yours.

Here are some examples of closing paragraphs that work.

Mr. Benefito, it's obvious you know your organization better than anyone does. But what may not be so obvious is how the ABC Corporation could help you realize similar or even greater results before the end of this calendar year. If you would like to take the first step, our complete team of experts can quickly determine each and every possibility.

Ms. Importanta, what does this information have to do with you and your operation? Perhaps everything, or nothing. Everything, if you determine that one or more of the results mentioned in this correspondence are relevant to your strategic initiatives for the balance of this calendar year, or nothing if you decide not to respond to this call to action. The choice is always yours to make.

Mr. Benefito, the possibility for your company to achieve similar or even greater results is difficult to determine at this point. One fact is certain—you are the one person who can initiate the call to action, and together we can quickly explore exactly what the possibilities are.

The Body Copy: An Overview

Naturally, you'll have to spend some time making sure these three pieces—tie-in paragraph, benefit bullets, and closing paragraph—fit together properly. Here are some examples of strong body copy that does the job.

Note that your name, company, and phone number appear beneath your name and signature. Your phone number must appear here—otherwise interested VITOs or their associates will not know how to reach you if they want to reschedule the time at which you will call. (By the way, as I mentioned before, this happens quite a bit.)

Here is another example of body copy—in other words, the letter minus the Headline Statement and the Action P.S.—for you to review. Please remember that the "right" letter for you to send to *your* prospects is the one that *you* develop—not my letter.

March X, XXXX

Mr. Benefito
President

Dear Mr. Benefito,

During the past seven years, we have worked with eighty organizations in the manufacturing industry including ABC, XYZ and BBB. Collectively, we've been able to increase revenues and efficiencies while at the same time, provide annuities that continue to increase shareholder value every month.

Are any of the following achievements on your list of goals, plans or objectives for the balance of this calendar year? If so, the good news is that while working with our business partners we have created a proven, repeatable process that is guaranteed to deliver results.

- *Our partnership improves Return On Assets* by actually reducing the asset base while at the same time making the balance of this base perform to extreme levels of efficiency.

- *Faster product shipments* by as much as XX days. Improved networking capital equals increased inventory turns and minimizes lost sales opportunities to competition.

- *Customer satisfaction is higher* because the information customers receive is more accurate, relevant and timely.

Mr. Benefito, it's obvious that you know your organization better than anyone does. But what may not be so obvious is how our organization could help you realize similar or even greater results before the end of this calendar year. If you would like to take the first step, we can quickly determine the possibilities.

To greater success,

Will Prosper
ABC Corp.
760-765-1321

That's less than 220 words, but they're words that count. They're VITO's words.

Putting It All Together

Now we've taken a look at all the text elements of the letter. Here's a template that will help you remember the way everything falls together on the page.

"Grabber" Headline Statement, taking the form of either a quote from a fellow VITO or a compelling statement of quantifiable success. Should not exceed thirty words.

Date

Mr. VITO Benefito
President

Dear Mr. Benefito:
Opening sentences that follow the theme of your headline. Focus on actual benefits, value you've helped deliver at real-life companies. Finish the story begun in the headline. Then continue with . . .

> **Your very best business benefit.**
> **Your next best business benefit.**
> **Your next best business benefit.**

One good way to close the letter is to leave open the question of whether or not the results you've outlined can be duplicated at VITO's company. Leave the ball in VITO's court and suggest that, together, you and VITO can work to determine whether or not the partnership you're suggesting will be likely to work out.

Sincerely yours,

(Your signature)

Your name
Your company name
and phone number
(NOTE: YOU MUST WITHOUT
FAIL INCLUDE YOUR PHONE
NUMBER HERE!)

P.S. Say here that you will call VITO's office at such-and-such a time on such-and-such a date. If VITO will not be in, or if this is a bad time, ask that VITO have (name of VITO's secretary) advise you of a more convenient time.

Now, that's not your standard business letter, I'll admit. But you know what? It works.

VITO *Can* Tell a Book by Its Cover

It's time to talk a little about the physical form of your letter.

VITO is called on to make dozens of important decisions daily. When it comes to issues VITO (or VITO's secretary, for that matter) considers to be less than earth-shattering, such as whether or not to read letters from new business contacts, *appearance counts.* Put more bluntly, if VITO *can* save a step by stereotyping your letter ("I know what this is; they're trying to sell me something") and ignoring your message, VITO will—usually within seconds.

If you send that letter, on which you have spent so much time isolating issues of specific interest to VITO, and make it look identical to your ordinary business correspondence, you aren't stacking the odds in your favor. As a matter of fact, you're practically begging for someone in VITO's organization to toss that letter out. Even if it does reach VITO's desk, you're still sending a *unique* message in a *deadly dull* format that, for VITO, might as well be a neon sign: "Like All the Others." Don't undercut that carefully crafted message. Don't undo all the work you've done. Make this letter look different.

You must assemble this letter in such a way that it includes little or no external or internal material identifying it as sales-related. This is not because you want to deceive anyone, but rather because you are following through on your commitment to project an image that is different from that of most salespeople. As a group, of course, salespeople are generally oblivious to VITO's real concerns. Accordingly, you won't be sending out letters that look like theirs.

Here are some of the most important guidelines for getting your letter opened—and routed all the way to an attentive VITO.

Don't Use a Standard Letter-Sized Envelope

They get lost in the shuffle too easily, because they look like everything else that comes over the pike. Use a large catalog-sized envelope, and place that unfolded single-page letter in it without paper clips, brochures, articles, or any other distracting materials.

Don't Use Envelopes or Stationery Bearing Your Company Logo

Instead, use plain white stationery and a plain white envelope.

I get a lot of static from sales managers on this one, but the results are worth whatever trouble you may have to go to in order to get this issue to come out your way. The question is not one of "projecting your company image," or "demonstrating quality and commitment to customers," or "standardizing everything that goes out of the office," or anything else that your company logo is supposed to do. The issue, instead, is *keeping this letter alive*. Logos cause preconceptions, and preconceptions cause people to "prioritize" correspondence. We don't want this letter prioritized (that is to say, put in a pile; that is to say, ignored). We want whoever sees this letter to conclude that there is no alternative but to pass it along the chain to VITO.

Let's say your company designs engineering software systems and is called Lightning Technologies. If VITO or anyone in VITO's organization sees "Lightning Technology Services, Inc." at the top of the letter, any one of the following thoughts may overpower your message.

- "We already have computers."
- "We don't need weather forecasting products."
- "We already have software."
- "We don't need consultants."
- "This is junk mail."

Your company's logo may be beautiful. It may have cost tens of thousands of dollars, and an army of consultants may have been required to develop it and place it properly on the company stationary. But on this letter, in this setting, with this objective, it *cannot* appear. Your initial correspondence with VITO must be free of any, repeat, any distraction from that painstakingly crafted message.

If people in your organization are adamant on the stationary issue (and a good many sales managers are), do what I do. Put together fifty letters according to the instructions that follow. Then put together fifty letters that are set up as the sales manager would do it. Then follow up by phone as outlined in the next chapter and see what happens. The nonstationary approach always wins. Always.

Don't Use Address Labels

You have written a customized message, not one piece from a scattershot mailing. Your letter must look the part. Type the address on the envelope, or write it out by hand (if and only if you have attractive handwriting). And, make sure you include VITO's title alongside or directly under VITO's name.

Don't Use Metered Postage

Stick regular *first class* postage stamps, preferably the peel-and-apply variety that's now available. (Did you know that each standard postage stamp you lick contains *eleven calories?* And believe me, you don't want to know what they make that glue from.) You're going for a personalized approach, so don't deviate from this. Bulk rate postage screams "sales message," "junk mail"; overnight delivery services may be effective, but they're awfully expensive considering that you'll be contacting dozens and dozens of VITOs. Express services are really your call; you may decide that using, say, two-day priority mail makes sense for particularly important VITOs.

Do Use a Return Address on the Envelope
But don't mention your company. Instead, use your name and the company address.

Don't Put Anything Else on the Envelope
Specifically, don't use trick phrases like "Personal and Confidential," "To Be Opened by Addressee Only," or any of the other cute phrases meant to keep people from opening VITO's mail as they've been instructed to do. We *know* someone besides VITO is going to open VITO's mail. (What's more, we know that these "privacy" techniques are likely to lose us points with VITO, who doesn't have time for games.)

Customize, Customize, Customize
You'll have to do work to develop a letter that will work within your industry. I want to emphasize here, though, that with the significant exception of the Action P.S., *everything* appearing in the letter to VITO must be customized to your unique selling environment. Work up a letter that's compelling because of what you know about your industry. Fine tune your letters to each of your solutions and each of the potential vertical markets within a given industrial category. Once again, *do not* try to send a letter that's "just like" the ones that appear here. They won't work for you.

Three True Stories
True Story Number One. I once followed up on a letter to a VITO in Florida by calling, as promised, at 8:30 A.M. Florida time. My office is in California, so that means I had to make the call at the crack of dawn! I reached VITO's secretary, who told me, "VITO is on the shop floor right now, but he's expecting your call. Let me have him paged for you." I waited a moment. VITO picked up the phone, but made no mention of the fact that I was calling at 5:30 California time. (VITOs run on a time zone of their own—VITO Standard Time—and everyone else is off schedule.) No, what I heard from the other end of the line was VITO asking me, "How do I know you're as good as you say you are?" I was delighted to tell him the success stories that demonstrated the point.

True Story Number Two. Luanne, a salesperson who worked for a very conservative investment firm, was dubious about drafting and sending the letter I've outlined in this chapter. She was afraid she'd get resistance from "the people upstairs." "If you do," I said, "just say this. You're trying a new program—one they paid for, by the way—that says it delivers the alumni 40-percent (or better) contact rate with top decision makers. You can't follow the program without sending the letter. Suggest a sample mailing of fifty letters, and then follow the rest of the program to see what happens."

A few weeks later, Luanne called to tell me she had done as I had advised, and had gotten the reluctant approval of "the people upstairs." "How are things going?" I asked. "Great," she answered. "I ended up talking to forty-three of the fifty people I targeted—and I have appointments with five VITOs this week." I said, "Ah, that's wonderful, Luanne. Listen, just out of curiosity, how many VITOs had you been able to set up appointments with before trying this technique?" "Well, Tony," she said, "I've been here for two and a half years, and by the end of this week, I'll be up to, uh, five."

True Story Number Three. Brian, a St. Louis sales rep, took my seminar and had a question about the Action P.S. He said, "Tony, I have to call nine VITOs at major local power companies, and I want to send all the letters out at the same time. What do I do about the time I mention in the P.S.?" I said, "Block out half-hour slots, assign each slot to one VITO, and just make the calls." He did—and he got through to seven of the nine VITOs. (It was a heck of a morning.) One of those seven contacts resulted in a $1.25 million sale, on which Brian received a $48,000 commission. That sale was finalized within three months of the day Brian sent out his letters—and this in an industry in which the average sales cycle is one and a half to three years!

What Now?

You've developed a compelling, customized letter for VITO that is likely not only to reach its destination, but to arouse interest in what you have to offer. Now what do you do? In the next chapter, we'll look at the specifics of your initial telephone contact with VITO.

PART 3

Making Your VITO Call

*"I used the Fax Recovery technique and the president
called me back in 5 minutes!"*
—Patrick Wilson

When you mastered this section you will have the ability to:

1. *Create and deliver your very best opening statement
   that will break VITO's preoccupation*
2. *Make VITO's personal assistant your permanent ally*
3. *Leave voice mail messages that will get a return call
   from VITO!*
4. *Break away from low level influencers that are limiting
   your sales performance and personal income*

═══ Key Thought ═══

VITO's are direct and to the point! You have eight short seconds to make your very best first impression. You'll know you've hit a bull's-eye when VITO gives you another eight seconds!

Chapter 11

Getting VITO's Attention by Phone

IN THIS PART OF THE BOOK, WE'LL BE EXAMINING THE PHONE TECHNIQUES YOU should use to follow up on the letter to VITO we discussed in the previous chapter. Because the call is most powerful when it follows a letter, my preferred method of dealing with VITOs who have not yet heard about what I have to offer is to send the letter first and call as promised. For VITOs who fall into other categories, you may decide to call first.

Not Just Any Call

Just as you took a little extra time and effort to research your letter to VITO, you must work a little harder to prepare for your phone follow-up than you would if you were contacting another person in the prospect's organization. Believe me, you don't want to let 7:55 roll around, pick up the phone, punch VITO's number, hear a voice say "VITO here," and proceed to use the standard opening statement all those sales books out there point you toward. VITO has heard it all before—and will quickly conclude that sharp letter you sent along was nothing more than an aberration.

No, your call will be different. Three to five days after you are reasonably certain VITO's office received your mail, you will, as promised and on schedule, initiate contact with VITO. *If you are serious about building a business partnership with this VITO,* you must be prepared for a rapport-building encounter between two professionals of Equal Business Stature. *If you are serious about building a partnership with this VITO,* you will be prepared for the first step on a journey with VITO's organization—a journey that begins the minute you make telephone contact with *anyone* in VITO's office—and will, if you are successful, have no end.

Let me be clear on one point. When I talk about establishing Equal Business Stature with VITO, I don't mean that you should try to mislead VITO into thinking that you are more successful than you are, and I certainly don't mean that you should exaggerate your organization's record of accomplishment. I mean you should present yourself as the knowledgeable professional you are! I mean you should take the leap from quota-chasing salesperson to businessperson! You are an understander of—and solver of—VITO's unique problems.

At this point in my seminar, there's usually a hand raised to ask a question: "Tony, what happens if I don't get through to VITO when I call at the time I mentioned in the letter?" Well, if you've done your job correctly up to this point, the odds are pretty good that VITO will be expecting your call. But, truth be told, not all your calls will result in direct contact with VITO that first time.

What if you get shunted out by others within VITO's organization? In the chapter that follows this one, we'll examine the best way to handle calls that result in contact with VITO's secretary and seem to stop there. I say "seem to" because far, far too many salespeople view being "stuck" talking to VITO's secretary as the end of the road. It's not, and once I outline the simple (but amazingly effective) technique for dealing with the personal assistants and secretaries who work for VITOs, you'll understand why! But more on that, and on the sometimes trickier question of dealing with people at reception desks and switchboard consoles, a little later. For now, we're going to examine what you should do when your first call does make it through to a VITO who is ready, or at least willing, to take your call. And trust me, if you send out enough well-researched, well-constructed letters like the ones we looked at in the last chapter, you're going to run into quite a few VITOs who'll take your call the first time.

Making Your Opening Statement Stand Out

You may be used to saying something like this when you call decision makers:

> "Hello, Mr. VITO, this is Will Perish calling you this morning from XYZ Associates. How are you today? Great. Hey, did you receive that letter I sent out to you on the twenty-third? Oh, well, it must have gotten lost. Listen, I'll tell you the reason for my call; we handle the world's largest widget accounts here, and I believe that in a brief twenty-minute meeting, I could show you some of the competitive advantages. Is Tuesday morning or Wednesday afternoon best for you?"

And so on. As familiar as you may be with that phone script or some variation of it, I want you to do yourself a favor and forget you ever used it. Toss it out the window, because it simply won't cut any ice with VITO. Once you develop your Ultimate Opening Statement, you'll be able to use a compelling, attention-grabbing statement that will remove the burden of "making" VITO do anything (which is impossible, anyway).

Here and now, we're going to break the conventional telephone habits that flash red "salesperson alert" lights at the VITOs of the world and make them disconnect from you. We'll hone and polish your current phone skills and develop the Ultimate Opening Statement—the opener that is your very best bet for winning interest and attention from a VITO.

The Ultimate Opening Statement: Definition and Goals

The Opening Statement is not the entire conversation.

It is not meant to sell VITO anything, or persuade VITO of anything, or convince VITO to meet with you.

It is what you say *until the other person begins to speak.* Period.

It must encourage VITO to interrupt you. You read right: that's the primary goal of the first fifteen to twenty seconds of your call. The secondary goal is to sound conversational. The opening statement must be delivered in a cordial, natural, and professional business tone. It must be said with conviction, passion, and enthusiasm—but it must not seem frenzied. Keep things relaxed, even if VITO doesn't. That means you will have to practice the statement we develop in this chapter until it sounds spontaneous and professional throughout. If it sounds canned, as though you're reading from a script, you lose. VITO will tune you out. If it sounds confrontational or abrupt, you lose. VITO will perceive you as someone who will waste precious time.

There's a fine line to walk here. Cordiality does not mean you abdicate any responsibility for participating in the conversation; being conversational does not mean that you are entitled to leap ahead to levels of intimacy with VITO that you have not earned.

Get interrupted. Keep the tone cordial. That's everything as far as the main goals of the Opening Statement are concerned. So you can forget about image-making, conveying important information, distinguishing yourself from your competition, and anything else you may be tempted to insert into this part of the call.

As a matter of fact, before we start crafting exactly what you're going to say, we should examine these goals in a little more detail—as well as what your Opening Statement must *not* do under any circumstances.

The Opening Statement Must Avoid, at All Costs, Pushing the Two Fear Buttons

The statement you use must *not* trigger the two greatest fears VITOs have about talking to salespeople. The first is that we'll waste their precious time, a legitimate concern that I think is pretty self-explanatory. The second is that we'll talk about something that they themselves are ill-informed about (and, not infrequently, couldn't care less about). When we do this, we challenge VITO's power, control, and authority, and that's something to avoid at all costs.

When we ask VITO something like, "VITO, have you considered the many advantages of a computerized de-fragmentation system for your document storage and retrieval pathways?" then attempt to close by asking something obnoxious like, "Is Monday at two or Tuesday at ten best for you?" guess what? We push *both* of these fear buttons. (That appointment-choice method, as you may know, is known as an "alternative close." Avoid it like the plague.)

When we say things like this, we sound exactly like salespeople—and VITOs know from bitter experience that the single best way to punch a hole in a busy schedule is to spend half an hour or so on the phone with sales-people who know nothing about the problems piling up on their desks. And in all likelihood, VITO neither knows nor cares about the possibilities of computerized de-fragmentation systems for document storage and retrieval pathways!

How's that for a shocker? VITO has no idea about the pros or cons of the features you have to offer. VITO *doesn't have time for details*. VITO hires people who *do* know and care about such things as computerized de-frag-mentation systems—namely, Seymours. To ask VITOs whether they have "considered" these things is to highlight nuts-and-bolts areas of the business about which VITOs generally know little or nothing. That's not the way to build business rapport!

The Opening Statement Must Permit VITO to Retain Power, Control, and Authority

Remember, your goals are to *get VITO to interrupt you* and to *keep the tone conversational at all times*.

To permit VITO to retain power, control, and authority, you must keep the focus on VITO's favorite person—VITO—and away from you. Of course, you will not, for any reason, interrupt VITO. But there's a lot more to the authority issue than that.

For one thing, you will never, never, never use the word "I" in your Opening Statement. And, just as in the Tie-in Paragraph of your letter, you will *not* begin by introducing yourself with "Hi, my name is (name), and I work for . . . " or anything like it.

Forget about VITO for a moment. When *you* get a call that begins with, "Hi, my name is . . . ." aren't *you* tempted to tune it out immediately? Now imagine you have an organization to run and a big staff meeting coming up in five minutes. How much time and attention are you going to give the call?

Let me be honest with you about what I'm proposing here. It's quite difficult. We're all human, and humans tend to focus on "I" first and others second. *Eliminating the instinct to open with some form of "I" takes practice!*

It's common practice for us to begin a call with "I'd like a few moments of your time," "I was just wondering," "I'd like to introduce myself," "I just wanted to know if you'd be interested in," "I'd like to tell you about," or any of a thousand other "I, me, mine" formulations. But you can't do it with VITO. I've said it before, but it bears repeating here: *VITO doesn't care about you.* So do whatever it takes to keep yourself from falling into the habit of opening with an "I" statement.

In addition, letting VITO maintain control means that you have to fight another salesperson's instinct: asking for an appointment. In your Opening Statement, you will use your time to provide solid business reasons for VITO to tell *you* to come in for an appointment. VITOs *like* to tell people what to do. That's what they do all day long! Fine, then. You're going to let them!

People may tell you to ignore my advice about avoiding the alternative close. After all, dozens of sales training books tell you to ask a question like, "Would Monday afternoon at four be a good time for us to meet, or would Tuesday morning at eight be better?" Is this really the kind of question you ask someone who enjoys telling people what to do? Of course not. But VITO hears it again and again. Offer a change of pace. Don't say anything of the kind. By the end of the conversation, VITO will have either decided not to work with you, told you to come in for an appointment, or pointed you toward someone else in the organization. (The first outcome is going to happen now and again, and if you've had any time as a salesperson that won't come as a huge shock to you; the second and third outcomes, of course, each represent a golden opportunity.)

Letting VITO maintain control means that you won't ask stupid questions like, "You *are* interested in raising revenues, *aren't you?*" You must never try to force a "yes" out of a VITO, or back VITO into a corner, or hold VITO hostage to an earlier remark.

The Opening Statement Must Help You Transmit an Unforgettable First Impression

You'll do this by focusing on *measurable benefits,* just as your letter did. In doing so, you'll distinguish yourself from the vast majority of VITO's business contacts.

You must come across as a seasoned, experienced professional who will stand by the results of the program offered—no matter what.

The Opening Statement Must Be Tightly Focused on Getting VITO to Want to Interrupt You and Find Out More

This call is your only person-to-person opportunity to convince VITO of the importance of meeting with you. That means you have no time to get side-tracked. Accordingly, you will *not* mention your benefit letter or ask if VITO has read it.

That's right. You are not going to reference your letter! You're going to avoid doing that at all costs. Think back. In your own experience, haven't you had the experience of saying to someone, "Hey, did you get my letter?" and having them reply, almost automatically, "No, I didn't." And where do you go from there?

If you ask VITO "Hey, did you get my letter?", you're really only doing one of two things. You're either challenging VITO by suggesting indirectly that the letter was never opened in the first place, or you're implying that VITO has a memory so poor that it can't retain a simple thing like having read a letter. Neither of these are particularly good places to start a business relationship.

By the way, I strongly advise against asking VITO *any* "yes-or-no" questions that sound even vaguely like closing maneuvers at this stage.

> You: "VITO, have you considered signing on with this kind of pro-
>   gram before?"
>
> VITO: "No. And I don't think I will now."

Why run the risk of exchanges like this? VITO is in charge, not you. Tossing off "yes-or-no" questions at this point makes the exchange a little too close to that of a prosecutor and a hostile witness. ("Now, VITO. Did you or did you not agree that you would consider using our widget service during our last meeting?") You don't want on-off responses from VITO. You want broad visions of what the future holds. You want VITO to do what VITO does best—expound on opinions, company goals, and objectives!

Because you will take every precaution against allowing VITO to get sidetracked, you will *not* discuss the ease or difficulty of getting through to VITO. And you will *not* appeal to any internal "referral" by saying something like, "Tommie said this would be a good time to reach you." You will stand on your own two feet, highlight your record of delivering solutions that provide measurable, memorable positive results, then get VITO's valuable opinion and direction. Period.

Always Remember: The Opening Statement Must Encourage VITO to Interrupt

Never forget that the primary goal of your Opening Statement is to get VITO to interrupt you. After all, the person who is speaking has power and control over the situation, and there should be no doubt in your mind now about who that person is when it comes to your interactions with VITO.

You will build in pauses to your Opening Statement, pauses that allow VITO to talk while you listen—and I do mean *listen*—to what is said. When VITO interrupts you, *you win,* no matter what is said. (Hard to believe, I know, but it's true.)

VITOs are lousy listeners. Yes, you read right. I'd estimate that, on their best days, they are less than completely attentive to what others have to say about 80 percent of the time. Managers get paid to listen to their valuable team members; Seymours *live* to listen, to compare, to contrast, to analyze. As you move up in the Network of Influence and Authority, you find that listening skills get worse and worse . . . and VITO, the worst listener of them all, is at the top of the heap. We're not going to fight that fact by asking an obvious question (such as "Are you interested in increasing your sales?") in a misguided attempt to stop VITO cold and force a "yes" answer. We're going to use the fact that VITO is a poor listener to our advantage.

(A side note: you may think that my observations on the listening habits of top decision makers are exaggerated. A study by Madelyn Burley-Allen, the nation's leading expert on listening, validates that VITOs are the very worst listeners in organizations.)

So—what *do* you say when VITO answers the phone?

Item One: The Sweetest Words in the English Language

The first words out of your mouth after you hear "VITO here" will be the most important words in VITO's life. Any guesses?

You've got it. VITO's name.

- "Mr. Benefito."

or

- "Ms. Benefito"

This usually break's VITO's preoccupation with whatever crisis has just descended on the office and probably wins you a second or two of interest. Use formal address ("Mr. Benefito" rather than "the first name") until you are invited to do otherwise. If VITO should answer their telephone by saying "VITO Benefito" or "VITO Benefito here," you would not want repeat their entire name! That would sound something like: "VITO Benefito." "VITO Benefito?" Is there an echo on this line, or what? Instead of that madness, I would suggest that you simply respond with VITO's title. Try something like this: "VITO Benefito." You: "The President of the ABC Corporation?"—and it's done.

Practice the Opening Statement we'll develop in this chapter until it becomes second nature to you. (And don't practice on VITOs. You'll lose appointments, sales, and business relationships.)

Item Two: The Pleasantry

Do *not* follow your natural instinct to supply your own name after mentioning VITO's. In fact, you will not, at this stage of the Opening Statement, offer any introductory material of any kind. Instead, you'll use a sentence that introduces a Pleasantry. I like to say something like, "Mr. Benefito, it's an honor to finally speak with you."

I cannot stress enough the value of the word "honor." It has a magic to it like no other word in sales. Here's an example of what it can do: One time, as I was concluding a conversation with a VITO, I said, "VITO, it was a real honor to speak with you today." And an amazing thing happened. VITO said, "That's an interesting word. I've never heard a salesperson use that word before—or anyone in this company, for that matter. Why do you feel it was an honor to talk to me?"

"VITO," I said, "you've given me an opportunity to look at things in your world, and now I feel very close to your organization. I feel that I really understand how I can help you in what you're wanting to do. And to me, it's an honor to be in that position."

If you can reach that point of understanding, you will be able to say— with complete honesty—exactly what I said that afternoon to that VITO. You'll be able to say it not only to your business contacts, but to others in your life, and you will be able to extend and rely on the kind of loyalty that really makes life meaningful. You'll be able to show that you truly honor your relationships. And that is one of the truest measures of success!

Here are some more examples of Pleasantries that work.

"Thanks for picking up the phone."
"It's a pleasure to speak with you."
"Your time is important, so let's get right to the point."

Don't ask "How are you today?" or any variation thereof! The ritual of asking our conversational partners this is part of our social conditioning, and the instinct to do so on the phone is extremely strong. Nevertheless, when dealing with VITO, we must reprogram ourselves, because engaging in this habit in this setting is a guaranteed way to turn off VITOs. You disagree? Well, what runs through *your* mind when a total stranger asks you something like "How are you doing today?" Do you stop whatever you're doing to be sure you don't miss a single exciting minute of the conversation that follows?

Sometimes, when I get a call from a salesperson who obviously knows nothing about me or my organization, who is obviously making a cold call, who butchers my last name because calling ahead to confirm the pronunciation is too difficult, and who asks "How are you today, Mr. Parionellio?"— sometimes, when I get a call like that, you know what I'll say? "Grab a big piece of paper, this is going to take us a few minutes. I'll tell you how I am. Okay. Now, we just got two little kittens, and we thought we had them trained to use the litter box, but as I got out of bed this morning, guess what I stepped into? I didn't really realize what it was until I took several steps across my antique Persian rug. As if that weren't enough, after I took my shower I went to use my electric razor, and darned if it hadn't broken. Just would not switch on. So that put me even further behind schedule this morning. Later I went outside to start my car, but the battery was dead. My wife had left the vanity mirror on. Anyway, this is the kind of morning I've had. So I'm glad you're calling to ask how I am today. Did you get all that?"

That's brutal, I admit. But to my way of thinking it's just as brutal to ask a completely insincere (and unconstructive!) question like "How are you today?"

You get the idea. Stay away from your (often intense) instinct to ask VITO "How are you?" Use a pleasantry that sounds sincere: one that doesn't ask a question you don't really want to spend time exploring, and that lets VITO know you have Equal Business Stature.

Item Three: The Conversational Bridge

After your Pleasantry (and, again, bearing in mind that you *want* VITO to interrupt you with a question or comment), you will be ready to use a Conversational Bridge that will lead you to your "Hook." The bridge will sound something like this: "During a conversation with Jane McLaughlin at Cambridge Light last week . . ."

Here are some more examples of Conversational Bridges that work.

- "While visiting Acme Corporation last week . . ."
- "As we speak, Acme Corporation is enjoying . . ."
- "Together with Acme Corporation, we discovered . . ."
- "Mark Houghton over at Acme Corporation said . . ."
- "Just the other day . . ."
- "Could you imagine . . ."

- "What would happen if . . ."
- "What do you think of . . ."
- "Let me ask you . . ."
- "What's your opinion . . ."

Keep in mind that the conversational bridge is a "connector" and ensures that your opening statement will have a conversational tone.

You should be ready to employ short bridges to get from any one phase of the Opening Statement to any other phase. However, you must not use the bridge to cut VITO off or to change the subject on an issue of importance. Remember, VITO must feel in control.

Item Four: The Hook

The Hook is a *verbal rendition of the Headline Statement in your letter.* However, you should never deliver it verbatim as it appeared in the letter. The Headline Statement is the written word; your Opening Statement is the spoken word. *Each requires a different formulation.* You could say something very vague in your Opening Statement, letting the listener draw conclusions and put pieces together. You can't afford to do that in your written headline! What we want VITO to think is, "Gee, this sounds familiar." We *don't* want VITO to think, "Here's someone who's got something memorized—there's probably a canned speech coming in about two seconds."

Here are some examples of hooks that work.

- "Jane told me she'd been able to reduce four major elements of ABC's overhead costs by 24 percent as a result of using our solution during the first quarter."
- "Acme Department Stores realized a $12,000 monthly reduction in retail unit costs. That money helped subsidize a new ad campaign—which in turn boosted their third-quarter earnings!"
- "Acme Construction decreased down time by 12 percent in the first three months using our solutions."

Keep the exchange conversational, but, in the absence of any direction from VITO, keep it moving toward this hook. The sooner you repeat the benefit VITO read about in the Headline Statement of your letter, the sooner you are likely to be interrupted with something along the lines of, "This sounds familiar. Did you send me a letter?"

IMPORTANT! When VITO says that or anything similar to it, whether at this point or at any other, *stop progressing through this Opening Statement* and say, "Yes. What did you think of it?" Look at what just happened! You got interrupted, which is exactly what you want. Then let VITO talk while you take notes in your VITO Journal! It's perfect!

If VITO does not interrupt you in this way, pause and continue with . . .

Item Five: The Introductory Phrase

This is the point at which you tell VITO who you are and who you work for. The phrasing is important here. As you are no doubt well aware by now, using "I" or "my name is" won't get you very far. Instead, say, "Mr. Benefito, Will Prosper with XYZ." Or, "This is Will Prosper with XYZ, the hardest working company in the Widget industry!"

Of course, if VITO asks your name at any point in the conversation before this, you will supply it. The advantage of waiting to *offer* your name and affiliation until this point is that VITO may be more interested in knowing who you are once you repeat the benefit you outlined in your headline letter. The dialog may sound something like this:

VITO: "Who is this?"

YOU: "Sorry, there's so much excitement buzzing around our office about what we can do for our (process manufacturing partners) I forgot to tell you. It's Will, Will Prosper with the XYZ corporation."

Item Six: The Ending Question

This is where you ask about VITO's specific business interests, or whether VITO feels your solution might be worth exploring further. *Do not ask for an appointment. Do not ask for a purchase decision. Do not ask an obvious question in an attempt to force VITO to say the word "yes."*

The Ending Question should incorporate the element of time ("this month," "this quarter," "this year"). This is very important. One basic way to ask this question would be to say, "VITO, are you looking for a new way to help you lower your cost of sales?" The better way to ask it would be to say, "VITO, are you looking for a new way to help you lower your cost of sales *by the end of next month?"* Do you see the difference? Now try to balance it out by integrating the other side of the equation. "VITO, are you looking for a new way to help you lower your cost of sales *without reducing customer loyalty* by the end of this month?"

And, of course, you should aim at getting VITO to speak while you listen closely to, and take careful notes on, what is said.

The question might sound like this: "Jane's results could be tough to repeat, but would you be interested in exploring a similar program for your organization between now and the end of the first quarter?"

Here are some more Ending Questions that work.

- "Does this touch on any of the top (three) issues that are of concern to you this (month, year, quarter)?"
- "Are you trying to accomplish something similar or even greater than this by the end of this year?"
- "Is this an issue that's important to you for this fiscal year?"
- "Is this something that's consistent with what you're trying to achieve this (month, year, quarter)?"
- "Are you interested in seeing if we could achieve the same or better results with your operation by the end of the second quarter?"
- "What would be the best way to see if we could help your company realize similar or even greater benefits this year?"
- "VITO, who on your staff would you like for me to continue this conversation with between now and the end of this business day?"

Hey, wait a minute—I know what you're thinking! Isn't that going to get you shunted right down to Seymour? Only if you let it! Later on, I'll explain exactly how you'll stop that from happening while you engage VITO in a brief conversation that will provide you with the ultimate, greatest qualification you could ever ask for!

Putting It All Together

Here's a "roadmap" of what the Opening Statement will look like.

Here's an example of what a good Opening Statement should sound like. Remember, though, that your Opening Statement, like your letter to VITO, must be customized to your VITO's unique business environment.

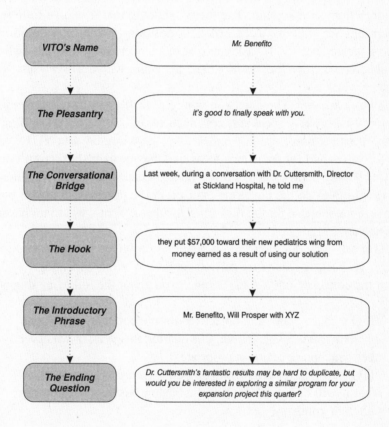

(*Do not* ask for an appointment. *Do not* ask for a purchase decision.)

REMEMBER! Your primary objective is to get VITO to interrupt at any point during this Opening Statement! The most likely interruption will sound like this: "This sounds familiar. Did you send me a letter?" When you hear this, you should always say, "Yes, what did you think of it?" Keep VITO talking while you *listen intently and take notes!*

Take some time now to develop your own Opening Statement before continuing with this chapter.

"That Can't Be All!"

Well, not quite. But pretty darned close.

It seems just a little too simple, doesn't it? If you feel that way, trust me, you're not alone. In fact, if you're like most of the salespeople I deal with in my seminars, you're getting a little worried about the problem of dealing with VITO's objections at this point. The fact is, though, that if you've followed the system this far, you are in an excellent position to leap over the initial objection stage and have VITO ask you—or more, accurately, tell you—when you should come by for a face-to-face meeting and/or whom VITO wants you to follow up with.

I'll tell you a secret. The objection you're probably most used to dealing with—price—is, broadly speaking, not much of an issue for VITOs. That's not to say that they don't watch pennies. They certainly do. But VITOs are looking for value, and for some new ideas that they or their staff haven't discussed yet. If they believe there's a reasonable chance you'll deliver these, they'll be willing to do the dickering later on in the process. (Or, quite possibly, have someone else do the dickering for them. That's what purchasing departments are for.)

If VITO asks you questions about potential problems with your product or service, go back to your first-call objectives. Without appearing to take control of the conversation, *ask VITO to tell you* about the following things:

- VITO's goals, plans, and objectives for the company over a *specific time frame.* (This month, this quarter, this year, or whatever other benchmark seems appropriate)
- VITO's criteria for establishing a new business relationship
- What it will take for VITO to establish a business relationship with your company

And if VITO *does not* pose objections at this stage, you should still ask the three questions above during your initial phone contact. (By the way, I'm not going to give you any specific order to follow in asking these questions. Just follow VITO's lead and ask the question that seems most appropriate given the direction of the conversation.)

"What's that, Tony? You mean I've got to come out and ask VITO these very pointed questions about the business on the very first call?" Yes. As a general principle, you really have to ask these three questions and your Ending Question directly and without equivocation the first time you speak to VITO. You have to ask each of them without offering fifteen different options and variations. You have to ask them openly, because openness is what VITOs expect from their partners. Count on it: You'll win serious points by asking these questions directly. The courage that's required to ask them is what VITOs, deep down, expect of every salesperson in their own organization.

Yes, it takes unshakable confidence to ask these three questions. But when you do ask them, confidently and with a sense of strong purpose, you will demonstrate to VITO that you are a provider of business solutions and a reliable ally in the daily battle to exceed company goals.

Don't ask VITO for everything! Focus your questions. If you ask something like, "What are your corporate objectives?" do you know what VITO will think? "Aha. Here's another lonely, behind-quota salesperson with absolutely no clue." And then VITO will say goodbye.

You must be very specific when dealing with VITOs. Ask, "What are your goals for *increasing efficiencies in the production department during the next quarter?"* That gives VITO something to go on.

It's worth noting here that these kinds of specific yet open-ended questions are ones VITO *loves to deal with!* You know why? Because VITO's own Managers *hate* to ask those questions! Managers know that if they ask VITO a question like that, all the decisions that were "finalized" during the last meeting will have to be tossed out the window, because VITO will have a new, grand, sweeping vision for them to implement. That means new training, new software, new policies, usually without any extra money in the budget—and that means the Manager will be even later and more over budget than usual.

Well, if the Managers don't ask VITOs questions like that, nobody else in the organization is likely to, either. Do you realize what that means? That means you're the only one VITO's going to talk to all day long who'll ask the kinds of questions VITO loves to answer! So don't be intimidated. Be specific—then stand back and let VITO do the talking.

The Toughest Question

Of the questions we've outlined here, by far the most difficult for most salespeople is the one in which they have to ask VITO directly about the possibility of doing business together. Let's spend a little more time on that question now.

As long as what you come up with is direct and to the point, you can formulate this question in just about any way. Here are some examples that work.

- "Mr. Benefito, (do you have/can you think of) any potential barriers to us doing business together (this year)?"
- "Is there any obstacle that you know of to us working together on something similar to this?"

- "Mr. Benefito, what's it going to take for us to do this for you by the end of the third quarter?"
- "Mr. Benefito, can you see yourself as a customer of mine by the end of the first quarter of next year?"
- "Mr. Benefito, would you do business with us if we were to develop a solution in this area that exceeded your expectations?"

Are you still nervous about saying something like this to VITO? If you are, it may be because your instincts are telling you that most prospects would not react well to being asked a question along these lines. Guess what? You're right! *Most prospects* you've spoken to over the course of your working career would disengage instantly if you asked them this. But *most of your prospects have been Seymours!*

Ask Seymour this question, and, yes, you'll go down in a fireball. After all, you haven't shown any charts yet! You haven't conducted seventeen feasibility tests! You haven't even had an in-person meeting to show off your nice color brochure and spec sheets! Seymour has no information to use in answering this question. So if you ask Seymour this, yes, you will get blown off.

But VITO is not Seymour!

If you ask *VITO* this question, odds are you'll get a straight answer. Isn't that a refreshing change of pace! How many hundreds of sales calls have you set in motion with some Seymour despite the fact that neither of you knew the answer to this question? Wouldn't you rather save your time and your prospect's by addressing this issue up front? Of course you would. And so would VITO!

It may help if you think of this first phone encounter as a job interview rather than a sales call. If a job were on the line, you'd probably have a lot less difficulty saying something to VITO like, "VITO, this position is a perfect fit for both of us. What do you want me to do to nail it down?"

Well, a job *is* on the line. It's yours! You're auditioning for a job as VITO's partner. And you have to act accordingly.

When I was having such terrible trouble meeting my quota selling computer systems, I didn't have time to dance around the issue of whether VITO would do business with me. I had a target to meet and I had no time to waste. I *had* to ask VITO: "Mr. Benefito, what will it take for you to do business with us within the next six months?" And the amazing thing was, that desperate, last-chance gamble of mine really was no gamble at all! It turned out that VITOs *appreciate* being dealt with in a straightforward manner. They *respect* a salesperson who will come out and ask this question directly. This is the question VITOs want their own salespeople to ask!

If I told you you had to ask this question if you wanted to keep your current job, you'd find some way to ask it. And you'd find, as I did, that there's really nothing to fear. Let's take a look for just a moment at the reasons that may be lurking behind your trepidation at asking VITO this question.

"If VITO says no, that may block off future contact with someone else in the organization." Yes! And that's exactly the point! If you're worried about stepping on the toes of someone with whom you already have a business relationship at VITO's organization, see the section in Chapter 14 on Pigeonhole Recovery.

"Maybe there's an existing vendor relationship that VITO values." Sure—maybe there is. But you're not asking VITO to give up on that vendor. This is not a closing call! If it sounds like a closing call, you're doing it wrong! This is an opening call! You're simply asking VITO *what it will take to work together.* Don't decide not to ask the question because VITO might well give you an honest answer! That's exactly what you want—and you want it now. Not months from now, when the "rubber stamp" Seymour is waiting for turns out to be not quite as routine a matter as you were led to believe.

"VITO might lie to me." Nah. VITOs are very honest. They don't have *time* to lie. It complicates things too much. They don't want to waste their own time, and they don't want you wasting the time of their key people, either. Plus, they tend to have a good deal of personal integrity. Trust me: Seymours lie a heck of a lot more than VITOs do. When VITOs tell you they see an opportunity for establishing a mutually beneficial business relationship, they mean it.

"VITO will be in a big hurry; I won't have time to fit this question into the call." True, calls with VITO tend to be very short. But take another look at that opening statement you've developed. It's lean and mean! You'll have time. When you do get in touch with a VITO, you should be prepared to go through everything you need to go through in five minutes or less. That may not seem like much time, but I'm here to tell you that, with practice, you'll find that it's more than enough.

"I don't feel that, at my level, I've earned the right to ask VITO that question." You mean you as an individual? Well, my experience has been that VITOs usually appreciate confidence and determination wherever they pop up, but for the sake of argument, let's say that you're right. You can still call VITO and ask this question. Why? You aren't making the call as an individual! You're making the call as a representative for your company! It's been in business for X years, has delivered Y results, and has paid Z dues over the years—and you're acting on its behalf. (Even if you work for a start-up firm, you're a professional offering your company's proposed solutions to a fellow

professional.) Your company has earned the right—now you must take action and exercise that right.

"VITO might say no." This is the big one, isn't it? VITO might reject your suggestion outright. Despite your best efforts and confident phrasing of the questions outlined here, VITO might blow you off. Fine. You get to make your next call to another VITO. (Or, if you're a true masochist, you can call Seymour and "try to start a groundswell." Good luck.) One way or another, directly or indirectly, you're going to get the "no" from VITO. Better now than after you've spent weeks, months, or years nurturing this prospect—and spending your precious time and your company's money all the while.

For my part, I do not consider VITO telling me "No, thanks" to be a rejection. Rejection, in my book, is the act of not reaching the right person when my product or service could be being used successfully—and getting cut off at the pass. Do you have to sell every single prospect in your territory to be successful? Of course not. Somebody has to say no. Don't get uptight about it. Move on. You *will* do better prospecting to VITOs than to Seymours.

There are other objections, but they all boil down to the same thing: Salespeople shy away from asking this question, but *businesspeople* don't. The first couple of times you ask it, you'll probably be a little nervous. But are you ready for a surprise? After a few times, you'll start to feel really great after making such a call to a VITO. By contrast, you'll probably agree that initial calls with Seymours tend to leave you feeling exhausted.

Warning!

Don't ask any other questions than those just outlined! Specifically, don't ask VITO to tell you "who's in charge of this" or "how purchases like these are handled." If you ask something like this, you'll be telling VITO that you're just another salesperson who knows nothing about business, nothing about the way an organization is run—and there goes your Equal Business Stature.

"VITO, I Don't Know the Answer to That, But We Have People on Staff Who Do!"

"Tony, get real! VITO isn't going to let me in the door without giving me a grilling over the phone. What do I say when that happens?"

No kidding. The only way to handle this is to *state your reasons plainly, be honest when you don't know the answer, ask VITO to talk to you about one or more of the three issues outlined earlier, and shut up.* And, strictly speaking, your initial call to VITO is not a success until you have either asked *all three* of these questions and received answers to them or gotten VITO to ask you in for a meeting. (In which case you will ask the three questions and more in person.)

Once again, the objective is for *VITO to do the talking and you to do the listening.* Follow the method as I have outlined it here and you will win meetings with VITOs.

Speak with confidence. Offer success stories when it's appropriate to do so. Discuss the three questions and don't ever forget that VITO's ego, power, and control are more important than yours. Let VITO drive the conversation. When you do that, VITO will want to hear more and will ask you in for a face-to-face meeting.

Words and Phrases to Use or Adapt in a Conversation with VITO

Energized
Superb
Unstoppable
Ecstatic
Excited
Fabulous
Excellent
Vibrant
Captivating
Passionate
Compelling
Perfect
Focused
Extraordinary
Brilliant
Confident
Empowered
Invincible
Driven to . .
Better than . . .
An organization like yours . . .
Discover . . .
Good
Our team . . .
Winners . . .
This month . . .
Next month's results . . .

Next month's reports . . .
Early March . . .
Early next quarter . . .
Fewer employee-hours . . .
Reduced costs in the (blank) department . . .
Plans are underway to . . .
How do you feel about . . . ?
The best part is . . .
They (other customers) surprised themselves with the results they got.
Is this something you're trying to do?
Is this something you've been thinking of?
Have you heard enough at this stage to suggest the next possible
action?

Words and Phrases to Avoid in Your Conversation with VITO

I
I'm with . . .
Fear
Failure
Fearful
Frightened
Disappointed
Impatient
Anxious
Insecure
Irritated
Reject
Stress
Stupid
Overwhelmed
Overloaded
Maybe
Perhaps
Possibly
Would there be an opportunity . . . ?
Is there a possibility . . . ?
We could . . . (Instead, say: Would you like us to . . . ?)
   We think . . . (This may seem safe, but it's much too close to hedging for
VITO. Say what you know and can prove.)

You may be familiar with . . . (If VITO is familiar with whatever you're talking about, this is redundant. If VITO isn't, saying this will only challenge VITO's power, control, and authority.)

If you are interested . . .

(Technical jargon of any kind.)

(Bureaucrat-speak of any kind.)

Profit . . .

Profitable . . .

Are you happy with what you have? (Or any closed-ended question likely to terminate your conversation.)*

Some Additional Hints for Phone Success

So much for the mechanics of the Opening Statement. It will probably come as no surprise to you that the mental preparations you make for the call will have as much of an impact on VITO as any script you assemble. Here are some suggestions on some other ways you can prepare for that all-important first phone contact with VITO.

- *Before you make your call, picture VITO's executive suite.* It's organized. It's calm. It's under control. Picture VITO dressed for success. Picture VITO calm, cool, and collected when calling an important business contact. VITO's office is usually quiet; get a good mental image of that office. You may not have an executive suite, but you *can* position yourself for Equal Business Stature with VITO.

---

* Please permit me a side note here on the issue of questions like "Are you happy with what you have now?" Not only should you not ask VITO this question or anything like it, you should not ask it of anyone at any level in VITO's organization. Sure, you may run into the occasional secretary who will give you an honest answer, but the reality is that most of your contacts, eager to move on to what they were doing before you called, will tell you the firm is ecstatic with what is currently in place, whether that's true or not. Furthermore, I don't believe I have ever encountered a Seymour who, when questioned in this way, would respond that there was a problem with a current vendor. If you stop to think about it, you'll probably conclude that this is your experience as well. Seymour is most likely the person who recommended the product. Therefore, they're not likely to say it's not doing the job.

True story: I once drove my classic 1957 Chevy pickup onto the lot of a truck dealership with the objective of spending money on a new truck. I was greeted by a salesperson who said, "Hey, nice truck. You've really taken care of that one, haven't you?" I thought to myself, "You know what? He's right. I really love this thing." I left the lot without buying. Six months later I drove to another dealership and was greeted by a salesperson whose first words after we exchanged pleasantries were, "Hey, how much do you pay in insurance on that?" I told him. Then he asked, "What's it like trying to track down parts for it?" I told him. Then later I drove a new truck off the lot. I didn't trade the first truck in; the sales rep had suggested I get a trailer hitch on the new vehicle so I could show the old Chevy off at car shows. I took him up on it.

- *Before calling VITO, clear your desk and put everything you need for the conversation at your fingertips.* That means your typed Opening Statement, a copy of the letter you sent to VITO, and a copy of the three questions you will ask during the conversation. You should also have ready access to a typed referral list of your best customer VITOs and their secretaries. Assuming that you have received appropriate permission, you can offer to fax this list to VITO. Having everything visibly ready ahead of time will boost your confidence and help make your delivery more compelling.

- *Mark points in your typed Opening Statement where you will pause briefly to give VITO the chance to interrupt you.* Never forget that this is the goal of your call. Plan to pause after every important point, name, number, or period of time.

- *Highlight important words and phrases in the Opening Statement that deserve special emphasis.* One of these should be VITO's name. Your research should help you to determine other items of interest.

- *Speak slowly, confidently, and authoritatively.* Speak at a rate that's easy for VITO to understand and interrupt.

- *Modulate your voice.* Vary the pitch. Keep your delivery interesting. Nothing turns VITOs off more quickly than a flat or sing-song telemarketing delivery from a salesperson. VITO has no time for amateurs, so don't sound like one.

- *Ask your co-workers to cooperate and minimize background noise.* If you have to, hoist a sign that says "QUIET PLEASE—VITO CALLS IN PROGRESS."

- *If possible, use a headset rather than a standard handheld receiver.* This will allow you to stand up while talking (which I strongly recommend), eliminate pressure on your diaphragm, and help you to relax your voice.

- *I recommend that you stand up,* but if you do sit, don't slouch. Sit up straight, all the way back in your chair.

- *Dress for success,* no matter what else you have planned for the day. Dress as if you were meeting VITO in person.

- *Practice, practice, practice your Opening Statement*—preferably with a friend or colleague *and* by taping it and listening to it. Ask your sales manager to play the part of VITO. When your sales manager is convinced, you're ready.

First and Last Impressions with VITO

We've already examined in great detail how the first eight seconds of every interaction with VITO will either get you another eight or result in a shunt to a lower-level person. How about the last eight seconds? Actually, when you get right down to it, the lasting impression or the last impression you leave VITO with may well be the one that makes it easier or more difficult to get you that next conversation or appointment.

Here are some pointers on how to close your interactions with a VITO:

- *Always add value.* This could be in the form of a new idea, a contact for VITO to exchange ideas with, a joint call between your VITO and another VITO, a recommendation, or an idea that is outside your area of expertise and products.

- *Always say "thank you" in a unique way.* Everyone says that they write thank-you notes, but very few people actually do it. "Doing it" means sending the hand-written note the same day that you had your VITO appointment. If you wait until you buy the card, fill it out, get the postage, and finally send it, VITO will not be impressed. As a matter of fact, VITO might say to him-selves (or for that matter, out loud): "If it took XYZ that long to thank me for a meeting, I wonder how long it takes them to make a delivery or fix a problem with one?"

- *Think about getting your VITO into the act.* Have your own president, owner or CEO send a thank-you note. Of course, you'll make it easy by writing these and getting your VITO to sign them.

- *Give or send a small gift.* This does not have to be expensive, but it must be useful. It can be a pen, paperweight, ruler—whatever! One of our team members, Catherine, suggested that we invest in a $900 machine that makes mouse pads. Now we can take the organization's annual report or other cornerstone document and make a mouse pad out of it, then send it along with my hand-written thank-you note. Do you think the next time I call or stop by to see VITO, he or she will be more available? They sure will. I am living proof of it!

In closing, let me caution you never to send a thank-you note to VITO's Administrative or Personal Assistant. Instead, send it to VITO. That's right—whenever you want to thank someone, send the thank-you to his or her next higher-up. Why? Well, just you imagine it: VITO gets the card, reads it, and then hand carries it to Tommie. Now, that's a real perk!

Chapter 12

The Gatekeepers

WHAT IF YOU CAN'T GET THROUGH TO VITO ON THE PHONE?

People whose job it is to keep salespeople from reaching decision makers have been the cause of a good deal of aggravation and rejection for salespeople over the years. As it happens, though, you can use a few very simple techniques to avoid most of that aggravation. Once you review the ideas in this chapter, my bet is that you'll wonder why you spent so much time in pointless phone battles with gatekeepers.

The secret of success in this area is to remember that no encounter with a gatekeeper has to turn into a conflict. In fact, when you use the tactics in this chapter and have the right attitude, you will be able to recruit one or more gatekeepers in VITO's organization as your allies!

The Two Types of Gatekeepers

For our purposes, there are two main types of gatekeepers. The first is the receptionist or other front-line person with the job of handling not just calls for VITO, but *all* calls to VITO's organization. The second is VITO's own personal secretary or assistant. Do not confuse these two types! If you have any doubts as to the identity of VITO's personal secretary or assistant, please stop reading now and return to Chapter 5 of this book. You will find there a technique whereby you can verify the identity of this important member of VITO's organization.

Confusing VITO's personal secretary with a "standard" gatekeeper is a tactical mistake you must avoid *at all costs*. Vastly different approaches are in order for each!

Connecting with the Executive Suite: "Standard" Gatekeepers

"Widget Company, how may I help you?"

Let's look first at the best ways to deal with "standard" gatekeepers: receptionists, temporary help, and other people who must deal with the switchboard at VITO's organization and field all those incoming calls from who knows how many sources.

You may be tempted to talk down to these people, but it's a big mistake to do so. Consider the following two important points.

- *Keeping track of the company's phone traffic is hard work.* If you don't think so, volunteer for switchboard duty for three or four hours at your own company. There's little time to think when things get hectic (which may be all day long). And when angry customers, salespeople like yourself, or other potentially hostile outsiders need someone to vent at, who do you think spends the most time standing in front of the fire hose? Not VITO. Not the Manager. Not Seymour. No—it's usually the first person to talk to that outsider: the switchboard operator or receptionist. All too often, the only feedback the receptionist or switchboard operator gets—even at today's supposedly "customer-sensitive" organizations—is negative. ("Why on earth didn't you tell me it was Mr. *Charles* Weenieburger? How am I supposed to know that I really should call him back if you just write "Mr. Weenieburger?") The sad fact is, receptionists are rarely if ever thanked by the companies they work for. For too many, the only time they hear the words "well done" is when someone tells them to order out for hamburgers.
- *Time is short.* Even if you were somehow able to track down a receptionist who *wanted* to engage in verbal sparring for the sole purpose of making your day go a little bit worse—which is highly unlikely—there'd be a dozen or more calls behind you blinking insistently. Receptionists really aren't out to get you—they're too busy.

All of this is by way of saying that there is simply no advantage in antagonizing switchboard and front desk people. So play it cool—don't tee off on the receptionist. Setting up grudge matches won't make your next call go any better, and it *certainly* won't win you any friends in VITO's organization. (Besides, VITO's secretary or assistant may occasionally sit in for the receptionist, so why take chances?)

Here, then, are the dos, the don'ts, and the what-ifs regarding making it past receptionists as you forge the telephone path to VITO's office. Your goal with these people is to avoid being grilled, screened, rejected, or disconnected.

You're going to reach that goal by being purposeful, self-aware, and *polite* throughout the exchange. And remember, every step along the way to VITO's office can and should be a rapport-building step.

Never Ask for VITO Directly

You went to all the trouble to find out the name of VITO's secretary to put together your letter. Now, you'll use that knowledge in your call.

If you ask for VITO directly, you may be subjected to a barrage of questions designed to keep you from reaching your intended destination. "Who is calling?" "What is this regarding?" "Is this a sales call?" "Oh, VITO doesn't handle that; you want to talk to . . . " You've heard them all before. Nine times out of ten, receptionists are under orders to ask questions like this when someone asks for VITO. If you've been making calls for more than a day or two, you're already quite familiar with the typical outcome of answering these queries and need no further instruction from me on the wisdom of avoiding them.

Instead of trying to get the receptionist to put you through to VITO, you will aim to be put through to VITO's secretary or personal assistant. You will specify this person's name. You will not volunteer your name.

Don't *ask* to be connected. Politely but firmly *tell* the person at the switchboard what needs to happen. Say, "Please connect me with Tommie in Mr. Benefito's office. Thank you." Do so with confidence and a strong sense of purpose. Note that I end my request with the words "thank you." There's a reason for this and it goes beyond an attempt at being courteous. I've conducted interviews with over 12,000 gatekeeper-receptionists, and do you know what they hate the most about us? You know it—we tend to lie. Or I should say we stretch the truth, pretending that we know someone when we don't, saying that we're returning someone's call when we're not. You know the usual stuff. But I also found out something that was a surprise to me. Ninety-seven percent of the individuals I interviewed were not "professional" career gatekeepers! That's right—they couldn't get the position they really wanted so, they were cooling their jets at the front desk until the marketing job or tech writer position became available. In other words, they were not receptionists by choice. They were receptionists by necessity. Anyone who is in a position of necessity will respond to an implied request much faster than someone who's in that same position by choice. That's why I use the words "thank you." It implies that they will take action. It completes the request in such a way that compliance is almost always assured. That's not the same as being overbearing. The point bears repeating: *Do not speak in an arrogant tone of voice, as though you were about to argue with Tommie about something.* If you do, you may not be put through. Speak simply and to the point. Speak as someone who knows what is to take place next. Here it is again: "Please connect me with Tommie in Mr. Benefito's office. Thank you."

Following this simple approach *exactly as I have described it* will resolve most of the problems you are probably used to encountering with receptionists and switchboard operators. Still, there are likely to be some times when your telephone partner tries to screen your call despite your best efforts to get through to Tommie. The following techniques may help you in these situations.

When Pressed, Do Not Get Flustered

If you are asked to identify yourself, or if you know that in your part of the country it is expected that you identify yourself, *calmly and confidently* say, "This is Will Prosper with XYZ. Mr. Benefito is expecting my call at 8:30 [just as your Action P.S. stated], and I'm running just a few minutes behind schedule. Please connect me." (Alternatively, you might say, "It's critical that I be on time. Please connect me.")

Never refer to your "letter." If you must say something about the reason VITO is expecting your call, read on. We'll be covering this in just a few paragraphs.

Don't Lie!

Never make it appear that you and VITO know each other. Not only is this unprofessional and not in keeping with your image as a straight-shooting provider of real-life solutions, it is extremely dangerous. You have no idea how large VITO's staff is or who talks to whom about what. And as I mentioned before, it's quite possible that VITO's assistant is *sitting in* for the receptionist. Talk about a credibility problem!

Don't cut corners. Tell the truth.

If You Are Still Facing Questions from the Receptionist . . .

If you follow the steps I have outlined, you will be assured of success in reaching VITO's office in the vast majority of your first calls. In the unlikely event you are *still* locked in the grip of a power-hungry receptionist, resist the temptation to turn the exchange into a conflict.

Your goal is to avoid being rejected or shunted to a lower level. You need to convince the receptionist that you have a valid business mission that's in the company's best interests.

Use a global hook that relates to the headline in your benefit letter to VITO. You want to give enough information for the receptionist to glean that the call is important, but not enough for him or her to be able to determine how the call should be handled. In short, you want to convince the receptionist that the person best suited to handle this call is VITO or VITO's secretary or assistant.

An example of this follows. Obviously, you will have to customize the part in parentheses to your business.

> Receptionist: "What is this call in regard to?"
>
> You: "It's about giving Mr. Benefito the opportunity that my company's other customers have had to (make revenue-generating employees as efficient as they can be)."

IMPORTANT NOTE: This is in fact the "Hook" portion of your Opening Statement that you are going to say to VITO.

Don't identify your product or service. (If you do, you'll be shunted to a lower level within seconds.) *Don't* use technical jargon in an attempt to confuse or intimidate the person on the other end of the line. You must without fail, however, use unmistakable VITO language that the receptionist will recognize as such. All the receptionist needs to shunt you over to Seymour is one syllable of feature- or function-speak! So don't talk like a Seymour. Talk like a VITO.

Now, let's say that in response to this last attempt, the receptionist says something like the following:

> Receptionist: "Hey—are you trying to sell VITO a fax machine?" (Or, "Are you selling long-distance service?" Or, "Is this about office equipment?")

At this point, you've been stereotyped. The receptionist has mistaken you for the high-pressure, low-follow-through salesperson you've worked so hard not to be. Rather than explain the intricacies of the business partnership you're trying to establish, respond with something along these lines:

> You: "Let's get realistic. If all I wanted to do was get somebody to (buy a fax machine), I wouldn't need to talk to Mr. Benefito, would I?"

In point of fact, you are trying to do much more than simply sell VITO (a fax machine). You want to work with VITO as a partner.

If the receptionist challenges you further, you have one last recourse for trying to get through during this call. Calmly and confidently say:

> "Would you knowingly stand in the way of Ms.
> Benefito's realizing the benefit that I just
> mentioned?"

OR:

> "Would you knowingly stand in the way of Widget
> Company's (gaining more market share)?"

OR:

> "Would you knowingly stand in the way of Ms.
> Benefito's (creating greater loyalty with existing
> customers)?

"Why Don't You Just Send Us Some Information?"

Whenever I hear this—and, thanks to the techniques I've just outlined, that's not very often—I say, "Certainly. I have a completely comprehensive and interactive package of information. If you stand it on its end, it's six feet one inch high, and it weighs 162 pounds. We call it Tony. When do you want me there?"

This line always gets a laugh. Use it if you're facing a real dead end. It may well get you past the gate and/or get you an in-person appointment.

"Can I Take a Message?"

> "Sorry, VITO's not in. Can I take a message?"

Some of your calls may reach this seeming dead-end—usually while you're talking to the receptionist, but possibly at other times as well. What do you do?

Say this: "Why, yes, thanks for asking! It's rather long, and it may take a few minutes. Have you got a big pad of paper handy? Or—you know what—I could save us both some time and get this important message out to VITO. What's VITO's fax number?"

You will get the fax number. In the extremely unlikely event that the person wants to take your verbal message, give your entire Opening Statement, including the ending question. Include specific times and days you'll be in the office for VITO's call. Then be there!

But let's be realistic. You can expect to obtain VITO's fax number in a flash by using this technique. With that number in hand, you will be ready to move on to the Fax Recovery. But before we look at that, let's talk for a moment about dealing with that other kind of gatekeeper: VITO's secretary or assistant.

Connecting with the Executive Suite: VITO's Secretary or Assistant

Many of the salespeople I work with are under the impression that dealing with this gatekeeper is significantly more complex and difficult than dealing with the front-line receptionist. Fortunately, they couldn't be more wrong.

Dealing with VITO's secretary or assistant is simplicity itself once you realize that this is the second most powerful person in the organization. Act on that assumption, and you'll be well on your way to building a business relationship that you can count on. Throw out the organization charts. Forget about the titles. This person knows as much about the goals, obstacles, and predispositions of this organization as anyone else. This person generally knows about changes in strategy and important business decisions *before* anyone other than VITO. This person is probably responsible, in large measure, for keeping VITO's little world from blowing up every day! This is a person you want—and must treat—as a powerful ally.

If you treat VITO's assistant as a minor functionary, someone incapable of comprehending the high-level message you have crafted for VITO, the doors will slam shut and, most likely, never open again. Treat VITO's assistant *as though he or she is speaking and acting for VITO* (which is, by the way, often quite literally the case), and the doors will swing open.

Give the Exact Same Opening Statement You Would Give to VITO

As you may already know, VITOs are never officially "in"—or at least that's how it seems.

When you've cleared the receptionist and VITO's secretary picks up the phone, I want you to picture this: VITO is dressed up in an official NASA-issue spacesuit. In fact, VITO has just blasted off the face of this earth and is now orbiting in the space shuttle! VITO's "out"—way, way out. So when you're talking to VITO's secretary, don't worry about VITO anymore.

Give the secretary or assistant the exact same opening statement you would give to VITO.

That's right. When you reach VITO's personal secretary or assistant, I want you to work through the Opening Statement in the exact same way you would if VITO were on the line. Pause for objections. Listen. Take notes. All of that. In other words, you are going to *talk to and treat this person as a VITO,* and you're going to mean it. Now, let me warn you: You can't do this if you have the slightest doubt about your ability to deal with the secretary or personal assistant as a business equal.

"Exactly like VITO?" Yes, exactly like VITO. The only adjustment you're going to make has to do with the beginning of your opening statement, your ending question, and the big three questions that follow. In these cases you will simply ask Tommie to speak for VITO.

That's it. That's the technique for turning around these supposedly fierce gatekeepers. And I'll tell you something: It works like gangbusters. All day long, secretaries of top decision makers across the country are forced to deal with people who don't acknowledge the pivotal role they play in attaining company goals. Your tactic is to *not be like those people.* Your tactic is to *assume that your contact can speak for VITO.* Nine times out of ten, you'll be right in that assumption, and the secretary will either forward your call to VITO or tell you when to call back for a telephone meeting.

In the overwhelming majority of cases—if you only remember not to patronize this person, to act with the same respect and deference you would accord VITO, to listen, listen, listen to what is being said—you will be successful.

Words to the wise: Once the business relationship is established, *always* keep the secretary involved in your efforts. You are not "using" anyone to "get to" anyone else; you are establishing a critical business alliance that should endure for as long as you have a business relationship with the organization.

Here's a story that will underscore the importance of treating VITO's secretary or assistant exactly like VITO. I was calling a VITO in New York City by the name of Joe Arthur; his secretary's name is Candy Overmeyer. I called at the appointed time; as it happened, Joe couldn't take my call because he was orbiting the earth in the space shuttle at the time. So when Candy answered the phone, I laid my Opening Statement on her. Candy said, "Did you send Joe a letter?"

I said, "Yes, I did. What did you think of it?" (*Not* "What did Joe think of it?") Then something magical happened. Candy said, "Well, Joe thought it was interesting that you focus on one thing, teaching people how to prospect for new business." And she proceeded to give me a blow-by-blow description of Joe's reaction to the letter.

I said, "Candy, is teaching your people to prospect for new business important to you?" Candy said, "Joe is concerned. We're coming out with a new product—and our people tend to go back to the same old accounts and neglect their prospecting work."

We went through the entire conversation this way. Finally, I asked, "Candy, what do you think we should do next?" Candy said, "Knowing Joe, I'll bet he's going to want to see an outline of your course." I said, "Candy, how many outlines would you like to see?" Candy answered, "Send back six—one for Joe and one for each of the five staff managers."

I sent Candy six outlines. Two weeks later I called her again and said, "Candy, this is Tony Parinello. What did you think of my outline?" Candy said, "Joe circled several things in your outline." And we went into an extended review of what Joe did and didn't like about my outline. After about ten minutes, I asked, "Candy, what do you think we should do next?" Candy said, "Knowing Joe, I think he'd want to have a few staff people sit in on one of your programs."

"Candy, that's going to be very difficult," I said, "because the programs I give are private corporate sessions. My customers don't like outsiders sitting in. But perhaps if you and Joe are getting together with the rest of the staff people, I could come in to give you a private two-hour presentation." I heard pages turning on Candy's desk calendar. Then I heard Candy say, "On June 14th, Joe will be having a meeting with all the vice presidents. Let me call you back." An hour later she called back and said, "Tony, you're on from ten to noon."

I never *once* asked Candy what Joe had to say about anything. I asked Candy what *Candy* had to say. And I got the appointment.

At the presentation, Joe himself, who at this point had never spoken to me, introduced me as follows: "Here's a guy whose expertise is prospecting for new business. He must be good, because he managed to book two hours of our time, and I've never even talked to him!" It went great. Twenty minutes into the presentation, Joe stopped me and said, "Tony, we'll take it." On the way out, after Joe had signed the contract, I stopped at Candy's desk, thanked her profusely, and promised to keep her informed at every step of the relationship. It was a promise I kept.

A few years later, I got a call from Candy. She told me she wanted me to know that Joe was leaving the company for another opportunity. Actually, as it turned out, it wasn't just Joe who was pursuing another opportunity. Joe was taking Candy with him. And you know who else he took with him? Me.

The Fax Recovery

The Fax Recovery is the technique to use if people tell you that VITO is in a meeting, out of town, on the way to a meeting, on the way to go out of town, or behind closed doors. (By the way, wouldn't you love to be able to sit in on one of these marathon, fate-of-the-Republic-hangs-in-the-balance meetings that always seem to happen just when you call? What do you suppose they're really talking about? Similarly, wouldn't you love to take a look inside that space shuttle they must always strap VITO into when you find out that VITO "just took off for the day" and thus can't take your call?)

There are two options to pursue in the event that VITO's gatekeepers or anyone else in the organization prevents you from getting through to VITO at the time you specify in your letter. In both cases, you must leave a message for VITO; both approaches involve use of the organization's fax number, which you will obtain using the approach I outlined earlier on page 121.

Option One: Send a Memo

But not just any memo! Did you ever see those little pink slips that fly around the office, the ones with "WHILE YOU WERE OUT" written across the top? You're going to take one of those, put it on the photocopier, and blow it up until it looks like it has a gland problem. It should occupy a full letter-size sheet of paper.

Put your neatly hand-written Opening Statement in the message area below the "WHILE YOU WERE OUT" banner. Include all the appropriate contact data in the spaces on the form, including your phone number. Fax it to VITO. Specify dates and times you'll be in the office for VITO's call. Be sitting by the phone at those times.

This is your cover sheet—don't dilute the effect by attaching a standard cover sheet to this form.

When VITO steps off the space shuttle, passes through all the debriefings and the medical checks, and makes it back to the desk, there will be three piles on that desk. One will be incoming mail. Another will be incoming messages. And a third will be incoming faxes. Take a wild guess as to which one VITO's going to look at first. Right. The faxes. When VITO sees that big "WHILE YOU WERE OUT" slip that looks like it's on steroids, you will have earned a "Wow!" You will have earned Equal Business Stature.

Date _____   Time _____

WHILE YOU WERE OUT

M _____

of _____

Phone _____

       Area Code   Number   Extension

TELEPHONED		PLEASE CALL	
CALLED FOR YOUR OPINION		WILL CALL AGAIN	
WANTS TO SEE YOU		PLEASE RETURN FAX	

Message _____

_____

_____

_____

_____

_____

_____

_____

_____

Option Two: Send the Letter

Fax an exact copy of your letter to VITO with the "While You Were Out" message as the cover sheet. Cross out the Action P.S. and write in the margin, "Sorry I missed you." (This is the reason you must leave lots of open space in your letter to VITO.) Fax this. Then specify dates and times you'll be in the office for VITO's call. Be sitting by the phone at those times.

Ask VITO and You Shall Receive

Whenever you ask, you will receive something. You may not get what you ask for, but you *will* get something!

I do believe that the more you ask, the more you receive and thus the more you sell. But what do you ask of whom? An effective, proactive salesperson might revise the famous quote from the greatest of all best-selling books to something like this: "Ask in the appropriate way, and at the appropriate time, and thou shalt receive what thou art after." Here's a short list of topics you should make a habit of asking about. If you keep on "checking in" in these key areas, the odds will increase that you'll eventually reach a position where you can ask the appropriate question at the appropriate time—and win what you're after:

- Ask VITO about his or her opinions and impressions. "What are your thoughts so far?" "Does this look like an idea that would work for you?" "Do you see/hear/feel anything that indicates this solution is not a good fit for you?"
- Ask VITO about his or her ideas for improvement. "What areas would you improve upon?" "If you were directing an improvement program for this solution what would you suggest?" "If budget were of no concern, what would you add to this solution?"
- Ask VITO about other members of his or her team. "Who is the person you trust the most to look into the details of this idea?" "If you could pick one member on your team to put this idea into action, who would it be?"
- Ask VITO for a referral. (You would ask this question only, and I really mean only, after your solution had delivered results to VITO.) "VITO, do you know anyone here in Hoboken, New Jersey (i.e., VITO's geographic area), in the insurance industry (i.e., VITO's industry) that you would like to introduce me to so that I might be able to help in a similar or even greater way?"

How's It Look?

If you execute all of the ideas in this chapter and find that you are still having difficulty getting through to and scheduling appointments with the VITOs you target, there is probably something wrong with either your delivery or the product or service you are offering. If it's the former, please review the steps for telephone success at the end of Chapter 11. You may find that you must revamp the way you are emphasizing benefits to VITO. (By the way, it's healthy to keep switching the benefits you highlight for the new VITOs you encounter. It keeps you from falling into a rut.)

Electronic Gatekeepers

Now, we'll find out how to use what we've learned so far to tackle VITO's voice mail system! The days of leaving just your name and telephone number are long gone. What you're about to learn is based upon my own research, which by the way has taken me ten years to complete!

Chapter 13

Voice Mail Messages to VITO

OKAY, YOU'VE MADE IT PAST THE GATEKEEPERS, AND NOW YOU'VE BEEN forwarded to VITO's phone line—but instead of getting VITO, you get connected to voice mail. Is this a stumbling block? Not at all! You've just been handed another golden opportunity.

Voice mail is beyond any shadow of doubt the most powerful sales tool available today. Second only to an in-person visit with VITO, voice mail will give you the chance to move your sale one step forward, qualify VITO's interest, underscore the value that you and your organization have to offer to VITO's and organization, and make your very best first impression. Let's look at that last point first. Every salesperson knows and understands the importance of "making a good first impression," yet how many of us leave voice mail messages that sound like a testimonial for Sominex?

More often than not, your voice mail message will serve as the first impression VITO is going to have of you. You should therefore treat it with great importance. Remember that you're on a job interview! And VITO is doing the "hiring." Sure, this is a tall order for a voice mail message, but it's been my personal experience that using voice mail properly can be an extraordinarily effective replacement for your personal presence in VITO's office.

The Competition Is Stiff

Picture, if you will, a day in the life of a Very Important Top Officer. On this day, VITO will be faced with over 128 unscheduled activities that include but are by no means limited to: emergency meetings, telephone calls, last-minute presentations, planning sessions, reading reports and other documents, interruptions, message slips, post-it notes, e-mail, and, yes, listening and responding to a barrage of voice mail messages—which, by the way, will include one from you. What guarantee will you have that VITO will take time out of this hectic, harried day to pay attention to you and your message? Only this:

What you have to say will demonstrate that you have Equal Business Stature—that you have one idea that will assist VITOs in the overachievement of one or more of their strategic goals—that you and your organization know how to deliver a solution that is rich in value—and that you are different from any other salesperson. Above all, you will do all of this using "VITO-speak," a language that only VITO understands.

To put it in a nutshell: This message will stop VITOs in their tracks and make them think to themselves or say out loud, "This person and his [or her] ideas are different. I want to know more."

Elements of Your Voice Mail Messages

Like all of the tactics we have discussed in previous chapters, your voice mail messages will follow a certain pattern. This pattern will take into consideration VITO's personality traits, the results he or she looks for, favorite agenda items, and all of the critical insights we've discussed in Chapter 4. Perhaps most importantly, your voice mail communications will trigger VITO's curiosity and quest for new ideas.

Your messages must be delivered with certainty, enthusiasm, and passion, because the simple fact is: *a voice mail system is an unforgiving thing.* If you sputter or repeat yourself, or trail off into silence, there's usually no way to call back or re-record the message. Sure, some of the more sophisticated systems will allow a second or even a third recording, but you can't leave something like this to chance. This is your first impression, and it could make or break your sales success. You only have to be burned once to know that voice mail is not a communications method designed for the salesperson who wants to wing it.

Speaking of "winging it," have you ever flown a glider or even flown in a glider? If not, then imagine this: When you're coming in for a landing, you only have one shot to do it right. It's not at all like a small prop-driven plane; you can't add power, pull back up, and take another approach. In a glider, if you don't line up properly with the runway on your "final" approach, then you're in very, very big trouble. With this image in mind, I'd like for you to consider that VITO's voice mail is like landing a glider: You've only got one shot at it and it had better be right on!

I have a wireless headset on my telephone. This allows total freedom of movement for both my arms and my feet, so I can be animated. When I get ready to leave a voice mail message for VITO, I stand up (this gets the pressure off my diaphragm and gives me a deeper, more authoritative tone of voice), then I visualize myself in the cockpit of a glider. Actually, I picture myself landing a glider—perfectly. Putting a positive image in your mind before you get ready to do something that's critically important will give you the edge you need to put you squarely in the VITO zone or on the runway!

Let's Create a Script

That's right. In order for your voice mail message hit the bull's eye, it must be well thought out. It must, in fact, be scripted. By the way, it's important to note at this point that we're going to create several voice mail messages, because VITO may not get right back to you after your first one. You'll be waiting three full days between your messages. (Please make note of this time period, as it's one of those little details that are so often responsible for a measurable, memorable outcome.) No response from VITO in three business days? Then you'll leave your next message, and you'll keep following this pattern until VITO calls you back.

How many messages will you leave all together? One every three business days until the end of time—or until VITO or someone on VITO's trusted staff returns your call. I have fifteen scripted voice mail messages at the ready. I keep very accurate notes on my computerized prospect management system as to what number message I last left. (By the way, you don't need to have a computer to keep track of anything—3 X 5 index cards work just as well. All you need is a little organization.)

It would be a career-limiting mistake to leave the same message twice or to stop leaving messages before VITO returns your call. When I first started to tap into the power of voice mail, an interesting situation took place. I had just left my fifth voice mail message for the president of a large computer company. Shortly after hanging up and taking off my headset, my phone rang. A voice on the other end of the wire said: "You've been leaving the president of my company voice mail messages. He's been putting a note at the end of them and forwarding the messages to me."

Not knowing who this was on the phone, I needed to ask a question that would reveal the company's identity. "Oh," I said, "That's interesting. What was the note he put at the end of the last one?" His reply led me directly to the sale: "He wants me to find out what it's going to take to have all of our salespeople here at DH leaving voice mail messages like the ones you've been leaving him." It was the Executive Vice President of WorldWide Sales for DH returning the call for VITO. Score one for a totally effective series of voice mail messages!

Your First Voice Mail Message

Let's revisit your Opening Statement for a moment. You'll recall that it started with VITO's name, was followed by a Pleasantry, continued into the Hook (a thin slice and verbal rendition of the Headline in your VITO letter), then your name and, if you so chose, your company name, and, finally, an Ending Question (one which should always include the element of time). Now, imagine that instead of VITO or Tommie answering the phone, you get plugged directly into VITO's voice mail, or Tommie answers but suggests that you leave a message in VITO's voice mailbox. Remember, you're standing at the ready. It's your big moment and you must land the glider—perfectly! So you could probably leave this type of message:

"Mr. Benefito, if you were in your office to take my call this is what you would have heard me say." And now you launch into the balance of your Opening Statement. That's right—the Pleasantry. For example, if you were going to use my favorite, "It's an honor to speak with you," you would make a small change and say "it's an honor to be leaving you this voice mail message today." Then you put out the Hook, followed by your name and company name, and finally, you leave the Ending Question. When you put it all together it might sound something like this: Please note, that in all of the Voice Mail messages that follow brackets [ ] are used to indicate where you must tailor your message to your target VITO.

"Mr. Benefito, this is Will Prosper. It's an honor to be leaving you this voice mail message. [Apex Corporation has created over $150 million dollars] of repeatable revenue while at the same time [lowering expenses.] By the way, they also have [less customer churn, less of a need to buy back the same market share time and time again.] All of this is a direct result of our proven ideas and business solutions. And what's perhaps more exciting, they didn't have to invest in [any technology], Mr. Benefito, we're doing that for them, too.

"At this point, our partnership with [Apex] is unstoppable. As a matter of fact, we are joining hands in developing a solution that is going to make their[customers' loyalty even greater.] What does all this have to do with you and your company? Everything and nothing. Everything because it's probably obvious that you would love even greater results and perhaps nothing because at this point it's too early to tell if we could make any contributions to your goals, plans, and objectives for this year.

"Mr. Benefito, you probably ask each of the associates on your staff to make one more call each and every day. Make your last call of the day to me. I guarantee that it will be the most surprising call of the day. And speaking of guarantees, if our team cannot provide similar or even greater results, we won't ask for the privilege of your business partnership. I'll be in my office accepting calls between [3:00 and 5:00 p.m. on Tuesday and Thursday] this week and I will be anxiously awaiting yours. Thanks for listening to my long voice mail message. Once again, it's Will. Will Prosper. My telephone number is 760-765-1321. Have a terrific day!"

"Tony," I hear you saying, "have you gone off the deep end? This is much too long. I thought VITOs were brief, direct, and to the point. What happened to our eight-second rule? Isn't this going to turn VITO off?" Well, sure, this voice mail message is longer than eight seconds, but you'll recall that each and every eight seconds must earn you the next eight, and so on. Furthermore, every eight seconds must be chock full of information that VITOs live for. When you couple this information with a delivery that is enthusiastic and passionate, you'll hit a bull's eye!

In addition, you must—I repeat, *must*—leave specific day(s) and time(s) that VITO can return your call. Do not under any circumstances leave out this important tactical element. I can just see your eyes rising. "Wait a minute, Tony! Do you mean to tell me that I have to schedule my 'office time' and structure my week around my voice mail messages to VITO?" Yep. You sure do—if, that is, you want to create and maintain Equal Business Stature. This means that you must treat your time with the same level of importance that VITO treats his or her time. And you must create a level of immediacy with the topics of your messages.

Voice Mail Message Number Two

Recall for a moment the Benefit Bullets that comprised the body of your VITO letter (see Chapter 10) and the individual elements of your Value Inventories (Chapter 9). Now imagine taking this critical value-based information and feeding it to VITO in a sort of "story-line." This will become the first in a series of voice mail messages that will eventually pique VITO's interest and prompt VITO into action. This is also what should eventually get you a call back. If it doesn't, you'll follow the three-day rule before placing your next call and the next and the next, until you do get a response.

In your second message to VITO, you'll add information and value to your first message. This will take the form of other areas in which your solution has a track record—that is, the information that you've extracted from your VITO letters and Value Inventories. However, be careful not to go overboard! You must "spoon-feed" your benefits one or two at a time on each successive call. Remember, we're building a series of messages, so you must not pile on too much information at once, nor must you ever repeat what you said previously. You will, however, create a "tag" to your prior message by using words and phrases that are associated with it. Here's an example of what your second voice mail message might sound like:

"Mr. Benefito, since the last voice mail message you listened to, not only has [Apex Corporation] created an annuity stream, but they also [shortened their time to market] while [reducing the cost of goods sold.]

"Mr. Benefito, are you happy with your [time to market,] or are you of the opinion that there's room for improvement between now and [the end of this

year]? Do you have all the [new business revenue] you want and deserve? Do you have all the fresh ideas that will help you overachieve your strategic goals? With just [six short months left in this fiscal year], do you think there is enough time left for any changes and the improvement that change can bring? If any of these initiatives are of interest to you, why don't you make your last business call of this day to me. I'll be prepared to answer any questions you may have about our ideas and solutions and how we might be able to put them both to work for you.

"I'll be in my office between [3:00 and 6:00 P.M. today] if you would like to return my call. Oh, I almost forgot, this is Will, Will Prosper with the ABC Corporation, the company that's totally dedicated to its business partners' greater success. My number is 760-765-1321. Thanks for listening to this long voice mail message. Good-bye!"

Still No Return Call?

Here's what needs to happen in your third voice mail message. Let's assume that VITO's voice mail system is functioning properly and they have received and listened to your first two messages. Now you have to prompt a little interaction.

In your third voice mail message, you'll review the major areas covered by your ideas and solutions, and then you'll synchronize this message with a fax that VITO or someone on VITO's trusted staff will be asked to handle. Your third message could sound something like this:

"Mr. Benefito, this is Will Prosper once again. There are [four strategic goals] that we consistently help our business partners to overachieve. The first is [creating new business revenue at a lower cost]. The second is [increasing efficiencies of mission-critical processes without any compromise to quality.] The third is [enhancing already high corporate images without having to launch expensive public relations programs] and the fourth is [assisting in the protection of existing market share.] Our business partners never [lose customers] unless they deserve to. Mr. Benefito, which of these four initiatives are most important to you and your team during the next [sixty days]?

"You can answer this question one of three ways. You can return my call. Or you can forward this voice mail message to the person you trust the most on your staff to over-accomplish the strategic initiatives I've mentioned. Or you can respond to the fax I just sent you. That fax contains an overview of our ideas and how they might apply to you and your company. I've included a short questionnaire on the bottom of the fax.

"Mr. Benefito, we are seriously dedicated to understanding how we could be of any assistance to you and your team. So the question becomes, do you feel we can make a contribution?

"You can call me, Will Prosper, right here at the [ABC Corporation,] between [3:00 and 6:00 P.M. today or Friday of this week.] In the mean-time, I'll keep an eye on our fax machine for your response. Thanks for lis-tening to this long voice mail message. The number is 760-765-1321. Have a terrific day!"

Am I pushing the envelope? Yes. Does this sound different? Yes. Can VITO take it? Yes. Does it work? Yes!

Still No Response?

Believe me, at this point VITO or someone on VITO's trusted staff is taking note! If you do not receive a fax or a call back, you will not give in or abort your efforts. Instead, you will intensify your campaign and launch one of two specific tactics. The first is one that I choose to call my "interactive voice mail message." In order to use this tactic, you must be geographically close to VITO's office.

Tactic Number One: The Interactive Voice Mail Message

"Mr. Benefito, this is Will Prosper once again. I am sure you recognize my voice by now. The fact that you haven't returned any of my calls I take as a good sign. Because if you didn't like what you've been listening to on your voice mail, you would have someone call me back and tell me to get lost! But you haven't done that. And because you haven't, I'll continue in my quest to add value to the overachievement of your strategic initiatives and at the same time take a positive step in reaching you. [Tomorrow at 3:00 P.M.,] I'll take the time to travel to your lobby and meet with you for [ten short minutes.] If [tomorrow is not a good time, or if 3:00] is inconvenient, please ask [Tommie] to call me by noon. I have no other appointments in your neighborhood tomorrow, so please, if for some reason you cannot have a brief chat with me, call by noon! I really look forward to meeting you at last and finding out if we can help you overachieve your revenue and cost-cutting goals before the end of this year. You can reach me, Will Prosper, right here at the ABC Corporation at 760-765-1321 and if tomorrow at [3:00] is not a good time, please call before [noon.] See you at [3:00 P.M.]! Have a fantastic rest of the day!"

"Tony, are you nuts?" Maybe so, but I am certainly not stupid. I know this works because I use it myself! At a bare minimum, this type of message will prompt action, and that's exactly what we want: *action*. But not just any action. We want "VITO" action—even if VITO calls just to ask who your pharmacist is!

On a more serious note: you must make sure that each and every message you leave is well planned, scripted, and delivered near perfectly. And if you do not hear from VITO by noon, you are by all means obligated to show up for the appointment! The very last time I used this tactic, I noticed two people sitting in the lobby as I entered VITO's building. I approached the receptionist and said: "Good afternoon, my name is Tony, Tony Parinello. I believe I have an appointment with your President, Ms. Importanta." The receptionist's reply took me by surprise: "She's sitting right over there with our Vice President of Sales, waiting for you." I just love it when everything works the way it's supposed to, don't you?

Now, that's the first tactic for your fourth voice mail message. If you can't take the interactive approach, however, what do you do then? With this tactic, we're going to switch our psychological gears. So far, all of our voice mail messages have offered a gain or an opportunity for significant improvement. This would appeal to VITOs who are motivated, who are in search of a positive result, and who want to see an improvement over current circumstances. In essence, they are moving towards a reward, a pleasure, and/or greater career and personal satisfaction. It would be shortsighted for us to think that all VITOs are motivated in this fashion (although I, for one, believe that most VITOs fall into this category). The fact of the matter is that like you and me and every other human being on this planet, VITOs can also be motivated by fear, concern over loss, or the experience of pain. It is also true that we can shift the reasons for our motivation on short notice. This is especially so in VITO's world, which is controlled by many different factors, the least of which is the competition, the economy, ill-performing sales teams, and the like. Therefore, in this message we shall position ourselves to reveal what VITO may be losing as a result of not taking action. This tactic taps into the simple fact that VITOs hate to lose . . . anything!

Your message might sound something like this:

Tactic Number Two: The Reverse Psychological Tack

"Mr. Benefito, this is Will Prosper [at the ABC Corporation.] You probably recognize my voice by now. We're stalled, and what concerns us the most about this is that while we wait, [fifteen] other companies the [same size as yours] in the same industry you're in are enjoying a total of [$95,000 of increased new business each and every day while they save a total of $42,000 every day.] Why should this bother me? No, I am not a shareholder in your company. It's because with every day that goes by that we do not take steps

to understand what we can do to assist you, the possibility exists that you are actually unintentionally wasting precious [revenue dollars]. To compound that causality, you may be spending [more time and money] than you have to in [five of your manufacturing operations]. There is really no need for this to continue! The number could not only be substantial, but it continues to add up even as you listen to this message.

"Mr. Benefito, every time I drive past your office, I am tempted to stop by and try to find a way to gain an audience with you. But for now, may I suggest that you ask the person you hold most responsible for your [manufacturing operations] the following questions. [How many engineering change orders require rework of finished goods? Has that number increased in the past year? And if so, what impact has it had on your cost of goods sold, reliability, and delivery commitments to your customers?] I've taken the liberty of faxing these questions to you. Just forward this message and the fax to the most responsible person on your team. I'll anxiously await the response.

"The name is Will Prosper. The company is the [ABC Corporation], and I'll be in my office between [3:00 and 6:00 P.M.] today looking forward to answering your return call or reading your return fax. My number is 760-765-1321 and the fax is 760-765-1326. Have a fantastic rest of the day!"

By now you know that I am very determined and serious about making sure that VITO understands my commitment to VITO, Inc.'s overall success. *You* must also be that determined. Your determination will be illustrated by your professional persistence and by putting all of your creative efforts to work.

The Voice Mail Message That Always Gets a Return Call

When all else fails, and my messages seem to be going into some voice mail void, I'll energize all the gifts that my maker has given me and resort to a bit of well-placed business humor. Here is my most powerful of all voice mail messages—the one that puts everything that came before it into perspective. Whenever VITO seems to be totally ignoring my messages, I'll put on my headset, stand up, take a deep, deep breath, picture myself landing my little glider, dial VITO's voice mail number, and say:

"VITO, every night before I go to bed, I talk to God. Why can't I talk to you?"

This works every single time I use it. Of course, if VITO happens to be a Buddhist, it's not going to be that effective!

Some Additional Words and Phrases

What follows is more food for thought—lines that can serve as the front bookends of your voice mail messages. Use them in the spirit of success!

First Voice Mail Message:

"Ms. Importanta, this is Will Prosper, and I am the member of the [Apex] sales team who could introduce you and your organization to a set of ideas and solutions that have a track record of . . ."

Second Voice Mail Message:

"Ms. Importanta, since the last voice mail message you listened to, [Big Name]'s organization has been getting their feet on the ground with the ideas and solutions we introduced them to. We are getting ready to conduct a tele-conference call with the leaders of [six] of our business partners. We'll be dis-cussing . . . [mention the benefits and areas of impact, then offer an invitation for this VITO to join in]."

Third Voice Mail Message:

"This is Will Prosper. You most likely recognize my voice by now. I haven't heard back from you, so I'll continue to add value to your day. Let me read you a direct quote from the President of the [Beachtree Company] . . . (read one of your many testimonials from happy customers)."

Fourth Voice Mail Message (two options):

"Mr. Benefito, I just realized that perhaps you have not received my last [three] voice mail messages, so I've taken the time to fax you..."

or:

"Well the [year] is moving right along. Could your team use a boost? Are you happy with their performance? Do you think there is any room for improvement? If so, please consider this . . . [list two or three of the major business areas your solution has had a track record in delivering]."

This next voice mail "bookend" could be used for contacting another division within an existing account:

"Mr. Benefito, the race is on. Who will be the next person at the [XYZ Corporation] to set the kind of records we've been helping one of your sister divisions accomplish, such as . . . [mention two or three specific areas that your solution is making possible]?"

Practice, Practice, and Practice

Here's the only way to make your voice mail messages perfect. First, you'll write them just as I did throughout this chapter. After you refine each one and you're satisfied with the words you want to use, you'll record them into a small cassette recorder. When you're done recording, listen to each message and write down what you're hearing. In other words, transcribe your words from your tape recording. Then erase your recording and re-write your voice mail message from your transcription.

Now repeat this entire two-step process five more times. When you're done, you'll have the spoken words written on a piece of paper in the way that works best for your personal style. Once you're ready to deliver your voice mail messages, you can either read from this spoken "script" or memorize what you have written. By doing this, you are converting every one of your written phrases into natural-sounding spoken words and phrases that will get results. Naturally!

Some Final Tips

Much like a speech, your delivery will account for up to 94 percent of the total message! I know that's hard to imagine, and it seems like a crazy thing to say, especially after I've spent an entire chapter on the importance of "word smithing" your voice mail messages, but according to all the research I've ever read, it's true. Here, then, are some tips for making the delivery of your voice mail messages the very best it can be:

1. Your rate of speech must be modulated during each of your voice mail messages. Once you have established your rate of speech, learn to modulate it slightly during your entire voice mail message—that is, it should be delivered with a consistent speed that varies by no more than 10 percent. Above all, make sure you do not speak too fast. If necessary, post a sign in front of you that says *Slow Down*.

2. Your pitch or tone must also vary. Please do not confuse this with raising and lowering the *volume* of your voice, which should always be at the same level. Instead, vary the inflections in your voice. For instance, you would raise your pitch at the end of a question and lower it at the end of a statement. Whatever you do, don't use a monotone voice that fails to convey any passion or enthusiasm, or sounds like you're reading from a script. In a sense, make sure you don't use a "sing-song" style. The best example of this that I can

think of is what you typically hear on an airplane's PA system as the flight attendant delivers the "safety demo."

3. Make sure you pause at the end of each sentence and after saying any critically important phrases that might include company names, numbers, or percentages.

4. Remember to smile when leaving your voice mail messages. VITO will be able to "see" it in your voice.

Here are some additional points for you to consider as you format your voice mail messages:

1. Always use a different beginning and ending for each of your messages.

2. Never, ever use techno words or phrases, product names or numbers, or industry jargon of any kind. If you use one single word that VITO does not understand, you'll get a call back all right—but it will be from Seymour, not VITO!

3. Never repeat the same message.

4. Always end your voice mail message with specific dates and times that VITO can return the call to you.

5. Your name and telephone number should be saved for the last words of your message.

6. Always include a call to action at the end of every voice mail message for VITO.

One last word: This is not brain surgery, nor should it resemble anything even remotely close to chewing aluminum foil! Think of voice mail as the golden opportunity it is—and have fun with it!

Sidetracked with Seymour?

A little later in the book, we'll be looking at the techniques you'll use for success during the in-person meeting with VITO. In Chapter 14, however, we'll examine a strategy you can use to get through to VITO if you find yourself, for whatever reason, dealing with Seymour—the person to whom salespeople are usually relegated when someone in the organization wants to stop the sales cycle dead in its tracks.

> *You're never rejected until you give someone
> or something the permission to reject you.*

The Pigeonholing Problem

SUPPOSE YOU'VE ALREADY STARTED YOUR SALES CYCLE WITH A SEYMOUR. YOU'VE done your analysis, collected all the data, bought a lunch or two, maybe sprung for doughnuts and coffee in the morning, visited a few sites, made a few demos, and now you're going in to give your presentation to Seymour. You're expecting to meet with Seymour and perhaps one or two associates, but often, when you actually make your way into the building, you find that there are six or seven Seymours waiting to greet you. (My theory is that Seymours multiply like hangers in your closet, but I could be wrong.) You give your presentation; it's one of the best presentations you've ever given in your life. All the Seymours are smiling and nodding their heads. You have few questions to answer, and the ones that do come up are easy. You get to the last slide; you put it up on the overhead projector and make your closing comments; you turn off the machine; flip on the lights; and you say to the head Seymour, "Seymour, as you can see, the facts are all here. Are you ready to work with us?" Then Seymour hesitates for a moment and says, "Well, I've got to see some more figures. We're talking to some other people. We have to crunch all the numbers on this end. Give me thirty days."

Bewildered, you walk from the conference room and out of the building. You get in your car and head back to your office. And you ask yourself, "How long is this going to last? How on earth do I turn up the heat under Seymour?" You get an idea—something that will necessitate another set of slides, but you can live with that—and you call Seymour the minute you walk in your office. But Seymour's not in.

And Seymour doesn't return your call that afternoon. Or the next day.

You call again the next day. Seymour's very busy.

After all your work, you're on the outside looking in again.

I'll bet you that this all sounds horribly familiar. I've just described the classic gridlock, the "I-loved-you-before-but-I'm-not-sure-if-I-still-love-you-now" problem we face all too often with Seymours.

When Seymour has either stalled you for the last two or three months (or years), or has simply given up on you and will not return your phone calls, you are, in a word, pigeonholed.

You want to get to VITO. You know that if you could, you would probably break through the logjam in the course of a single meeting. (VITOs, as you have probably gathered by now, aren't big on wasting their own time or that of anyone else in the organization, and are big on straight-ahead assessments of whether it is worthwhile to do business with someone.) How do you talk to the person who can make things happen for you—-without appearing to go over Seymour's head?

The Pigeonhole Recovery Letter

Right now, we're going to take a look at a letter you and your sales manager can put together. If you follow the procedures I outline, this letter can get you out of the pigeonhole and into VITO's office. It won't make anyone angry or leave you looking underhanded.

Important note! The letter you'll see in this chapter is industrial-strength stuff, but it will *not make sales materialize where none would otherwise exist.* It will simply deliver the same result you would have gotten anyway from Seymour—but a lot sooner. If you were going to win the deal, you'll win it in a hurry. If you were going to lose the deal, you'll lose it in a hurry.

If you follow my instructions carefully, you will not jeopardize your relationship with Seymour.

What's the Goal?

The Pigeonhole Recovery Letter's aim is to either open up the relationship by pointing you toward VITO's office—or smoke Seymour out and help you determine that you're looking at an account that simply isn't worth pursuing anymore, no matter how much Seymour is enjoying all those free lunches and big colored charts. The letter really works. I know, because it's worked countless times for me. The *reason* it works is a simple one. Rather than *fighting* with Seymour, the Pigeonhole Recovery Letter allows you to move up the chain by making *heros* out of Seymours—if they can handle it.

As a practical matter, this letter will be written by you. But your manager will sign it, and others in your organization will approve it. Like the letter you developed for VITO, this one must make use of a Headline Statement showing the benefits of the proposed solution. This Headline Statement, however, *must* be a quote, and it must be signed *by a person in your own organization who outranks both you and your sales manager.*

Exactly who this person is depends on the relative importance of the VITO you're after. If the organization represents a multimillion-dollar account your firm's president has been salivating over, tracking down the president to approve the quote probably won't be too tough. In other instances, a quote from a regional vice president or other high-ranking officer may be more appropriate.

The first step is to consult with your manager about the proposed letter. The idea here is that, after signing and sending the letter, your manager—not you—will conduct the follow-up call referred to in the Action P.S. at the bottom of the page.

Once you've secured your organization's cooperation on this (and it shouldn't be too hard), develop a Headline Statement referring to initial work you have done in collaboration with Seymour. The quote will indicate that this work has identified a specific, quantifiable solution to a problem in VITO's organization.

For the Pigeonhole Recovery letter to work, it *must* feature Seymour's name in the Headline Statement. Other than that, it's just about identical in form and content to the standard letter for a first-time contact with VITO.

Here's an example of a Pigeonhole Recovery Letter that works.

"Seymour Jones and my team have completed an in-depth study. The results show that your corporate personnel costs can be reduced by 36 percent—over $18,500 returned to your bottom line annually."

Jim Smith
President, XYZ
December 14, 1994

Mr. VITO Benefito
President
Dear Mr. Benefito:

Your Widget Department Specialist, Seymour Jones, has been working with my account manager, Will Prosper. We've studied your business. We understand your unique needs. We're prepared to take action.

These are three of the many benefits we have provided for other customers:

- An average 16 percent reduction in quarterly unemployment claims
- Absentee rates at or below 5 percent within two months
- In the words of Mary Jackson of Ellis Enterprises, "a staggering increase in the efficiency of support staff"

We stand ready to move forward with the solutions to your personnel cost containment problems.

Sincerely,
Joan King
Sales Manager
555-1244

P.S.: I will call your office at 9:30 A.M. on Monday, December 19. If you will not be in, please ask Tommie to advise me of a more convenient time.

The Pigeonhole Recovery Process: Protocol and Diplomacy

Now, you never send a Pigeonhole Recovery Letter to VITO without inviting Seymour to take a look at it first. Call, fax, or leave a message for Seymour. Say something to this effect: "Hi, Seymour. My manager is getting ready to send a letter to your president. It has your name at the very top of it. I'd like to share it with you before it's mailed. Please call."

If Seymour knows the name of the health club you work out at every night, he'll be there waiting for you. If Seymour knows where you live, he'll be in your driveway when you get home that evening.

When Seymour returns your call asking to see the letter, be as polite as Emily Post would require—but don't get into the details of the letter. Instead, fax it or hand-deliver it. See what happens.

If Seymour likes the letter but wants you to hold on to it for a week or two, you've got a good sign. Seymour is probably interested in taking action but is too busy to do so. You can either wait (which may be understandable if you're dealing with a potentially large account), or say something like this: "Seymour, I understand your concern on this, but I can't wait forever. My manager has been asked by our VP to write all of our best prospects. Everybody reports to somebody, right? I'll tell you what, though. If I play my cards right, I may be able to stall her for forty-eight hours. I'll see what I can do." The result: You will probably get an up-or-down decision in short order.

If Seymour responds *negatively,* with something like "I don't want this letter to be mailed!" you have two choices. You can stop the letter and be right back where you started, or you can say something like this: "You know, Seymour, I really don't think I *can* stop my manager. If you and I don't want it to go out, you might have to call my boss and tell her not to send it." (The wording there is important: "If *you and I* don't want it to go out . . .") Now, Seymour probably won't call your manager—in which case the letter goes out to VITO—but if a call does come through, your manager should be prepared to tell Seymour about the "pre-sales" dollars your company has spent on pursuing this opportunity—what with all the lunches, demos, analyses, and demonstrations—and the necessity of making a business decision on what action to take next. Your manager should then offer Seymour the opportunity to join in a three-way conference call with VITO.

If Seymour *ignores* messages from you about your plan to send the letter, you can either continue your attempts to reach Seymour (which probably won't get you anywhere), or simply send the letter to VITO, with a copy going out to Seymour as well.

If Seymour calls you in hysterics after the letter arrives on VITO's desk, you might decide to do a Say What: "Say *what*? My manager sent *what*? Oh, I'm so sorry . . . hey, Seymour, what can I say, I can't control what my manager does. I thought she'd wait until you and I could talk! We know how it is, Seymour—everybody reports to somebody, right? Listen, Seymour, my manager is an animal. I've seen her on the grill before. She doesn't stay there for long." Now, maybe this does represent a *teensy* white lie—and you may decide that it won't be appropriate with the Seymour you're trying to get a decision out of. Then again, if you've reached this stage of the sales cycle, and Seymour won't do you the simple courtesy of telling you that, no, there's no point in pursuing things any further, you may conclude that you'll still be able to sleep at night after using this technique.

Before Your Manager Follows Up with VITO by Telephone or in Person . . .

Give your manager all the paperwork you have on the initial call to VITO, including the three big questions that follow. Ask your manager to try to arrange a meeting *for you* with VITO. At the conclusion of the conversation, your manager might say something like, "VITO, would you like to meet our account rep, who has been working with Seymour to uncover all of these savings?"

If VITO says yes, you can then tell Seymour that your manager has arranged a meeting between you and VITO—and that Seymour's really going to look like a hero when you get your solution implemented. (Which, of course, is quite true.)

Nailing Things Down

The technique described in this chapter will, in most cases, either get someone from your firm, preferably you, into VITO's office—or help you isolate and stop working on an account that's going nowhere. That last option might not seem like much of a blessing, but it is. After all, the point of this system is not to get sidetracked with Seymour, but to spend the lion's share of your time identifying and speaking to new VITOs.

I admit that this technique is not for the faint of heart. The Pigeonhole Recovery Letter is a tactic that should be used sparingly. If you send them out too often, you'll send the message to others in your own organization that you can't conclude your sales calls, and that you're consistently calling too low in the organization. Once again, let me warn you never to send anyone a Pigeonhole Recovery Letter without first securing the approval of all the people in your organization whose names appear in it.

If the account turns out not to come your way, so be it. Once you finalize where all your pigeonholed accounts really stand, you can focus all your efforts on prospecting to the top person in the organization.

The good news is that you'll only have to use the tactics I've discussed in this chapter one time. Thereafter, your initial efforts and ongoing sales work will include contacting VITO first and then Seymour. When you live by that simple rule, the classic "pigeonhole" problem disappears. Forever!

PART 4

Meeting VITO and Keeping VITO Involved

"As a former CEO for 15 plus years I can say Tony hit the nail on the head."
—Jeff Petrizzi

When you mastered this section you will have the ability to:

1. Develop a presentation that will be unique to VITO's needs
2. Deliver a presentation that will leave a lasting impression of the value you can add to VITO Inc.
3. Maintain a mutually beneficial business relationship with VITO
4. Get "VITO to VITO" referrals that are worth their weight in gold

════ Key Thought ════

Your VITO presentation must be directed towards VITO's goals. Skip the usual "our company started in 1947 in Hoboken, New Jersey. . ." Vito cares about VITO, Inc., and not a whole lot more.

Chapter 15

Preparing for Your Presentation to VITO

IN THE FOLLOWING CHAPTER, WE WILL BE DISCUSSING THE FINER POINTS OF making a presentation to VITO. It should go without saying that this will entail a great deal of homework and advance preparation on your part. You will have to know who will be taking part in the meeting and what to expect. You will have to make decisions about how to set up the meeting room, what display tools to use, and whether you'll be doing a product demonstration. You will have to assemble an agenda, a discovery agreement, and all your supporting materials and handouts. You will have to anticipate questions and objections and prepare your responses. And as if all this was not enough, you will have to make sure that you are fully tuned in to VITO.

What do I mean by this? I'm not talking about the things we've already discussed about who VITO is and what VITO wants. I'm talking about the things that VITO will respond to on a physiological level—that is, all the verbal and nonverbal cues that you will give to and get from VITO, cues that will provide that all-important "connection" between you and allow you both to communicate freely and comfortably.

A Word about Zones

Have you ever noticed what a nuisance it is to jockey for position when you queue into the local multiplex cinema for "open seating?" Or when you inch forward with a mass of other people, waiting for your "zone" to be called during the boarding (or herding) of your flight? These words are really misnomers, because in neither case does the seating arrangement leave you feeling very "open" or in the "zone" at all.

If you're like most people, you feel a certain degree of concern, discomfort, or even anxiety on occasions when you're being "hemmed in" from all sides. Usually, this sensation doesn't last more than the few minutes it takes for you to snag your seat for the next big screen epic or white-knuckle flight. What's happening in these situations is formally called "incursion on one's territorial zone." That is, when other individuals violate the physical space around our bodies, it automatically causes stress.

Honoring another person's personal space, on the other hand, can help build a mutually good feeling that will ensure a great first impression and the building of business rapport. By understanding the workings of our territorial zone, we can totally avoid any feelings of discomfort caused by "space invasion" during our VITO presentations. Let's take a look at this.

In or Out of VITO's Zone

Imagine there's an invisible 18-inch barrier surrounding your body. Actually, you probably don't have to imagine too hard, because there almost certainly is an invisible 18-inch barrier around your body. We call this your "confidential" zone. Here in the United States, this is the area most people hold as essentially private, a space only to be occupied by one's spouse, one's significant other, one's close relatives (children for example), and one's domestic pets (pythons excluded). Entering thoughtlessly into another person's confidential zone is generally the equivalent of a physical challenge.

However, there are three other zones of which you should be aware. The first is the zone located between 18 and 32 inches from your body, known as the "individual" zone. This is the region where most Americans are comfortable interacting with people they know on a social or business level. The next zone lies between 32 and 44 inches from your body and represents (for Americans) the "sociable" zone. It's about the distance between VITO and you when you're sitting in a chair in front of VITO's desk. In this zone, most of us are comfortable interacting with people we do not know very well yet. Finally, there's the region outside the confidential, individual, and sociable zones. This is known as the "common" zone, the area where we Americans are comfortable with (or at least occasionally prepared to accept) unexpected entrances or intrusions into our space from others.

Let's assume, for now, that you're making a presentation in VITO's office. You must always—I repeat, *always*—ask for VITO's permission before you make the transition from the common zone (just outside their office) to their sociable zone (inside their office). To do this, say: "May I come in?" or something that's darn close to that. After a period of "getting acquainted," you must then ask for permission before you place any material on VITO's desk. Putting your briefcase, a binder, brochure, sample, or anything else on the desk or an equivalent area means that you've entered the individual zone, and you can't do that until you've been granted permission! You must, and I do mean *must,* enter the zones *one at a time,* and then only with permission. This includes remaining standing until you receive an invitation to sit—and even then, asking, "Is this seat okay?"

This bears repeating: *Do not take up residence in the sociable zone (32 to 44 inches) without permission.* I've watched many a well-researched presentation collapse because the salesperson:

1. Took a seat without being invited to do so, and/or
2. Treated VITO's desk as though it were his or her own desk, and/or
3. "Hemmed in" VITO by consistently operating in his or her confidential zone.

These three classic presentation mistakes represent violations of the sociable, individual, and confidential zones, respectively. If you don't think the heedless act of ignoring these invisible "borders" can affect your commission check, you're sadly mistaken. Play it safe, play it smart, and above all, don't act like you own the place! Gain permission at each appropriate zone's border before proceeding.

Here is an example of how you might gain entry into a closer zone with VITO. Let's say you're giving a presentation and you are using a dry erase board or chalkboard. At a certain point (you'll know when the time is right), ask VITO to join you at the board. Give VITO a colored marker; this brief point of contact within VITO's confidential zone should encourage him or her to become engaged in the "chalk talk." With a little luck, VITO will move up next to you and occupy the sociable or (even better) individual zone as you outline your points on the board.

Of course, all of this changes a bit if VITO comes to your office for the presentation. This will give you greater control, but it will also present some added challenges. Since VITO will be entering your "common" zone, you need to make the situation a comfortable one. If you're waiting in the presentation room and VITO is escorted in, stop whatever you're doing and immediately invite VITO in: "Please come in, I've been looking forward to meeting with you today. Here (making a motion with your hand), I have a seat for you." Then motion VITO to the front of the room. From this point forward, you'll be using the guidelines we discussed earlier for VITO's sociable, individual, and confidential zones.

A Simple Handshake

If you've been paying attention, and I know that you have, you're most likely thinking: "Hey, Tony! What about shaking hands? Isn't that an intrusion of VITO's confidential zone?" Actually, it most certainly is, but here in the United States and in most other countries, a handshake is an acceptable and even welcome "intrusion" that is an exception to the rule.

The handshake is so important that it's worth a comment or two. There are three things that must go hand in hand (sorry) with your handshake:

1. You must always smile whenever you shake VITO's hand.
2. You must always make eye contact when you shake VITO's hand.
3. When you clasp hands, you must always follow VITO's lead
   - in firmness
   - in motion
   - in direction
   - in the length of the handshake itself

I know that this must sound a bit strange, but if VITO's handshake is limp, your return grip should be limp; if it's firm, yours should be firm, and so on. I want you to forget the "power" shake rule whenever you're meeting a VITO. Once the handshake is over, you must return to the process that I've outlined earlier.

See It, Hear It, Feel It

A great deal of research has been done in an attempt to find out if the language people use has any relation to their decision-making process or feelings they have. For example, it was assumed that the stronger and more descriptive the language, the stronger and more powerful the decisive thought or feeling. However, what researchers really discovered was quite different and surprising!

Have you ever talked to a prospect until you were "blue in the face"? Used every single one of the words you knew, but they still didn't "connect" with what you were trying to say? (If you happen to have a teenager in your family, you'll know the feeling well!) For that matter, have you ever tried to get a point across to someone by doing a "hands-on" demo? For example, you may want to show them how to use a new word processor or how to access their e-mail—"Just start typing, push several different keys, and you'll get the hang of it"—but they couldn't grasp it until they read the manual.

Finally, have you ever tried to get a prospect to "feel" what you wanted them to feel (or perhaps what you were feeling yourself), but they weren't able to get to the same emotional point that you were? If you've experienced any of these situations and frustrations, then you can understand the reason for the research that was done by Richard Bandler and John Grinder. A psycho-linguist and a mathematician respectively, these two men found in the course of their psychological research that there are three basic groups of people, as follows (and by the way, since VITOs are people, they will definitely fall into one of these groups):

1. People who show emotions, make judgements, come to decisions, and understand through a more *visual* display—i.e., "Seeing *is* believing!"
2. People who show emotions, make judgements, come to decisions, and understand through *auditory* input—i.e., "Just *tell me* the facts!"
3. People who show emotions, make judgements, come to decisions, and understand through *kinesthetic,* emotional input—i.e., "I've got the *feel* of it now!"

During your presentations, it's important to know which category each member of your audience falls into. Why? Because if, for example, VITO and the rest of the audience happen to be visually oriented and you spend most of your time talking, you'll be sure to miss the mark. If you go about thinking the world at large and your audience in particular are just like you, then you could certainly miss the mark by miles and miles! Let's take a look at each of the three categories in a bit more detail.

Visual: These individuals can see things clearly in their minds. They can put the pieces of the puzzle together without the assistance of an instruction manual. Try to "picture" this: *a white sand beach, crystal clear water, a beautiful sailboat sitting quietly just outside the surf line.* Can you *see* it? Can you *visualize* it? Did your mind paint the picture? If not, don't be disappointed. Perhaps you're someone who needs to connect with the sounds of that picture, in which case you would be more of an—

Auditory: These people would prefer that I played a tape recording of the sounds of the palm trees rustling in the breeze, of a gentle surf lapping against a sandy beach, and the creaking a boat makes as it rocks slowly side to side. If I were to introduce the call of a distant seagull, you would *hear* it clearly in your mind, wouldn't you? No? Well, then, perhaps you're someone who connects more with the feeling of the moment, in which case you would tend to be more—

Kinesthetic: For a moment, close your eyes. Can you *feel* the warm breeze and the sand in between your toes as you walk to the water's edge? And now, the tingling that salt water makes when it first touches your dry skin and gets into your eyes as you begin to swim? Your muscles start to get into the rhythm of your swimming and before you know it you're alongside the boat—*your* sailboat. The hot aluminum on the first step of the boarding ladder almost burns your hand as you pull yourself up. Now you stand on the deck and your companion hands you a soft fluffy towel and a cold drink. You look up to the sky, and the sun warms your face. If this *feels* like paradise, then, my friend, you show emotions, make judgements, come to decisions, and understand through a more *kinesthetic,* emotional way. You've got the *feel* of it now, don't you!

So What's VITO's Preference?

It's not hard to figure out what VITO's preference is, or anyone else's, for that matter. Like many situations in your sales work, if you're paying close attention, then you'll observe the clues that will lead you directly to someone's visual, auditory, or kinesthetic preferences.

VITO the Visual

Visual individuals have some "pet" words and characteristics they frequently use or display. Here are some of the words they like: *picture, show, see, view, perspective, bright, vision, imagine,* and *look.* Listen for phrases like this:

1. "I get the *picture.*" or: "Do you get the *picture?*"
2. "Can't you just *see* it?" or: "Yes! Now I can *see* it!"
3. "What's your *point of view?*" or: "Here's my *point of view . . .*"
4. "Why don't you just *show* me?" or: "I'll be better off if you just *show* me."
5. "*Imagine* this . . ." or: "I am having trouble *imagining* this."
6. "That's a *brilliant* idea!"

Be careful, though. Don't be too quick to judge people just on the words they use or respond to. You also need to understand that individuals who are "visual" *look* a certain way! Have you ever noticed how some people gaze at you with a blank stare when you speak? They almost look right through you, don't they? If this is the case, then that person is actually "seeing" what you are saying (or dozing off—I prefer to focus on the first assessment). People who have a visual preference can be fun to communicate with, because you can almost tell what's going on in their minds by watching their eyes. For example, ask a person with a visual preference something that pertains to the future, and they will usually look up and to the right. If you ask: "VITO, where do you picture your organization's position in the marketplace by the end of this year?" and VITO looks up and to the right, she is most likely "seeing" her ranking.

Generally speaking, when visuals look up and to the left, they may be preoccupied with something in the past. For example, if VITO responds to your question while looking up and to the left, she may be thinking of or recalling what happened last year. If you observe this, the answer you get may be somewhat inaccurate, and you may want to ask another question to check or confirm her information.

If VITO happens to look straight ahead with an almost unfocused gaze upon his face, he may be undecided or trying to internalize your request. If this ever happens, you should immediately begin to use more visual words to better describe or restate your request, such as: "Perhaps if you're in search of some additional *bright ideas,* I could *show* you how our other business partners are realizing their *vision.*" If it still looks like you're not getting your point across to VITO, you can increase the use of your physical gestures, become more animated as you speak, or increase the use of eye contact as you make your presentation.

Remember: If you want "visuals" to understand your ideas and your enthusiasm, they must "see" it in *their* minds. Once they *see* it, they will *believe* it. You may want to show a video of testimonials from other VITOs (your very best customers) speaking about their experiences with your company.

VITO the Auditory

An auditory's preference will be sounds. The way in which you deliver your message will be critical to getting the "auditory" on your side. The tone of your voice, your pitch, and your rate of speech are all critical to establishing belief. I mentioned earlier in the chapter on voice mail the importance of each with suggestions for improvement. You must use very descriptive words, but more importantly, you must emphasize the words you want them to remember by using intonation, inflection, and pauses throughout your presentation.

To reach mastery with your presentation style and in gaining an auditory's attention, I'll suggest again here that you may want to invest the time and money to join and participate in Toastmasters. They are masters in teaching effective communication skills with which the auditory is certain to connect.

VITO the Kinesthetic

Many VITOs will be prone to "feel" your message; their belief or passion will begin at the "gut" level. They can and will become emotional and draw on their instinctive interpretations of your message, becoming hot or cold to you and your belief. They are also "touchy-feely" people. They generally have a longer handshake, and often will touch you on your forearm or shoulder with their left hand, while shaking with the right. There is no emotional fence-sitting with this VITO!

If you want to get your enthusiasm across to VITO the kinesthetic, then you should get close (remembering to ask permission before entering the individual zone), use plenty of eye contact, and use words and phrases during your presentation like: "VITO, do you *feel* at this point that you can personally *help me get a handle* on other divisions and departments that could possibly gain from our ideas and solutions?" or "Could we *touch* base between now and the end of next week or do you *feel* differently about it?" or "By the way, afterwards we could place a call to the president of one of our other business partners. I *promise* you'll *enjoy the experience!"*

It's All about VITO

My intent here is not to get all wrapped up in any sort of "psychological warfare" during your VITO presentations or during any other part of your sales work. It's my belief that if you do, you'll create more problems than you'll solve. But on the other hand, I do feel very strongly about using the proven behavioral research of Richard Bandler, John Grinder and countless others to our advantage while we serve VITO's best interest. The key here is *serving VITO's best interest.* Don't get obsessed in your quest to figure out what VITO's communication preferences are. Just factor these tactics and observations into your day-to-day sales work and before long you'll be tuned into VITO's world almost automatically—and you'll be better prepared for any presentations you have to give!

Chapter 16

Delivering Your Presentation to VITO

YOU'VE NOTICED, I HOPE, HOW FAR ALONG THIS CHAPTER IS IN THE BOOK. There's a reason for that: Far too many salespeople rush the presentation process. I don't want you to be one of them! Why? Because when you make a presentation to VITO, you must be certain that you have a complete understanding of the value that your solution can deliver to organizations like VITO's and, perhaps more importantly, what value you can offer *this* VITO.

In this chapter, we'll take a look at what you'll need to present, how to prepare for your presentation, and how to actually do it—both one-on-one presentations with just you and VITO and those where VITO's trusted staff will be joining in (which, by the way, will happen quite often). We'll also explore the pros and cons of display tools and product demonstrations, as well as the dos and don'ts of delivering presentations and how to deal with questions.

The Value of Your Presentation

I would venture to say that VITOs have sat through far too many presentations given by far too many salespeople that pitched products, company capabilities, success stories, guarantees, and so much more that didn't relate to VITO or what VITO needed to do with their organization. The key words here are *their organization*. At each and every step along the way as you plan your presentation, you must be preoccupied with VITO's world and the results they want to realize—*not* the accomplishments of your own company. As we move forward I want you to focus on the two VITO fears that we mentioned in Chapter 11. Do you remember them? I'll remind you: VITO's two greatest fears are wasting precious time and being engaged in conversations that include or refer to topics that are unfamiliar. If you trigger either of these fears during any part of your VITO presentation, both the presentation and the sale will be over.

Failing to customize your presentation is another way to doom the sale. If you've been given a boilerplate presentation which you give to your prospects time and again without any variation, or a presentation that contains only minimal customization based upon the particular VITO or organization you'll be talking to, then you're not going to reach your maximum potential as a salesperson. That's a guarantee!

Should you know your stuff well enough and be able to think on your feet to improvise your way through an emergency like a burnt-out bulb in your projector or a laptop melt down? Absolutely! Just about every salesperson has a story to share in this area. During my seminars, I often run into salespeople who ask me whether or not it's "really necessary" to do customized research for each and every new VITO presentation. I tell them there is always a choice and here it is:

> *Winging the presentation or a winning presentation.*

I prefer the latter, and I hope you do, too!

Who's Who?

Whether you'll be making your presentation only to VITO or to several people on VITO's staff, it will be much better received if you take the time necessary to figure out exactly who is in your audience. It's true you'll never be totally certain who will join in at the last minute[*] but by this point you should have more than a basic idea of who will be evaluating what you have to say during your presentation and what you need to know about their organization or specific department. What follows is a checklist for this purpose. If you can't answer these eight "Who and What" questions with a very high degree of certainty, then you're not ready to start working on your presentation.

1. Have you met or at least spoken by telephone with each person you know will be in attendance at your presentation?
2. Do you know the correct spelling and pronunciation of each person's name, as well as their title? Has anybody been promoted recently, or is a promotion in the works? Double and even triple check all of this information. An error here can and will be disastrous!
3. Have you an idea of each person's personality style? There are plenty of great books available that will help you in this area. In fact, one of them is by an author you already know—me! Its title is *The Power of Will.*

---

[*] If someone enters your presentation at the last minute, or if there is someone in attendance whom you did not expect, you might handle it this way: "Let's take a moment before we get started [or continue] and make sure that we have everyone's interests at hand. Excuse me, I don't believe we've met. My name is Will Prosper (as you hand them a copy of the agenda), and I'll be leading the discussion of the points we've just reviewed. Would you like to make any changes before we proceed?"

4. Have you developed a reliable working hypothesis as to each person's role in the Network of Influence and Authority? A reminder: Consumer, Intellect, Director, and Leader.

5. Do you know exactly why each person is attending? Does he or she want to be there? Does he or she have to? What is their agenda?

6. Do you know who your supporters and advocates are? If so, what part(s) of your solution do they support? Who are your adversaries? Do they have an ax to grind? What part of your solution do they have a problem with? Which individuals will be indifferent?

7. What is currently being done at VITO's organization to solve the problem you propose to solve? Who recommended the incumbent solution? How long has their current solution been in place? What's not working with it? What is?

8. Who besides yourself will be playing an active part in your presentation? Your sales manager? Credit manager? Specialist? Your own VITO? Furthermore, who on your prospect's VITO team will be asked to speak, and why?

If you have the answers to these eight questions, then you can proceed. If you have any additional work to do, stop reading now and do the necessary research. This will serve as a learn-by-doing experience that will save you time and ensure that you develop a stellar presentation. I can assure you that by taking the time to answer every single part of all eight questions, you will improve your chances of getting the sale by at least 60 percent!

Environmental Controls

Where will your presentation take place—on VITO's turf or yours? If VITO is coming to you, then you have some work to do, and I don't just mean getting your presentation ready. You also have to make sure the meeting room is set up just right. Environment has an extraordinary effect on human behavior, and that means your room setup will have an extraordinary effect on the way VITO will perceive your presentation.

It's easy to wait until the last minute to get your meeting room ready, but take my advice: It's far better to get it done the evening before than to try to assemble everything you'll need on the morning of your meeting. After all, you'll have plenty of other things to do right up until the time your guest(s) arrive! By using a little bit of lead time, you can exert control over the environment and put all the right elements to work for you. That said, before you even start thinking about where to put the tables, charts and refreshments, you should work your way through the following meeting prep checklist:

VITO Presentation Checklist

1. Make sure the room is well lighted. A dingy, poorly lit room will affect everyone's internal clock—including yours! It might even cause your audience to tune out what you're saying. Virtually all human beings start to lose their mental edge when they're kept confined inside a poorly lit room. Brighten your presentation room up as much as you can—but keep the curtains or blinds drawn if you can. You don't want people daydreaming and staring out the window. Never—I repeat, *never*—dim the lights during your presentation for any reason!

2. Keep outside and adjoining room noise to an absolute minimum. Unplug all phones; turn off any speakers, beepers, and pagers; and let your neighboring officemates know that you've got an important VITO presentation in progress between the hours of X and Y. It will probably help to post a sign to this effect.

3. Remove all clutter ruthlessly. The presentation room is no place for stray computers or boxes that have nothing to do with your meeting. When VITO walks through the door, the room should be completely clean and absolutely free of unsightly clutter.

4. Arrange for refreshments. When VITO and others enter the room, they should have immediate access to coffee, tea, juice, soda, and water. You may care to offer an array of healthy snacks—fresh fruit or breakfast/energy bars. Skip the high fat/sugar "treats." They're not as popular as the ad agencies think they are. This is a wonderful way to show your audience that you're truly grateful for their presence. If possible, offer mugs and glasses with your logo on them as a gift item upon their departure.

5. If there are several members of VITO's staff attending, always use name tents in your presentation room, and always place VITO's name and company name on a marquee in your lobby.

Once you've attended to these matters, you'll be able to arrange the tables and chairs for maximum advantage. I favor a "U" shaped setup for groups of five or more because it promotes interaction, and a standard rectangular table for smaller groups. If you are using a rectangular table, make sure that you sit where the "X" is shown below. If it's just you and VITO, you should sit on the same side of the table.

X (You are here)

Starting Your VITO Presentation

Typically, presentations are begun by offering information about your company: its mission statement, commitment to the marketplace, products, history, and so on. But this is not going to be a typical presentation. This is a presentation to VITO! For that reason, it must not follow guidelines established for typical presentations. Remember, you're on a job interview whenever you interact with VITO, and your presentation is no exception from this rule.

There are two jobs to be done during your VITO presentation:

> *Your job is to talk.*
> *VITO's job is to listen.*

You must make sure that VITO doesn't finish before you do! That's no small feat, especially when you consider the fact that VITO's are poor listeners! The VITO you're meeting with and presenting to is special, and so is the organization he or she built. This is an individual with unique problems and opportunities, and you have to remember that at all times.

You've worked hard to learn all you can about VITO's particular situation, and that hard work is going to be evident in the customized portions of your presentation, which will, in fact, form the heart of your presentation outline. Keeping in mind the variations posed by the answers to our eight "Who and What" questions, then these customized portions will include the following:

1. A Discovery Agreement (more on this shortly)
2. An interactive discussion on the Benefits, Advantages, and perhaps even Features and Functions of your solution, depending on who is in attendance, co-mingled with value statements at appropriate points

3. Responses to prior specifications, studies, or forecasts with which you've been asked to comply
4. Responses to issues, questions, and other inquires that may have surfaced during your earlier meeting with your prospect(s)
5. Responses to specific questions that arise during the presentation itself
6. A logical, on-line summary of key points, and a conclusion complete with your recommended "next-step" action plan

That first all-important element—the Discovery Agreement—is worth visiting in greater detail. This is basically a proposed agenda for your presentation that gets VITO talking first and gives VITO (or anyone else in attendance) the opportunity to make any last-minute changes to the agenda before you start talking. The Discovery Agreement offers concise summaries of each key point you plan to cover during your presentation. You'll be asked to review each point in chronological order, and you'll be getting buy-in on each point before you move on to the next one. Yes, this will take a bit of time at the beginning of your presentation, but it's time well spent, because when you get right down to it, we have only two critical elements to work with: time and direction.

Los Angeles: Summer 1969. There I was, barreling down the highway with a friend, smiling from ear to ear behind the wheel of my '66 Corvette Sting Ray convertible. We had the top down. We had the music blasting. We were exceeding the speed limit. Life was perfect. Suddenly my companion noticed a sign hurtling by. A look of concern came over her face. She said something, but with all the delicious wind, I couldn't hear her. I shrugged my shoulders and put a hand to my ear. "We're lost!" my friend yelled at the top of her lungs. "You're going in the wrong direction!"

My response? "Who cares? We're making great time!"

That was way back in 1969. A lot has changed in the world and in my life since then, but this important fact remains unchanged: Time and direction will always determine the outcome of life, relationships, careers, and, yes, presentations to VITO.

Here's an example of what a Discovery Agreement might look like. Note that the document below does not reference products, services, solutions, product numbers, or any techno-babble. Nor does it make any claims of what's right or wrong. It is simply an accurate, detailed list of what you found out—in essence, discovered—during the interviews, sales calls, and other pre-sales activities. This document should have the look and feel of a working document, with plenty of space for notes and comments. If it looks too formal, VITO will think your attempts at getting a buy-in are insincere.

Discovery Agreement for the ABC Corporation, Inc.

Pacific North West Operations
Persons interviewed:
Jane Collins, President/CEO; Robert Palmer, VP Finance; John Casisa, VP Operations; Brenda Barnes, Accounting Manager
Findings:

1. Time to market is slipping—12 percent in the past year.

   _____

   _____

   _____

2. Payroll errors due to time and attendance errors are at an all time high of 24 percent.

   _____

   _____

   _____

3. A/R backlog of 14 weeks is typical.

   _____

   _____

   _____

4. A/P backlog of 6 weeks is typical.

   _____

   _____

   _____

5. Customer data base is outdated and used only once each year for back-end sales opportunities.

   _____

   _____

   _____

6. H/R benefits manager has the retirement program as well as the 401K plan on hold.

   _____

   _____

   _____

Discovery Summary:
Everyone at ABC who was interviewed was in favor of an outsourcing solution that would remedy each of the six issues listed
above. ABC wants to retain all control; therefore solutions considered must have on-site services. ABC also has requirements in the
manufacturing department for temporary services, but these are a
lower priority. ABC has stated the need for a total single solution for
all their needs which ideally would be completely installed and fully
functional by year end.

Please remember that the Discovery Agreement provides an overview of
what you know about this organization's goals, plans, objectives, and challenges. It also summarizes what you've established or accomplished to date
by working with particular team members.

It is important to remember that the Discovery Agreement is not an outline of what you can do to help VITO's particular situation, nor is it a detailed
outline of the presentation that will follow. Its primary purpose is to validate
the following statement:

> *If you don't have consent, you can't present!*

After your review of the Discovery Agreement, you'll take the time to
gain acceptance or agreement from everyone in your audience before you
proceed to the next item on your presentation's agenda. What you say could
sound something like this: "Ladies and gentlemen, do you agree that I accurately described the current challenges that you face in your manufacturing
and accounting departments, or would you like to make any modifications
before we begin?"

No matter what anyone says, you win. With a question/statement like
that, you'll either gain immediate acknowledgement and acceptance of your
assessment, or you'll find out exactly how much you've missed the mark.
That's certainly good to know, right?

Of course, sometimes certain people in attendance will want to tinker with
the wording of your Discovery Agreement. When this happens, be sure the suggestion is in the best interest of everyone in attendance—i.e., "Is everyone in
agreement that we should also discuss Robert's suggestion of a time and attendance reporting and data capture solution?" If the answer is yes, then add it to
the agenda and make sure you plan time to cover it. If it will require additional
time, or if you can't cover it because you don't have the necessary material, say
so up front (although the latter might cost you some credibility).

It's been my personal experience that in the vast majority of cases (especially if you've done your homework well), you'll simply get the green light to proceed to your planned agenda with perhaps one or two minor adjustments. I suggest summarizing the outline of your presentation for everyone's benefit, and as you move through the agenda, ask, "Ladies and gentlemen, have we covered this item to your satisfaction?"

By the way, throughout your presentation, you should never say: "Are there any questions?" Let's face it, no one likes to look stupid, especially VITO. It's far better to say: "What questions do you have?" (Important note: Whenever you say this, silently count to ten before you continue. And during this countdown, make sure you are scanning your audience and establishing eye contact with everyone in it. Especially plan on starting and ending your audience "scan" with VITO.)

What Comes Next?

After winning consent for your Discovery Agreement, you'll move ahead to the all-important "discussion" phase of your presentation. The order in which you address the points in this section can make all the difference, since it depends on which members of your audience fit into what part of the Influence and Authority Network. Remember, each constituency will want to learn more about a particular aspect of your product, service, or solution. You'll recall from Chapter 7:

VITO, the leader, needs to know about Benefits
Directors need to know about Advantages
Seymour, our friendly Intellect, needs to know about Features
Consumers need to know about the Functions of our solutions

You should be able to recite that analysis of the Network of Influence and Authority in your sleep by now! Why? Because that's the exact order of your presentation. You'll start with Benefits, the highest place on the network, and work your way down. If Directors are present, you'll dive into Advantages. If Seymour is there, you'll hit a few Features, and lastly you'll mention Functions for any Consumers that are in the audience.

The general rule of thumb to follow is: The lower on the network, the less time you'll spend in that topical area. For example:

When VITO is present, be prepared to address VITO's concerns and topics first. Highlight and discuss the Benefits of what you have to offer. Your beginning comments may sound something like this: "Within six short months of using our solution, it's possible to realize an additional $15,000 in new business revenue while observing a reduction in your fixed expenses normally associ-ated with that magnitude of new business growth." You may continue with: "This is based on the use of our solutions with over forty-five other investment firms [in VITO's industry] within the past three years." The key here is to be totally focused on either hard, tangible results or soft, intangible benefits and results (review Chapter 7 if you need to) that impact VITO's top, middle, or bottom line. At the end of each Benefit, always pause and ask for questions. If VITO should ask, "How are such results possible?" or if any one of VITO's directors are present, then you would continue with advantages.

Advantages will be given as short explanations of how your solution would be tailored to meet the unique needs of VITO's organization. For instance: "What you may find interesting is that your sales procedures will only be modified in the areas that directly impact on forecasting and bud-geting. All other procedures will be identical, and we'll do it all without any capital investment on your behalf." Be sure you address the Advantages to all departments that will be involved. This is also a great place to introduce new information that perhaps hasn't been discussed before. For example, let's say that your total solution can address more than one of VITO's departments, but you're only presenting your solution for a single "early adopter" department. You could add (as you make eye contact with VITO): "VITO, you'll be pleased to know that as soon as we see the desired results in your sales depart-ment, we can discuss ways in which we have delivered similar, or even greater measurable results in the marketing and customer services departments." Here again, before proceeding, always ask: "What questions do you have at this point?"

If our friend Seymour is in attendance, we'll have to address some of the wonderful Features of our solution. *Proceed with caution!* Remember that VITO will most likely tune out during this part of your presentation. To avoid any break in continuity while at the same time making your presentation appeal to all persons in attendance, ask for permission or make a statement that sounds something like this: "At this point we'll be discussing some of the tech-nical aspects of our solution as they apply to the results you can expect." Then, after mentioning two or three Features, you should immediately tie them back into the Benefits you stated earlier. For example: "Our reporting system allows for incorporation of your existing spreadsheets that have a maximum of 344 cells. You'll be happy to know, VITO, (once again, establishing eye contact) that this allows us to increase the time your salespeople will be able to spend with your prospects or customers." (It is key to mention VITO's name as much as possible, since that will help to keep attention levels at a maximum throughout your entire presentation. Caution: do not overuse VITO's name.)

Finally, if there are any consumers present, be prepared to address their concerns regarding Functions. Once again, you should tie Functions to Advantages and/or Benefits. For example: "Your programmers will simply request the forecast report by pressing the 'Print Forecast' key before they leave for the day. This will give your sales management the precise information they need to effectively deploy each salesperson for the next selling period."

To summarize: You should plan to address each player in the Network of Influence and Authority that will be attending the meeting. Mind you, we're talking about a rough outline here, not a script that must be adhered to at all costs. If VITO wants you to focus on a particular area—do so! If Seymour is asking too many questions, suggest that a smaller group meet to discuss the topic in greater detail at the end of your planned agenda. Do not—I repeat, do *not*—go into overtime under any circumstances! It's best to say something like: "Seymour, let's roll up our sleeves after our brief meeting today so we can explore all of your areas of interest." (Notice that I use the word "interest" here it's best never to use the word "concern" with Seymour.)

Display Tools

There are plenty of tools you can use during your presentations to add drama, variation, and visual interest to what you have to say. As a general rule, you must not allow any of the tools you select to overpower or "upstage" your part in the presentation. Whatever visuals you choose to use must be brief, direct, and to-the-point, with no more than eight to ten words on each display and/or handout.

Depending on the size of your audience and your budget, you'll most likely be faced with choosing from the selection listed below. I've also listed what I view as the pros and cons of each method. Keep one single and critically important fact in mind: If VITO is in a high-tech industry and provides cutting-edge electronic solutions to the marketplace, you'd look pretty smart showing up with a laptop and projector rather than a three-ringed binder! One time I witnessed an excellently prepared presentation that failed before it started. The consultant/salesperson stood in front of the president and staff members of a large document processing company with his overhead projector. As he placed his first black and white overhead on the projector, he said, "We have studied your business and are pleased to say that our solutions have much in common with your strategic direction." Exactly three minutes later, the president quietly left the room.

With that in mind, here are your choices for display tools, and I strongly advise you to choose carefully!

1. **Three-ringed binder.**
   Advantages: Portable; no electrical power necessary; can be modified very easily; color can be inexpensively added; very easy to use.
   Drawbacks: Very low-tech; high touch image (sometimes an advantage if your audience is high-tech adverse); useable only with one or two observers; shows wear and tear easily and must be maintained.

2. **Flip-charts.**
   Advantages: Great for small to medium-sized audiences of five to ten people; again, no electrical power is necessary; versatile; high visual impact because of its size; can be very interactive and impromptu, since both you and your audience can write upon it.
   Drawbacks: You must have excellent handwriting and you must be able to spell (that leaves me out, on both fronts—how about you?); because of the size, they are very difficult to transport and they damage easily, which makes for a relatively short life span; if you plan to write on them during your presentation, that takes time and is also distracting, especially since you'll most likely be talking to the flip-chart when you're writing, rather than to your audience (yet another no-no!).

3. **Overhead projectors.**
   Advantages: Easy to use; bright and clear; great for medium-sized audiences of ten and higher; transparencies are very interactive, since you can write on them; audiences can follow along with identical handout material; and (perhaps the best "pro") you can easily jump forward or backward to answer questions, which may speed up your presentation.
   Drawbacks: Projectors require a screen; they're electrical, so can break down; they have a dated "low-tech" appearance; the lights must usually be dimmed for best viewing and whenever you do this (which I strongly suggest that you don't), you run the risk of losing eye contact with your audience and thus the ability to "see" if they are still connected with your topic.

4. **Laptop, computer-controlled presentations.**
   Advantages: Great for high-tech, animated presentations; entertaining to watch and participate in; can be customized to your audience by scanning in logos or other documentation; any existing video, graphics, or whatever can be added in (albeit sometimes not too easily—I am here to tell you that these laptops and the software they use to create presentations have personalities all their own!).

Drawbacks: Requires a high investment; the learning curve may be lengthy; again, computers can and will break down; they are big and heavy to lug around, even if they only weigh four pounds; they require cables and connectors which have a tendency to grow legs and walk off minutes before your presentation.

5. **Video-teleconferencing.**

   Advantages: Very up-to-date; has a cool image but when you get right down to it, using these gizmos takes plenty of technical know-how.

   Drawbacks: I for one feel that the VITOs of the world enjoy the personal commitment that is inherent in a physical appearance. The only exception to this is if VITO's company is the supplier of such equipment.

Tips on Handouts

VITOs think fast, love to be in control, have short attention spans, and love to participate. With all of this in mind, you should plan your handouts accordingly. Here are some helpful tips:

1. Handouts should look identical to the presentation material that you are projecting on the screen, on the flip chart, or in the binder.
2. They should have plenty of room for "doodling" and taking notes.
3. At several different times during your presentation, you should specifically ask VITO and everyone else to "do" certain things with their handout material. One of my favorite and most successful presentation tactics is to provide my audience with a small set of colored markers (which, of course, have my company logo on them). Throughout out my entire presentation, I ask everyone to use certain colors to highlight certain elements on the handouts: "Please take your yellow marker and highlight the areas which are of greatest concern to you between now and the end of this quarter." "Now . . . on this next page, take your red marker and please flag or add the words that present extreme problems and are causing you to lose market share opportunity." At the end of my presentation, I'll say: "Let's take a moment and recall all of the red flags we set during the time we've spent together." By the time I leave, VITO and I and everyone else have an extremely clear understanding about what course of action is necessary to take the next step and open up this relationship. Besides, color has been proven to increase

information retention by more than 250 percent! I am sure you agree that this is a very, very powerful tactic.

4.   Also provide a small binder so that handouts can be stored easily for future reference.

Should You Make a Product Demonstration?

I'm sure you agree that most activities in life have advantages and disadvantages. Product demos are no exception! If you sell a solution that lends itself easily to an in-person demonstration, you may want to incorporate it into your presentation. However, the operative word here is "easily." I've seen far too many a good presentation turn into a downright disaster because of a demo gone bad. Here's a good rule of thumb to follow to make your presentation and product demo a "ten:"

> *If your demo can be conducted in ten minutes or less,*
> *And be understood by a ten-year-old,*
> *And you've been successful with it ten out of ten times,*
> *Then by all means— do it!*

Here are some of the most important advantages of performing product demonstrations:

1.   Demos let your prospect actually see, hear, or feel what it is that they have the opportunity to invest in.
2.   Demos are rooted in direct experience, so are more likely to leave lasting impressions.
3.   Demos give prospects the opportunity to converse about what would (or will) happen after their investment takes place.
4.   Demos give prospects something "concrete" to talk about after they return to their facility or workgroup.
5.   Demos have the potential to give you an insurmountable edge over the competition (especially if your competition does not give a demonstration, or attempts to give one and executes it poorly).

This last point is worth expanding upon. I make it a habit to never announce to my prospects beforehand that I plan on performing a "demo." This is especially critical if my competition is making their presentation first or is the incumbent provider. Information has a tendency to "leak," and therefore might influence my competition to take the opportunity (or risk) to do a demo, as well. Keeping my intentions to myself gives me the upper hand. However, all of this applies only if my previously mentioned rule of thumb applies.

Here's the flip side—the disadvantages in the demo debate:

1. Demos can go wrong—perhaps disastrously wrong. You'll run into some sales reps who take the view that nothing that's plugged into an AC outlet while a prospect is watching cannot be counted on to function properly (and you can add my name to that contingent).
2. Demos whose execution you delegate to a colleague may, if things go haywire, cause that colleague to lose composure and say something everyone (especially you) will regret. "Oh, the factory just told me that they are fixing this problem in our new release, which will be available next May . . ."
3. Demos may not engage the prospect as much as you think they will.
4. Demos may alarm the prospect as to the difficulty level of your solution.
5. Demos may engage the prospect too much and leave you unable to make the sale because of some variation of the request, "Can I see (it all/some more/a full-scale example) before I make my decision?"

What's the bottom line? If you're really, really confident in your ability to execute the demonstration crisply, professionally, and proficiently, it may just be worth the risk. However, two final words of advice are in order. First, develop a backup strategy—something you can do or say just in case the widgets don't rotate or synchronize in quite the way you've promised. (That strategy should never include the phrases "this has never happened before" or "when this happens, all you have to do is cycle the power off and on.") Second, make sure you (or whoever is conducting the demonstration) get plenty of rehearsal time in before your actual demo. Having said all of this, what it all comes down to is that you should never stray too far from the following fact of life and sales:

> *All the product knowledge in the world cannot
> make up for a lack of people skills.*

Once You're Rolling

Keep all of the following important guidelines in the forefront of your mind as you move forward in delivering your VITO presentation:

During your presentation, you should:

1. Set clear starting and ending times and stick to them. If topics or questions arise that will put you into "overtime," say so and gain

permission to either cover the additional material or table it for a later meeting. By the way, I most certainly prefer the latter option, since it's a great reason to make that all-important follow-up call.

2. Plan on using index cards or some other form of notes to keep you on track and to make sure that you cover all of the topics on the agenda. When you're on a roll, you don't want to make the mistake of jumping ahead or missing some critical points. Believe it or not, referring to prompting notes is actually a compliment to your audience. It says: "You're important and this topic is important. That's why I don't want to forget anything."

3. Try to use two different types of visual media, such as a laptop-generated presentation and a flip chart for interactive topics.

4. Make sure that your handouts follow the principles that I've outlined earlier.

5. Gain and maintain eye contact with all participants throughout your presentation.

6. You'll probably get thirsty, so keep a pitcher of water or your other favorite beverage (nonalcoholic, of course) at close hand.

7. Remember to count to ten after you ask: "What questions do you have?" During that countdown is a great time to take a sip of that beverage.

8. Get in the habit of repeating each question for clarification and making sure that everyone, including you, understands it before you give your answer.

9. Have a notebook and pen handy at all times so you can take notes.

During your presentations you should not:

1. Read statements verbatim from a piece of paper.

2. Talk to the screen, flip chart, overhead projector, or anything other than the audience.

3. Interrupt any member of your audience who may be speaking.

4. Continue to hold a pointer or marker or anything else after you've used it.

5. Carry change in your pockets or fidget with any part of your garments.

6. Exceed sixty minutes without a break for your audience.

7. Let anyone enter the presentation room and interrupt you for any reason other than notification of a bomb scare!

8. Leave the presentation room while another one of your team members is presenting.

Dealing with Questions

During the course of your presentation to VITO, you will no doubt have to answer a question or two. Simple enough. But have you ever been asked a question and answered it, only to have the other person say: "That's not what I asked?" This sends a clear message to the person asking the question that we didn't listen, understand, or care about their concern—or even worse, the answer we offered turned their question into an objection!

To get a better handle on how to answer questions, let's take a closer look at why VITOs ask them in the first place:

1. VITO wants additional information, or validation of facts already known.
2. VITO didn't believe something presented by you or your organization.
3. VITO has a more specific requirement that he or she wasn't addressed.
4. VITO is not totally convinced that you fully understand VITO's particular requirements.
5. VITO is of the opinion that you haven't put forward an acceptable presentation, and is giving you a chance on the spot to revise it out of the goodness of his/her heart.

With VITO (and almost everyone else, too) it's hard to tell immediately which one of these or any other factors may be in play. Fortunately, there is a three-step process that you can use to evaluate any question. By working your way through this process (which, by the way, never concludes until VITO says, "You've got it"), you'll be playing it safe. But in reality, if you did your homework, up-front questions resulting from three of the five reasons above will never happen! Can you figure out which ones they are?

When VITO asks a question, you should:

1. Always—I repeat, *always*—restate VITO's question using your own words. This is not the same thing as repeating the question verbatim. That's called an insult! By the same token, you should never waste time restating obvious or nonessential answers. As an example, VITO might say: "I am concerned about reliability. What type of warranty period comes with your Pathfinder solution?" A typical wrong response: "You're concerned about reliability, aren't you? That's why we at Pathfinder, Inc., have taken the time to develop the best products in the industry . . . blah, blah, blah." A correct response: "VITO, Reliability is one of the top three goals of our

manufacturing process. As good as it is, there is always room to make it better. In the meantime, we offer an extended 2-year warranty that will cover complete replacement of your solution within twenty-four hours of the report of a catastrophic failure! Does this sound like an acceptable solution to you?"

2. Present "social proof" to substantiate your answer. Social proof is real-world evidence that your proposed solution works. It can be based upon the experience of other organizations, other VITOs, or your own in-house experts. Here is an example of using social proof:

   VITO: "Our delivery process gets very complex at times. We have customer orders coming from six different locations! If one of your units were to break down, we may not be able to wait a full 24 hours. How would you handle that requirement?"

   A response using social proof: "VITO, multiple location fulfillment was a nightmare for our own company until we applied our on-site depot to solve the problem. Here, allow me to share with you two different ways this works. One is with an organization similar to yours, the other is with a totally unrelated industry. However, they both share the same methodology." After VITO takes a look at the one that's closest to VITO's industry, he or she will be convinced.

3. Ask whether your answer was sufficient by using a question that influences the direction of the conversation. At the conclusion of your response, you're going to request feedback from VITO, but you're going to do it in a very specific way. You'll never ask if VITO "understood" your answer! For the same reason, you wouldn't ask your sales manager if she understood the verbal status report you just gave her. Here's a better way: "VITO, do you think our methodology would give your facilities the flexibility they need?" This accomplishes two distinct goals: First, it solicits VITO's opinion, and second, it gives VITO a way out. If VITO isn't sure, he/she can always say: "I'll share my thoughts with my VP of Operations and have her give you a call and discuss this further."

---

*Whenever you leave important questions unanswered
or you answer them ineffectively, you leave the door open for
a reasonable question to turn into an objection.
Don't become your most fierce competitor!*

One Final Word

After two and a half decades of selling and twelve years of public speaking, I'll pass along my last piece of advice which is comprised of six words when preparing for and giving epic presentations to VITO:

Join Toastmasters and participate in it!

Chapter 17

Meeting with VITO by Phone and in Person

BY NOW YOU'RE PRIMED TO MEET VITO BY TELEPHONE OR IN PERSON. YOU understand the Influence and Authority Network; you've learned how to build rapport and achieve Equal Business Stature by focusing on solutions. You've developed your first-call objectives and your initial letter to VITO, including that all-important Opening Statement.

But wait! What if VITO tries to shunt you over to Seymour? What if VITO is absolutely in love with another supplier? What if VITO is impressed enough with your call and letter to ask you to come in for a brief meeting—but won't even give you the time of day once you show up? What on earth are you supposed to *say* to VITO once you show up?

We'll be addressing all those issues—and the ever-popular topic of dealing with objections that arise during the sales cycle—in this chapter.

But before we do, take a few moments to go back to Chapter 3 and quickly review the section on building business rapport and the pitfalls to avoid. These are all important points to keep in mind as you prepare for your in-person meeting with VITO.

What's Really on VITO's Mind?

You need to be prepared for anything and everything VITO can throw at you during that first face-to-face meeting. To be in the best possible position to react to the questions and challenges that will be coming your way, you'll have to take a closer look at the way VITO thinks.

VITO—like others within the Influence and Authority Network—has a personal agenda relating to business decisions and actions. The origins of that agenda can be found in the surrounding circumstances VITO faces at any given time: the current financial status of the business, recent moves by competitors, future goals, personal considerations, and, perhaps most important, what VITO perceives and believes about the world as a result of past experience.

Not surprisingly, VITO is going to tend to move toward things that seem to advance items on that personal agenda—and away from things that are seen as obstacles to those items. In fact, at any given time, VITO is likely to be moving either *toward a positive outcome or away from a negative outcome.* (No, VITOs don't usually stand still!) You must be in a position to understand which direction VITO is moving in—and why—during your encounters, so you can chart your own proper parallel course.

The Four Mindsets

You are likely to find VITO (indeed, you are likely to find anyone in the organization) in any number of different mindsets. At this point, we're going to examine the four most popular ones. Your own experience within your industry may give you some further insights. Of course, your overriding goal when communicating with VITO is to determine which mindset is currently predominant and adjust your approach accordingly.

What follows is broadly applicable to phone encounters with VITO, as well as in-person meetings. A word of warning seems appropriate before we examine these four mindsets. You can't assume that VITO's attitude on any given issue is necessarily shared by others in the Influence and Authority Network. Where VITO sees potential (in expanding into a new market, for instance), Seymour and others in the organization may well see only danger and problems (in the form of increased production rates, shortened production cycles, conversion problems with existing software, and a host of other issues).

This is an extremely important point. *A goal for VITO is not necessarily a goal shared by others in the organization.* We may be used to thinking in terms of VITO defining the broad mission statement for the company, and this is certainly accurate enough, but it's a big mistake to assume that *all* of VITO's goals are shared by others in the Influence and Authority Network. Similarly, something VITO perceives as a victory—say, a proposed update of technology that will streamline a bloated organization—may be viewed as a potential catastrophe by others you come in contact with. As a general rule, the higher the person is in the organization, the more likely that person is to share in VITO's perception of what constitutes a "win." Managers and directors tend to see things in generally the same ways that VITO does; Seymours and Consumers typically do not.

That having been said, the necessity of *finding out* how VITO is thinking about the ideas you're discussing remains. When you ask VITO something along the lines of, "Mr. Benefito, what are your [growth, consolidation, asset expansion, etc.] goals for Widget Inc. over the next three months?" pay very close attention to the answer you get. It will almost certainly point you toward one of the following categories.

Mindset One: Opportunity

In this mindset, VITO is open to new ideas. The thought process runs something like this: "All right; our next step is to capture the Asian market for our widgets. How do we make that happen? What do we need to do to make sure that it happens by the end of the fourth quarter?"

Typically, this mindset arises when things are going well. Perhaps new products have been released and are meeting with some initial success in the market. Perhaps VITO's company has increased its market share. Perhaps the new mission statement has lit a fire under everyone in the organization. VITO is moving *toward a positive outcome.*

You're in a great position! VITO's looking for new ways to achieve goals, and is perhaps on the lookout for the edge that will strengthen the company's position even more.

Here are your goals for a conversation with a VITO who is in the Opportunity mindset.

- Support and nurture the current mindset.
- Help VITO understand how the total solution you and your company have to offer translates into *specific benefits* that will advance, even ensure, successful completion of VITO's present and future mission.
- Take this opportunity to sell *expanded solutions* with *near-term add-on potential.* (In other words, take advantage of the fact that the Opportunity mindset is the best one in which to establish the framework for an ongoing partnership with VITO.)
- Be prepared for an average or slightly-longer-than-average sales cycle. VITO is not in a crisis mode and is likely to want to take all the time necessary to make a solid decision. VITO will likely want to check all the angles before signing up with a new business partner who is capable of fulfilling future growth plans.
- Remember that price will *not* typically be a major issue.

Mindset Two: 911

Put out the fire! In this mindset, VITO is trying to correct a crisis situation. The thought process runs something like this: "We're losing ground here."

Maybe the competition is getting an edge. Maybe the economy is sour. Maybe the customer base is shrinking. Whatever the emergency, VITO is dialing 911 and reaching for the nearest extinguisher. VITO is moving *away from the negative result* of a pressing problem.

Here are your goals for a conversation with a VITO who is in the 911 mindset.

- Recognize that a crisis almost always prompts the need to fix this particular problem *now*. Focusing on just about anything else will not win you any points with VITO at this stage. Don't pursue fancy proposals, endless studies, full-blown analyses, or anything else. Sell the scaled-down solution to the crisis at hand, period. (Remember: When the bell rings, firemen don't talk much; they *act*.)
- Recognize that a crisis sometimes dictates buying for price and buying *fast*. And if you've been selling for very long at all, you probably already know that selling on price is a way to establish a *short-term* business relationship—one that is likely to end when the crisis goes away and a lower price comes along.
- Recognize that a crisis often necessitates rapid decision making, and an accompanying acceleration of the sales cycle. This means that VITO may not be taking all factors or potential later disadvantages into account. You must move faster than your competition and be up-to-date with exactly what that competition is offering.
- Upgrade the relationship once a solution is found and successful. After you hand VITO the fire extinguisher, you should never walk away and consider the sale closed. (Remember, we don't close VITO. We open doors!) If you help VITO solve this problem, you will have earned a good measure of loyalty and respect. Immediately after the fire is out, return with your long-term solutions. VITO will probably revert to the Opportunity mindset and may become open to learning the total scope of your solutions.

Mindset Three: "All Set"

In this mindset, VITO is trying to save time by sticking with an existing vendor or supplier—but the conviction that the vendor or supplier is the best partner is not etched in stone. The thought process goes something like this: "Hey, I've got no needs. I believe my current source of supply is taking care of everything." After all, if VITO or his people walked through what every potential vendor or supplier had to offer, nothing would ever get done.

Here are your goals for a conversation with a VITO who is in the "All Set" mindset.

- Understand that VITO's *believing* the company is "all set" with the current source is not the same thing as VITO's being *convinced* the company is "all set" with that source.
- Be willing to professionally but firmly challenge VITO's "all-set" opinion. (We'll look at this in more detail later on.)

- Know the difference between this mindset and the next one, in which there is little or no chance of establishing a business partnership with VITO.

Mindset Four: No Daylight

In this mindset, VITO is set in a firm conviction that the current vendor or supplier is the right one for the organization. Unshakable loyalty exists. The mindset goes something like this: "I've spent a good deal of time looking into this and I've studied all the angles. We've made the best choice, and our current team has it handled. I'm convinced we're going in the right direction already."

In this instance, VITO or someone VITO trusts has gone to the trouble to determine that the current vendor or supplier is definitely the one to stay with.

You are extremely unlikely to win this VITO's account. However, if you want to try making a presentation, it probably can't hurt.

Here are your goals for a conversation with a VITO who is in the "No Daylight" mindset.

- Expect a very long interest-building cycle before the sales cycle begins in earnest.
- Try convincing VITO that you have a better solution by broadcasting your very best references, and by passing along, very slowly and skillfully, a large number of staggering testimonials from customers who are willing to back up what you are saying by talking to VITO on the phone.
- Invite VITO to various business events. Expose VITO to the other VITOs who are your loyal customers.
- Arrange to be awarded a Congressional Medal of Honor if you eventually win this VITO's account. In the vast majority of cases, it will not happen even if you follow the steps just outlined.

Remember—There Are Two Categories Here

On the one hand, you may be dealing with the VITOs who head up companies in your *existing customer base*. On the other hand, you may be dealing with VITOs who lead organizations that you have never contacted before.

For the first group, your aim is to quantify and broadcast the continuing benefit—preferably in dollar terms—of doing business with you. For the second group, your aim is to *listen* for current requirements, and then to highlight your past successes and explore the possibility of a mutually beneficial business partnership.

Most of what follows is designed to help you make the most of your meeting with VITOs at companies you have not yet worked with. We'll talk more about VITOs at your current accounts a little bit later.

The First Few Seconds

You've probably heard it a thousand times: You don't get a second chance to make a first impression. If that's true in business in general, it's doubly so in dealing with VITOs, especially ones that represent potential new accounts for you. What do you do to make sure that you stand out from the pack as a different kind of business professional when you first make it into VITO's office?

You may remember that I came down very strongly against using company stationery or other identifying material in your initial letter to VITO. That was a letter—this is a meeting. Now is the *perfect* time to use your company logo to advantage. Here's what you do.

During your first meeting with VITO, pass along a three-ringed binder with your company logo on the front. You might decide to make the first page a copy of your initial letter or of any other correspondence you have sent along before this point. Explain that your gift to VITO has a practical purpose. You'll be sending along updates on your progress with others in the organization on a regular basis—and VITO can include each within the binder. This is a very strong, highly professional way to begin your first meeting with both VITOs at companies you have not yet worked with and those in your current customer base. Taking this approach will automatically distinguish you from the vast majority of salespeople VITO has met with.*

---

* There is another method exclusively for use in first meetings with VITOs in existing accounts. This is an existing account to which you've been delivering some undeniable hard-dollar (say, lower production costs) and soft-dollar (say, improved employee morale) results. Order a custom-made coffee cup that prominently features your company logo and colors. I find a large executive-size cup and a matching coaster works best. You'll probably spend fifteen dollars on this, but believe me, it will be money well spent.

Attach a small tag to this item. On this tag, detail the measurable, quantifiable savings that you've been able to achieve in VITO's company. Wrap the cup in a little box and give it to VITO as an introduction present. When VITO unwraps it right then and there and sees the beautiful cup, you'll probably see a smile and hear something like, "What's this?" That's when you say, "VITO, working with Seymour, we've been able to quantify that our business relationship has (increased revenue, increased efficiencies and effectiveness of revenue-generating/mission-critical employees and/or mission-critical processes, helped protect existing market share, created add-on business from that existing market share, decreased expenses)." Sound familiar? And you will have planted a permanent "silent sales rep" that will sit on VITO's desk for the length of your partnership.

Here's a powerful illustration of how anchoring your results to a coffee cup in this way really can make a huge difference in the way VITO perceives your organization. One rep I know, named Frank, gave VITO the cup after having implemented his company's program. The tag on the handle read, "Increased production for third quarter: Net Benefit to Benefito Industries, $650,000." That cup stuck around the office for a good long while, a constant reminder of exemplary performance. But the story gets better! The rep made a routine visit to VITO three years later and noticed that the handle on the cup had broken. VITO had glued it back on. "VITO," Frank said, "why don't you let me get you another cup?" VITO said, "Don't you dare touch that. That's my $650,000 cup!" Imagine—three years later, and VITO still remembered!

So. You walk in the door. You look VITO in the eye. You say, "Mr. Benefito, it's great to finally meet you." Following VITO's lead and style, you shake hands firmly and confidently. You pass along your notebook and/or coffee mug. What next?

Beyond the First Few Seconds: Opening Your Business Conversation with VITO

VITO is usually rushed. Don't be discouraged. Be like VITO: brief and to the point. Whether on the phone or during an in-person meeting, proceed to your Opening Statement. As always, pace yourself so that VITO can interrupt you and do the talking. When VITO talks, *listen and take notes* in your VITO journal, of course!

In general, follow all the rules for phone contact with VITO that were outlined in Chapter 11.

"I don't have much time. What's on your mind?"

Regardless of which of the four mindsets your VITO is in when you encounter each other, and regardless of whether you're talking on the telephone or meeting in person, you're likely to hear something like these two sentences at the outset of your exchange.

First of all, remember those two big fears VITO has about salespeople. You must not waste time. And you must not ask VITO idiotic questions.

- "Who's your long distance carrier?"
- "How much have you spent on overseas calls this quarter?"
- "Are your people happy with their office equipment?"
- "Do you have a service contract on your copiers?"
- "How long have you been buying floppy disks made in Pakistan?"

VITO doesn't know the answer to these questions, and if you ask them you'll be seen as a challenge to VITO's authority.

"What Happens After I Say My Opening Statement?"

Following are some examples of different conversations that could conceivably follow your Opening Statement. Parts that must be customized to your selling environment are set apart (in parentheses).

The following conversations are provided as guidelines only! Please do not attempt to march lockstep through the conversation, with these conversations as your "scripts." It won't work. VITO never knows the lines! And keep in mind that your conversation will last only as long as VITO wants it to last. VITO is in complete control; all you can do is influence the conversation with the proper questions and answers, and stay away from features and functions—the "F" words that will trigger VITO's second fear of salespeople and cause VITO to automatically disconnect from your conversation.

Opening Statement Response #1: "I'm Interested"

> VITO: You know, we were just talking about that this morning at our staff meeting. It sounds great. Tell me all about it!

Sounds like a dream come true, doesn't it? Be careful!

At seminars, when I ask salespeople to tell me how they'd respond to this request of VITO's, there are two answers that come up more often than any others. The first is, "Press for an appointment. Tell VITO you'll be in the area on Monday morning at 8:00, and ask if that's a good time. After all, if he's that interested, he'll want to spend some time with you to discuss it." The second is, "Tell VITO everything about the product, service, or solution. After all, you've just been asked to tell VITO all about it!" Both of these answers represent big problems for you if you follow through on them!

Meeting with VITO is great, and there's a time and a place to do it—but your objective is to get VITO to tell you to come in, not the other way around. As for going all-out on a description of your product, service, or solution, *you just don't know enough* about VITO yet to do that. Remember, we salespeople tend to talk too much, particularly during phone encounters. Sometimes it's hard to tell if what we're passing along is really engaging VITO and addressing the needs of the organization, and sometimes we stray from our objective of discussing benefits with VITO, and fall into the trap of discussing features. So to avoid that, I'm going to suggest that you resist the temptation to do a "product dump" at this stage.

Here's what you should do when you hear VITO say something like "Tell me all about that (product/service/solution) of yours." Give VITO a choice of three things to talk about, attach a time line, and then follow along. This brings us to an important call objective: determining VITO's goals, plans, and objectives over a particular period of time. But you don't do this by asking, "VITO, what are your company's goals for this year?" That's much too vague. VITO isn't going to take time to educate you about all that! Instead, try this approach.

> *You:*   VITO, the other (manufacturing clients) that I deal with tell me that these three things are of paramount importance to them. In the next quarter, will you be focusing on . . .

Then you list for VITO no more than three *benefits you are able to deliver to others in VITO's industry.* Here's another example of what it might look like.

> *You:*   Our (retail customers) say they're focused on (increasing
>   employee effectiveness, consolidating operations, and
>   assuring the highest level of customer retention and satisfac-
>   tion). Are you looking at any of these areas in the (next
>   quarter)?

These three things may in fact be the same three things that are listed in your letter. But they *must be benefits.* Stay away from features at all costs! If VITO picks one, go into more detail *about that benefit,* citing success stories from your company's past where appropriate.

Let's say that you lay out three benefits, A, B, and C—and VITO says none of them are of interest. Don't throw out another three! Ask for VITO's guidance one more time.

> *VITO:*   What you just outlined is not what we're focusing on here next
>   quarter.

> *You:*   Well, there are a lot of other areas we could be looking at.
>   What will you be focusing on next quarter?

Opening Statement Response #2: "Oh? How Do You Do That?"

Suppose you begin to move toward your success stories, but VITO cuts you off at the pass.

> *You:*   Mr. Benefito, we've done a lot of work with companies in your
>   industry, and I am certain we have a few new ideas to get your
>   product to market quicker without sacrificing quality.

> *VITO:*   Oh? How do you do that?

Be careful! Don't lecture VITO on Features over the phone. In person, you can monitor reactions more closely, but over the phone, you'll have no idea how VITO is reacting to what you have to say.

Features bore most VITOs to tears. I make it a personal rule never to mention Features to a VITO during an initial phone contact, and only to do so in person after I have seen persuasive evidence that I am dealing with a VITO who has a genuine Seymour outlook on the world. These are pretty rare, but they are out there. Otherwise, I stick with Benefits and, if those seem to have made an impression, the related Advantages. (You might want to take this opportunity to review one of the Network of Influence and Authority charts featured in Chapter 7. Feel free to draw an arrow from BENEFIT to ADVANTAGE on the chart—and then draw a vertical line to the *right* of FEATURE. This will help you remember that it's always permissible to move from a Benefit to an Advantage in talking to a VITO on the phone, but very dangerous indeed to talk about Features.)

If you're pressed on this point during a telephone conversation, you could tell VITO that you have people on your staff who handle the technical parameters, and that if VITO likes, you can have them drop by for a quick briefing with VITO's technical staff. Talk about Equal Business Stature!

Alternatively, you could tell VITO that a technical discussion will require several charts and spec sheets, and that the resulting conversation may last upwards of fifteen or twenty minutes. Then conclude by saying, "If you want, I can have someone here fax the specs to you directly. There's about four or five pages, and we should use them as source documents, because this could get into a somewhat lengthy technical discussion." I guarantee you, this will refocus the discussion.

Stay on Benefits and Advantages and you will never go wrong.

Opening Statement Response #3: "But You're Not the Lowest Price"

> *VITO:*   I've heard you guys are not the lowest price in town, and I always buy the lowest price.

> *Note:* What comes next takes unshakable confidence, but do it anyway.

> *You:*   VITO, could you please define "price"?

> *VITO:*   What do you mean by that? "Price" means the lowest number.

> *You:*   Well, others in (VITO's industry), such as (use specific names), have defined "price" as . . .

Be prepared to provide examples of how your other customers in VITO's industry have defined price. "Mr. Benefito, the other manufacturing clients, such as ABC Corporation, tell me that price includes higher effectiveness and better attitudes among key employees, especially as this relates to total quality management. Other elements of price I've heard about would be lower turnover and increased process control. Are these factors part of *your* price equation?" This approach would probably fail spectacularly with our binary friends, the Seymours. VITOs, however, will understand what you're getting at.

Opening Statement Response #4: "Sorry, Not Interested"

VITO: I have no interest whatsoever in this.

You: I really didn't expect you to have any interest. If you did, you would have called me!

Warning! This takes practice. You cannot run the risk of sounding sanctimonious or sarcastic. Here are two alternate approaches:

You: It's not that surprising to me to hear you say that, Mr. Benefito. You know, most of the top people I talk to aren't interested until they realize exactly how we can become a partner in helping them achieve important goals for this (quarter/fiscal year/whatever).

OR:

You: You know, it is amazing to me that I have the (2,000) customers that I do, Mr. Benefito. Because they *all* said they had no interest at first. But then they took the time to take a look at how we could help them with a few of their most important goals.

Again, listen and take notes to whatever VITO says in response. If what VITO outlines leads you to believe your solution can in fact help, follow VITO's lead and supply appropriate success stories that are directly tied in to the problems he identifies. If your solution really can't help, but you know of another solution that can, by all means tell VITO about it! I call this *building value-added rapport,* and it turns VITOs into long-term business allies. You will probably have an open door to call VITO at a later date to find out whether or not VITO used your suggestion and how things worked out. Remember, you'll need business three months from now, too.

Opening Statement Response #5: "It's Not My Priority Now"

VITO: What you just said is not a current priority.

Retain your Equal Business Stature, then bail out. As a businessperson, you must be willing to accept that what you have to offer may not be at the top of VITO's list at this point in time. Ask one solid question, follow up, and back off.

You: When do you feel this will become a priority—(one month, two months, three months) from now?

VITO: (Perhaps peeved by your persistence.)

You: (Very conversational.) I apologize for being so bold, Mr. Benefito, but we've helped (44) other firms in your field to achieve (mention one or two of your very best benefits). Sometimes I get overly enthusiastic about giving everyone that edge. Maybe my solution isn't right for you at this time.

If you still get a negative reaction after an exchange such as this, odds are good that you are dealing with a VITO who is in a No Daylight mindset. Don't try to push; it won't work. Just disengage, thank VITO for the time, keep the contact active, and check in by phone or mail every now and then to see whether your message will be likely to be greeted with more interest.

Opening Statement Response #6: "I'm All Set, Thanks"

The following technique is for when you're trying to determine whether or not VITO's loyalty to the current supplier really is unshakable. Like much of the rest of this book, it's not for the faint of heart, and it does take unshakable confidence. But you may find that it works wonders for you.

VITO: I'm extremely happy with my current source of supply. They take care of all our needs. I would never consider changing.

You: Mr. Benefito, would you be interested in knowing what your loyalty is costing you? (Or: Would you be interested in knowing how much your loyalty is costing you?) (Or: Would you like to know if you're missing out on anything as a result of this loyalty?) (Or: Would you like to know if your organization's loyalty is costing you anything?)

You've just challenged VITO's world. But you know what? VITO can take it. But you have to be ready for what's coming next; you have to be prepared with quantifiable results to back up your challenge.

VITO: What do you mean by that? Even if my loyalty were costing me something, I'd never go through the nightmare of converting everything. All that time, effort, and energy counts for something, too.

Don't be vague in your response! Cite specific amounts that you have been able to save others in VITO's industry.

You: Would it be worth ($22,000)? One of our customers found that loyalty to another supplier was costing them ($22,000) yearly in direct costs alone. Now, that's the hard dollars. There were soft dollar costs, too: (employee turnover, poor response rate to customer complaints, lapses in quality control). Mr. Benefito, would you like an opportunity to discover what your hard and soft savings could be?

You: Mr. Benefito, the ABC company was able to (decrease their average time to market with new products by 12 percent) by working with us. I don't know how much your loyalty is costing you now—but would you be interested in going to the next step so we could find out exactly what your savings could be?

STOP TALKING! Wait for VITO's reply. It may take a while, and you may feel a powerful urge to fill in the gap in the conversation. Don't do it. Stand your ground and let VITO respond to this question . . . then follow VITO's lead. If you get a negative response, you are in all likelihood looking at a No Daylight mindset. But the conversation may well proceed along these lines:

VITO: What would it take to find that out? (Or: What are you talking about? How would you get that kind of information?) (Or: What is this "next step" you're talking about?) (Or: We don't plan on changing, but just out of curiosity, how would you go about finding something like that out?)

If you get any response along these lines from your challenge to VITO's loyalty, it will be the biggest sign of interest you'll ever get from someone who's said "not interested." You must be ready with the exact action plan that will help VITO determine how much that loyalty is costing. If you *cannot* lay out all of the steps of your action plan, do not challenge VITO's loyalty in the first place!

You: Well, Mr. Benefito, first I'll need (fifteen minutes) of your time to go over a few business issues, then (four hours) with (Seymour, the CFO, the manager of the department, whomever), then eight hours back in my office to put it together—and if we start today I can be back to you by (4:00

> P.M. on Thursday) with a complete summary of the benefits
> and hard- and soft-dollar savings we can offer you.

Of course, where you see the information in parentheses, you should insert your own time frames. You must customize them to your own experience within the industry, and you must be able to stick to what you say. Don't ever promise VITO a five-minute meeting that can't be conducted in less than twenty.

Important Note! VITO's "How-would-you-find-that-out" question and your "Here's-what-I'll-need" response marks the successful outcome of your first visit with VITO! This exchange is the unspoken aim of *all* of these sales dialogues. Of course, you must first *wait* for VITO to ask you the question. Once you hear it, though, you should set out what you're looking for in a straightforward way, establish the dates and times, ask VITO the *broad* questions you need to ask, then get off the phone or out of VITO's office and get to work. It bears repeating that you must not at any stage of your relationship with VITO, and certainly not at this one, pepper VITO with questions about past contract history, specific prices, service contracts, or any other mundane details.

Opening Statement Response #7: "No Way You Can Help Me"

> *VITO:*   I really doubt that you people can help with any of our corpo-
> rate goals.

Important note: In dealing with this and other responses from VITO, remember that you're looking for base hits, not home runs. Highlight a specific, demonstrable benefit for VITO, even if it's not the kind of benefit that turns an industry upside down. The VITOs of the world today are looking in every corner of their organization for savings and increased efficiencies. Base hits—dollars, cents, minutes, seconds—count!

> *You:*   The president of (Rogers International) initially questioned
> our ability to handle diverse tasks. She was surprised to see the
> real difference we made in cutting down on inventory without
> the worry of stock-outs.

STOP TALKING. If VITO does not respond within five seconds, proceed with something along these lines:

> *You:*   Her results may be hard or even impossible to duplicate,
> but would you like to take the first step to find out if you
> might be able to realize a similar or even greater benefit?

Opening Statement Response #8: "I Know All About Your Company"

> VITO: I've heard of your company. We really have no interest in pur-
> suing this.
>
> You: Mr. Benefito, do you not have the interest—or do you not have
> the time?

It's been my personal experience that there's a tremendous difference between not having interest and not having time. Highlighting the distinction may well win you a hearing. Both of these responses come from an initial misunderstanding on VITO's part as to the actual reason for your call and the benefits your solutions can offer. If you run into this objection time and time again, you should examine your opening statement more closely. (In the event, you may want to try to rescue the situation by saying something like, "VITO, maybe *I* didn't do a good enough job explaining exactly what this call/visit is about and what my company has to offer.")

Opening Statement Response #9: "Talk to Seymour"

You must master this response and overcome it if you want to sell to VITO. In all likelihood, you will find that this is the single most popular response to your opening statement.

You are not doing your job if you accept this shunt to Seymour without getting the answers you need.

> VITO: I'm way too busy to talk about this. I have people on my staff
> to look at these issues. You want to talk with Seymour Jones in
> our design and development group.

Whether VITO says something like the above during a call or an in-person meeting, you *must* find some way to salvage the situation. During a telephone call, this kind of response presents a particularly tough challenge, as VITO will be tempted to connect you to Seymour without asking you your opinion on the matter. If you let that happen, or if you let VITO steer you out of the office and toward Seymour's, you will not have accomplished your objectives. Try this.

> You: Before Seymour spends his valuable time and your company's
> money talking with me, let me ask you—what are you looking
> for in a business relationship?

Trust me. This is a show-stopper. Only VITO can answer this question; the response you get will give your business relationship with VITO two immediate and powerful benefits. First, you will quickly build Equal Business Stature by showing VITO that you understand the importance of conserving employee time and expense. Second, you will develop insights on how VITO makes decisions and looks at the issue of spending capital.*

"Here's What I Look for in a Business Relationship, but . . ."

I was granted fifteen minutes with the president and founder of one of the largest photo developing companies in the country. I had prepared for the meeting for days. What would I say? What would VITO say? How would the conversation flow? What should we discuss? Let me tell you here and now, this question about business criteria was not on my list.

Well, the time for my meeting rolled around, and I was escorted to the president's suite. (As you might imagine, this man's office had more than a few spectacular photographs on display, but having already learned my lesson on "icebreakers," I did not comment on any of them.) I sat down, ready to discuss the president's plans, goals, and objectives for the upcoming year.

The meeting rolled along pretty smoothly. At the end of the fifteen minutes, the president shook my hand and started to walk me out the door. I stopped in the doorway, looked him in the eye, and said, "VITO, it was an honor to meet with you today, but I couldn't help noticing the painting over your credenza. Can I ask you what the significance of that painting is?"

It was a large oil painting of QualComm Stadium in San Diego. The stadium was filled with people waving colorful flags and holding up banners. The bleachers were packed. In the foreground was a two-door 1961 Chevy Impala. The front wheels were off the ground, but the car was not moving forward. It was bouncing up and down. There was a man standing alongside one of the front wheels with a yardstick. Another man was leaning over, apparently to determine how high the car was bouncing.

It was a very strange painting.

---

* The technique for adapting this to VITO's secretary or assistant should, at this point, come as no surprise. If VITO's secretary ever says that you're being transferred to Seymour, say, "Before Seymour spends his valuable time and your company's money talking with me, could you get VITO's answer to one question? What does VITO look for in a business relationship?" Trust me on this one too! Say it with conviction and a sense of responsibility, and this will prompt an immediate response from VITO's secretary, something like, "You mean you're not going to speak with Seymour until I get this question answered from VITO?" To which you can reply, "Well, wouldn't it be a shame if Seymour spent all his time with me only to find out that I'm not able to satisfy VITO's critical business requirements?" Now you can have a very casual conversation with VITO's secretary about the importance of you and your organization totally understanding VITO's goals and exactly how VITO selects a business partner. It would almost be irresponsible to shunt you over to Seymour without nailing down this essential information!

The president said, "Tony, there's a contest here in San Diego. Car buffs set up their cars with hydraulic springs and compete to see whose car can bounce the highest."

And I asked, "Well, how does that fit in with your business?"

You know what the president said? He said, "Tony, I have a yardstick of my own. When people come into my office with new ideas, the person who registers the highest on my yardstick wins."

And it was then that I asked a VITO for the first time: "Could you please share with me the elements of your yardstick?" In other words, what exactly are you looking to measure with that yardstick?

We talked about his priorities for a solid forty-five minutes. This at the conclusion of my scheduled fifteen-minute meeting! I left that office knowing exactly what I would need to do to work with that VITO. In the months that followed, I focused on what he'd told me and nothing else. And I won that account.

When you ask VITO about the criteria for establishing a new business partnership, you may get an answer like this:

> *VITO:*   Well, I look for a supplier/partner/business partner ready to take responsibility and solve problems. When a new solution becomes available, I want a proactive team to be watching out for me and making sure that I'm getting the very best value and solution for my needs. In brief, I want new and creative ideas. I want a partner who's into total quality management. So, now that I've cleared that up for you, you'll want to talk to Seymour Jones, who makes all recommendations in this area for me.

STOP! You still can't let this happen until you've gotten your answer to the big question of whether or not VITO would do business with you. If VITO tries again to shunt you to Seymour, you must keep this from happening.

Here's what to say.

> *You:*   Mr. Benefito, if my company can measure up to your business criteria and satisfy Seymour's technical needs, could you picture yourself as one of our customers by (the end of the next quarter, the end of the fiscal year, or the end of some other, similarly specific time period)?

If VITO says no firmly and without reservation, you've got the ultimate qualifier. But this is rarer than you might think. After all, VITOs don't get to be VITOs by passing up opportunities! (They also don't tie up the time of key people in their organization by making them spend time with salespeople who don't offer something of value.) You are more likely to hear an answer like this:

VITO: Well, we have a lot to discuss yet. But if you could satisfy my staff, and if I could get an edge using your solution, maybe I could see myself working with your organization. (Or: Well, I'm never one to pass up a good business opportunity, but I'm just not sure if you're right for us. It's too early to tell.)

Important note! Never ask VITO "why," especially when you've been presented with vague statements like "just not sure" or "need to feel more comfortable" or "not certain." Pressing VITO for specifics at this stage is usually a bad idea. Similarly, you should never try to make VITO "understand" something you think has been missed at this stage of your relationship.

Many salespeople ask me questions that miss this fundamental point. They ask, "How do I make VITO *understand* that he's overlooked an important point when he answers this question *without knowing all the facts*?" You don't! You can't! If you attempt to do so, you will be robbing VITO of ego, power, control, and authority, and your Equal Business Stature will be gone forever!

The key is to put things in VITO's language and work from there. If you have an opportunity that VITO feels is legitimate, you will get results. If you don't, you won't. Period.

Let me tell a little story that illustrates my point. Many years ago I was working to sell a large computer system to a company, and I had the president come in for a demonstration. My systems engineer, my manager, and I were there, giving a demonstration to the president of this company on a relational database. Now, relational databases are very complex animals, and if you're not familiar with them already, I hope you'll forgive me if I don't try to explain them to you here. This president was sitting there, shoulder to shoulder with my systems engineer; the demo started; the systems engineer launched into his explanation; and as he went on, I saw VITO get more and more confused about exactly what was taking place. How could I tell? He got more and more quiet! He stopped asking questions about twenty minutes into the demonstration.

Well, the systems engineer's fingers were flying across the keyboard. He was chattering away, expounding upon all the features of this relational database. We reached a point where the systems engineer had to take a deep breath before diving into another ocean of technical information. During that brief pause, VITO looked at me and asked, "Tony, how much memory does this machine have?"

I think he asked me that because it was the only question he felt comfortable posing—and notice that he didn't pose it to the systems engineer, but to me! Now, my manager (who thought everything was going great) expected me to answer VITO in a certain way. And the systems engineer (who was happy to have a chance to show off all he knew) also expected me to answer VITO in a certain way. What they both expected was for me to say something like, "VITO, this machine has two megabytes of main memory, expandable to eight. And then we could put on an accelerator, which would add another two megabytes, and even that doesn't include the on-line storage, which goes up to three gigabytes." But I didn't say that.

What I said was, "VITO, this machine will never forget anything you tell it."

When I said that, the president started to smile. Then he said, "Finally—something I can understand!"

The systems engineer's eyeballs rolled back in his head. My manager's ears issued forth with clouds of steam. At the end of the presentation, the president shook everyone's hand and went home. My manager called me into the office and said, "Tony, this is a technology-driven organization. When you are asked a question by the president of a company, I expect you to give a proper answer. Don't be so cute. Next time, give the proper technical response to a question like that."

A few months later, when I'd sold that system, I went to my manager's office, slid the $265,000 purchase order right on the desk, and said, "This is for the machine that never forgets."

Whenever you feel the temptation to get VITO to understand, stop—unless you want to see how VITOs act when they feel insecure. (And you'll never want to see that more than once in a lifetime.) Knowledge is power, and VITOs, as a rule, don't like to be in any situation in which they feel they know less than the other people in the room.

It's a funny thing about salespeople. Our first instinct is to talk change, change, change, to our customers. That's a brick wall! VITOs know they know their business better than you do. When you tell them they have to change, or that they don't understand—you lose big time.

So what *do* you say? Let's assume you get a less than iron-clad "no" at this point to your "would-you-buy-from-us" question, a "no" that sounds like it might have a little daylight around the edges. Try something like this.

You: Mr. Benefito, your advice is important to me. If the president
         of a company that was *your* best prospective customer said no
         at this point to one of your best salespeople, what would you
         expect your person to do?

That's the technique that works best for me, and I strongly suggest that you use it. But if you—or, perhaps, your sales manager—feel you must, despite my warnings, ask about the *why* behind VITO's objection, try this approach.

> *You:*   Mr. Benefito, you obviously have good reasons for saying no at this point. Would you please share them with me?

If there is daylight in the sale, you will know it after using one of these two approaches.

Four Rules

There are four cardinal rules for dealing with VITO early on. They are:

1. Be specific.
2. Use time lines.
3. Always deliver what you promise.
4. Never challenge VITO's ego, power, control, and authority.

Things are likely to get pretty hectic in a meeting with VITO; you may have difficulty taking down notes or remembering where you are in the cycle. Here is my promise to you, though: If you remember the four rules I've just outlined for you, none of that will matter.

Never Be Late for a VITO Appointment!

When you make that all-important, in-person first appointment, make sure that you show up early! Double check your directions and plan on getting to VITO's lobby at least ten to fifteen minutes early. Why? First of all, it will reduce the stress normally associated with getting somewhere on time. Secondly, it will give you some time to take a look around. Are there plaques on the wall celebrating high achievements in quality, customer service, or sales? Is there a list of famous clients, or letters from satisfied customers? Pull out your VITO journal from your briefcase and write down all the pertinent information. Is there a company newsletter you can keep to which you might submit an article for future inclusion? You can even take some time to circle VITO's facility before you take that parking space. Do you notice any of your competitor's names? Are there any product boxes lying around bearing names that look familiar? It's amazing what you could learn by observing who is pulling up to the loading dock. Finally, if there is a visitor's sign-in log, take the time to flip a few pages and see who's been calling on whom. Grab every opportunity you can to observe and learn!

Where Do You Go from Here?

We've now covered the basic outline of your initial contact with VITO, whether that contact takes place in person, on the phone, or a combination of the two. In the next chapter, you'll find advice on the best ways to involve VITO in the sales cycle as it progresses.

Chapter 18

Keeping VITO Involved

LET'S ASSUME YOU RECEIVE POSITIVE FEEDBACK FROM VITO AFTER ASKING YOUR initial questions, but have been told in no uncertain terms that you must deal with Seymour. This is not an uncommon result, and it's nothing to get discouraged about. The message you're getting is a simple one: VITO is a prudent business person who values the opinions of the people in the organization. That's fine. Your objective is simply to *involve VITO in the process from the beginning and be in a position to broadcast your findings to VITO throughout the entire cycle.*

Warning! The tactics we'll be examining in this chapter will not, repeat, *not* work with municipalities, government agencies, or similar groups. When government bodies buy something, they go out to bid; when the bids are sent out, the doors are closed. Period. You cannot get in to see these people; in fact, you will probably be breaking the law if you try to do so. Other vendors can file complaints if you try to meet with people making purchasing decisions after the bids are opened. In such instances, you will, alas, be unable to bring VITO—or anyone else—to the plate as your ally in the same way you would be able to (and with perfect confidence in your propriety) in other settings.

Keeping VITO Apprised

Within two or three days of your first meeting with your Feature-hungry friend Seymour, which I'll assume you need no coaching on, call VITO. Ask if you can drop by alone to chat briefly and provide an executive briefing on your meeting with Seymour. You should probably specify that the meeting will last less than, say, five minutes. VITO probably won't have patience for anything much longer.

If you have followed the steps outlined in the previous chapter, correctly identifying VITO's mindset and asking appropriate questions, VITO should agree to meet briefly with you. After all, you've got Equal Business Stature!

While in VITO's office, incorporate something like the following into your conversation:

You: Looks like Seymour and I will be spending a lot of time together pursuing some ideas for your organization. Could you do me one personal favor? When the decision is made for or against my company, would you grant me the honor of an in-person visit with you?

If VITO agrees, make a note of the date of your request and put it in your prospect file.

If VITO rejects your request for a meeting, say:

You: VITO, my company will be spending some pretty significant time and resources over the next (several months). Meeting your criteria is of the utmost importance to us. If we fail to earn your business, my company has to continue to learn.

My own experience is that, if the work leading up to this point has been done properly, VITO will almost always agree to your request for a meeting when you frame it in these terms. Good thing, too, since this promise for a meeting is of the utmost importance in your later management of the sales cycle. (In the unlikely event that you cannot win an agreement for a later meeting, your only option in the event of trouble will be the Pigeonhole Recovery Letter described in an earlier chapter.)

Loss Recovery

If, at any point during the sales cycle, you detect any signals that you're losing, call VITO for the face-to-face meeting.

You: Mr. Benefito, back on (exact date when VITO promised you a meeting), you promised me the privilege of an in-person visit, whether your decision was for or against my solution. Will you honor your promise and grant me that visit tomorrow?

VITO: Guess I did promise you. Come on in at 10:15.

If you've done your job correctly up to this point, which includes keeping in touch with VITO throughout the sales cycle, you should have no trouble getting a positive response of some kind to your request.

Don't get nervous about setting this appointment. (In fact, nervousness in asking for it is probably a bigger obstacle than anything VITO has to offer.)

VITO is, as a general rule, quite honest—perhaps the most honest person in the organization—and will keep promises. You should not have to work too hard to win your hearing.

You must now get your manager involved in the sale—or perhaps another person of higher rank in your organization. For our purposes, we'll refer to this person as "your manager" here.

Prepare your manager to assist you with this meeting, your last chance to win this account. If possible, prepare a compelling visual presentation of your solution. See Chapters 15 and 16. *Keep it simple.* Don't deal in abstracts or intangibles—find something concrete, something hard or soft, hot or cold, or wet or dry that VITO can hold. Then, with your manager, isolate your best success stories and endorsements, and stand back and let the Guiding VITO Principle come into play.

What, you may ask, is the Guiding VITO Principle? It's a simple idea that underlies everything we've covered so far.

> *You can't sell VITO. Only VITO can sell VITO.*

What's more, VITOs *love to convince themselves that they've made the right decision.* Let this predilection of theirs work in your favor.

Don't press. Don't panic. Don't shower VITO with a blizzard of supporting documentation—that's Seymour stuff. Spotlight your successes, make it tangible, make it *stick* . . . then stand back. If there are silences, *wait them out* and hear what VITO has to say.

If this final attempt fails, at least you got a last shot. And as you leave VITO's office, you'll hear your manager say, "You did the best you could; that wasn't the right deal for us." Even if it doesn't come down your way, you'll be a hero in your manager's eyes.

Win Broadcasting

As the sales cycle matures, you may see clear signals that you're winning. Now is the time to broadcast this very likely possibility. This is the time for a trial commitment to opening a business relationship with VITO. Remember, you are not "closing a sale!" (To my way of thinking, the only way you "close" a sale is to lose it.)

Follow the same principles outlined above in securing a meeting with VITO. When you sit down with VITO, outline all the progress you've made with Seymour.

Make Seymour a hero in VITO's eyes. You'll have everybody smiling, and you will have laid the groundwork for a long-term partnership.

Show VITO all the potential savings you and Seymour have identified together. Quantify everything. Speak openly and specifically. Do not equivocate. Blow your own horn and be straightforward in the results you foresee delivering to VITO's organization.

At some point in the meeting, say something like this:

You: Mr. Benefito, as you know, we're absolutely committed to developing a long-term partnership that benefits your organization. When my competition—(and here mention all the competitors you know have been calling on this account)—finds out that you're favoring our solution, they may come in here and try to pull a few fast moves. Are you going to be able to resist them and those tempting "special deals" they're going to show you? Are you going to be able to resist their sly little "special offers"? Will you say "no" to them?

Now you must watch VITO's body language with a very critical eye. Your "sure order" may be in serious trouble, even at this late stage.

At the conclusion of your meeting, strive to leave the door open for a return visit. *Never, under any circumstances, leave your VITO alone during the last few critical weeks of the sales cycle.* If you can't arrange a meeting, call!

Once again, if you manage the endgame correctly, you won't have to worry about "closing." (And isn't *that* a relief.) During your Win Broadcast meeting, VITO will in all likelihood *tell* you when to start and what to do next. That's exactly where you want to be.

PART 5

Success!

"The fastest method I've seen to sales success!"
—Brian Carlson

When you mastered this section you will have the ability to:

1. *Exceed VITO's expectations of a business partner*
2. *Get to VITO in all of your existing accounts*
3. *Use guarantees as a winning sales tool*

═══ Key Thought ═══

Success has many different definitions. If you focus on VITO's definition first, you'll achieve your success sooner rather than later!

Chapter 19

Success!

YOU GOT THE "YES"! CONGRATULATIONS. YOU'VE DEVELOPED A BUSINESS relationship with VITO's organization. You've opened a new door and established a new partnership.

As I have reminded you throughout this book, you must not imagine that you can "close" a sale with VITO and then walk away.

You must personally see that the results you promised are delivered. You must maintain contact with VITO and with all other important influencers in the organization *throughout the lifecycle of the account.* In this chapter you'll find some ideas on how to do that.

Formalize the Partnership

Look around the American business landscape today. Which companies are in trouble? The companies that

- Got complacent
- Took customers for granted
- Read their own PR materials and believed them
- Thought the words "market share" were some kind of magic incantation that would ward off customer-focused competitors
- Depended too much on high-priced marketing plans

All those companies are dead or dying. The companies that are going through the roof are the ones that are committing to becoming partners for life with their customers. Show VITO which category your firm falls into.

After the bottom line is signed and the widget delivery is scheduled, if you have not already done so, prepare a blank binder with your company logo on the front. Either schedule a formal "good-to-be-working-with-you" meeting with VITO—or, if this doesn't work out, briefly pop into VITO's office while you are visiting with someone else and hand the binder over. As we outlined earlier, VITO will probably say something like, "What's this? It's empty." And you'll say, "It won't be for long. You'll be getting progress reports in the form of value inventories (see Chapter 9) from me by mail at least (every month)." Then you update VITO with success stories, written in the same concise, results-oriented style you used in your initial letter. (If you have already presented VITO with this binder, use the "good-to-be-working-with-you" meeting to drop off a brief summary of your goals for the project.)

Be sure all the letters you pass along to VITO are three-hole punched, so that they fit in the binder. Every time your product or service keeps a disaster from happening, saves money, or results in a more efficient workforce, you send another memo in VITO-speak. Where do you get the information? From Seymour! At first, you can put together a simple questionnaire about your service. Ask Seymour to do "a quick analysis." (Seymour *loves* to do analyses!) Then make a point of scheduling regular meetings so you can keep tabs on all the wonderful successes Seymour is implementing . . . with your help.

This is not an exercise in creative writing, or an effort to show VITO how well you work with Seymour. You must focus on results. You must anchor your benefit in VITO's consciousness, and you must do it on a regular basis. That's what your new partnership is all about. Be unlike every other sales-person VITO runs into. Make sure VITO gets the message from the front line. Take the time and trouble. Send the memos.

Take Advantage of the Fact that VITO Knows You're a Damned Good Businessperson

Let's be honest. You've done a hell of a job here, and VITO knows it.

Inevitably, VITO will say something good about you during an in-person meeting. Right then, at that very moment, write the comment down on your notepad. Put quote marks around it, hand it back to VITO, and say, "VITO, would you mind personalizing this for me?" VITO will say something like, "What for?" Show VITO a copy of the same benefit letter you initially sent. Then say, "I want to include that quote in a letter that's going out next week to fifty (manufacturers) in (Chicago)." (Of course, you should never be so foolish as to ask permission to use VITO's words to sell to a direct competitor.) Be ready to give VITO a list of companies you'll be sending the letter to.

Nine times out of ten, VITO will agree to your suggestion. *Ten* times out of ten, VITO will wish there were more salespeople like you working for VITO, Incorporated.

You may worry that a move like this will seem presumptuous on your part. Well, it might with Seymour. It won't with VITO. In VITO's eyes, you can only *earn* points by being a good businessperson.

As you leave your "good-to-be-working-with-you" meeting, ask, "VITO, is there anyone *that you would like to introduce me to* that I might be able to help in a similar or even greater way?" (Note that you don't say "anyone that I could call . . . ." That's too self-centered.) Get ready to take down the highest-quality category of referrals a salesperson can get.

"Yeah," VITO will say, "Jane Smith over at ABC might be a good person to call." Write down the information. But don't stop there! Ask, "VITO, what's Jane Smith's secretary's name?" VITO will smile and say, "Jamie." Return the smile and say thank you. Shake hands. Leave.

VITO just did your prospecting work for you. Make a beeline for your word processor; draft a letter for this new VITO. This type of referral represents the only time that you should adapt or adjust the formula for your postscript. When VITO identifies a prospect for you in this way, add a sentence to the beginning of the Action P.S.: "VITO Benefito of VITO, Incorporated, suggested that I give you a call . . . ." Jamie will see VITO's name in the headline and Action P.S., and will more than likely recognize that name. You're in!

No, you don't have to worry about getting referrals to Seymours from VITOs. My experience has been that VITOs refer VITOs, and nobody but. And those referrals carry weight!

Personalize

I've already spoken briefly about the danger of loading VITOs down with technical drawings, manuals, schematics, or other Seymour-friendly communications. Instead, leave your "good-to-be-working-with-you" meeting with VITO with a color picture of your company's smiling staff, gathered in front of the headquarters building. Make it abundantly clear that VITO has signed on with a group of *businesspeople* who are committed to delivering results.

If you must leave something in the way of written material, keep it brief (one page is best) and make sure it's in color. I've found that color pie-charts work especially well.

Do What You've Promised—and Stay Tuned

When VITOs go places, they take along the people who helped them. That means that, if you make absolutely certain you deliver the goods, you may well get a call two years from now—when VITO leaves to take an even bigger job at an even bigger company! This sort of thing happens to me all the time. One of my very biggest accounts came from a call that took place in just this way!

Guarantees Are Powerful—But Be Careful!

Salespeople love to make guarantees because they have the potential of providing a significant competitive edge. And "guarantee" is one of the words that makes VITO's ears perk up! Sometimes guarantees deliver great results for your company's bottom line and your commission check. But sometimes they backfire. If your organization has authorized you to make guarantees to your prospects and customers, there's somebody who should make a habit of reading the fine print of your contracts backwards and forewords, and it's not your prospect. It's you!

There's a wrong way and a right way to tell VITO about your organization's guarantee. Consider this example: "VITO, our solution is guaranteed. If you don't like what you see within the first 120 days, you'll get your entire investment back." Now, I'd be the first person and VITO would be the second to agree that this sounds great—but is it accurate? You'd better find out! Will your organization really refund all of VITO's investment if VITO doesn't like the way your solution performs? And the words "like what you see" are very, very subjective. I doubt that any well-written contract uses terms such as this. In addition, that phrase "entire investment" is a disaster waiting to happen. What if VITO had to modify the ventilation system in six manufacturing facilities in order to accommodate your solution? Would you be willing to bet that a hungry attorney wouldn't be able to convince someone somewhere that the ventilation system should be included as an element of VITO's "entire investment"?

The odds are that your company has spent a good deal of time and legal brainpower developing the language of your contracts and the guarantees they state. Read it! And when you talk about the guarantee to VITO, avoid sweeping statements you can't back up. I recommend sticking with something like this: "VITO, our widgets are guaranteed. Let me go over our policy with you when we're finished here, and then I'll give you a copy of your own so your legal or procurement department can review it in greater detail." I am sure you'll agree that this or something darn close is a more professional, responsible approach that will win more points with VITO and ensure that you build and maintain Equal Business Stature.

Here are ten helpful hints for staying out of trouble when it comes to making guarantees, dealing with complaints, and staying on the right side of sales law. By the way, I am not a lawyer, and I don't know about the specifics of your organization's promises or selling culture, but I'll assume you realize that no one can guarantee you'll never run into problems with lawsuits. I can promise you one thing, though: If you don't adhere to the following list, you'll end up regretting it someday!

Tony's Top Ten Ways to Stay out of Legal Trouble

10. If a VITO ever asks you to sign something, explain that your legal department has to review all such documents prior to your (or anyone else) signing anything. When you come right down to it, that's what sales managers and vice presidents are for!

9. If VITO or any other person in their organization should ever suggest that you speak directly with their lawyers, politely decline the invitation. (News flash: lawyers live to start trouble. That's their version of prospecting for new business!)

8. Follow the rules your company has established for handling any type of customer complaint or escalating customer problems. In other words, don't ever improvise under any circumstances and don't promise to fix something that you don't have the authority to fix! Doing this will just prolong and complicate any resolution.

7. Never, ever make any claims to VITO beyond the limits of your sales role. Translation: Don't pretend to be in charge of anything you're not, and don't pretend to know anything you don't, no matter how tempted you may be to assume the mantle of the expert.

6. Be completely familiar with any regulatory issues that affect your industry and the solutions you supply; and, of course, you must abide by all of them—repeat: *all of them.*

5. Know all of your organization's policies, down to the letter.

4. Don't make any attempt to rewrite any of your organization's policies. They're there for a reason, and you don't have the authority to summon a one-person emergency meeting of the board of directors. Warning: Violation of this rule means you can get both your manager and the law mad at you, which is not a pleasant situation and tends to lead to career-limiting circumstances!

3. Put your customers first when they're right, but let them know, tactfully, when they're wrong. VITOs can accept when they are wrong and expect to be told so. They don't live by the saying "The Customer Is Always Right" and neither should you.

2. Always do what you say you're going to do. There's no substitute for follow-through! It builds goodwill and keeps people out of court. As a general rule, always under-promise and over-deliver to VITO.

1. Always tell the truth. Honesty and integrity, as the old saying has it, have distinct advantages over falsehood. The truth is always easier to remember!

I've developed this list from my own experience of doing what's right and doing what's wrong. I must admit that at the time I did the latter, I was certain it was the "right" thing to do. But, as you can imagine, it never was.

> *If you're doing anything other than actually engaging in a sport that uses a scoreboard, fixating on "beating the other side" will lead to rigid, inflexible patterns of behavior that will eventually hurt your cause.*

Chapter 20

Some Final Thoughts on Your Current Accounts

NOW THAT YOU ARE FAMILIAR WITH THE FUNDAMENTALS OF THE SELLING TO VITO system, I want to share some final thoughts on dealing with Seymours. Specifically, I want to look at the problems you face, not in new accounts where VITO is the initial contact, but in existing accounts where you may currently be dealing with a Seymour as your sole contact.

You may remember that, at the outset of this book, I urged you to take another look at your existing accounts, and to make an effort to meet the VITOs in your current customer base. As we move toward the final portion of the program, I'd like to take this opportunity to remind you of the importance of doing this—and to caution you against complacency when it comes to dealing with accounts you've "already sold."

Implementing the advice I'm offering on this score may be among the most difficult things for you to follow through on. I know, because I've been there.

I realize that, once you get the commission check, you don't want to "mess with a winning formula." And I can certainly acknowledge that it's tough—initially—to talk yourself into going to a "closed" account and asking to talk to the top person. But it is nevertheless essential to your long-term success as a salesperson. You must move beyond Seymour, even in your current accounts.

"Come on, Tony, a Sale Is a Sale. Why Make Such a Big Deal about This?"

Because a sale is temporary. A partnership is long-term.

Some sales are essentially matters of short-term mutual convenience. Some sales are long-term partnerships. In today's business environment, if you confuse the former with the latter, *you lose.*

Why should you take the trouble to "VITO-proof" your current customers? Because it's a heck of a lot more expensive—both for you and for your company—to find new customers than it is to hold on to and develop existing ones. And when I say "develop," I'm talking about expanding your partnership to include add-ons as well as completely new solutions to problems in the organization.

In the long run, VITO is either going to be your ally and business partner or your enemy—the one who makes things happen for you in the organization, or the one who scans the printout, sees something that looks vaguely like the "fat" the accountants have been whining about, has to make a decision, and cuts you off. (An even more frightening scenario, of course, is the one in which VITO doesn't know you exist—and cuts you off when your competition makes one of those "special offers.") You are going to run into VITO one way or the other. It's better on your terms. Believe me; this is experience speaking.

"But I Sold Seymour on the Bells and Whistles!"

I hear something like this at just about every seminar I do. "Tony, you said earlier that VITOs like Benefits, and Seymours like Features. Well, I closed this sale by pointing Seymour toward all the fancy new gizmos and whatnots and double-insulated thingamabobs. VITO doesn't care about those! What's more, VITO's going to *ask* me how those bells and whistles translate into Benefits—and I don't know!"

Find out. Or, if you prefer not to, don't be surprised when you lose the account.

It really is that simple. If you've sold things to Seymour based on a feature set, and no one, including you, has made the business argument to VITO or, at the very least, VITO's close friend the manager, about the benefit to the organization, you are exposed on a critical front. Your long-term relationship is in jeopardy.

When the competition shows up on your customer's doorstep and offers a brighter gizmo, a bigger whatnot, a triple-insulated thingamabob, guess what? You're history—in less time than it takes to say "Seymour!" And that's just the most likely scenario. When the competition shows up on *VITO's* doorstep and makes a compelling case for a new widget that will actually deliver a tangible benefit to VITO's organization, you're history in less time than it takes to say *"I should have listened to Tony."*

Yes, VITO has the ultimate veto power. If VITO doesn't understand the value of what you have to offer, even some rinkydink company with some rinkydink product or service can knock you out. Why take the risk? Because it's simpler to do nothing? Maybe so. After all, when you come right down to it, it's simplicity itself to lose an account—and, for that matter, your job! It's the consequences that are so difficult.

Where to Start

Many salespeople avoid the steps I'm suggesting in this chapter because they are intimidated by the thought of approaching VITOs at the most tenuous accounts on their list. Don't worry about those accounts at first. Start with the ones you know you're delivering results for.

Pick out the nicest, happiest, most approachable Seymour you know, the one who works for a company that is absolutely ecstatic about what you do. (Later, of course, you'll adapt what follows so that you can work your way through your entire customer list—or, at any rate, the ones you want to keep for a while.)

At one of your many meetings with Seymour, say, "Seymour, your company is one of my best customers. My president/sales manager/regional vice president (align the title to the size of the account) has personally asked me to identify ten of my top clients, and I've identified you as one of those. I've been asked to set up a meeting between me, you, and your president, Ms. Benefito, to thank both of you for the value of our relationship."

In some cases, Seymour will agree to arrange the meeting for you without giving you any static at all. (This is particularly likely when you are dealing with an account to which you are delivering solid results, and Seymour wants VITO to know it.) In other cases, Seymour will ask, "What's up? Why do you want to meet with her all of a sudden?"

If Seymour asks this, whip out a long, official-looking list. Yes, the list must be on paper. Remember, Seymours love substantiating documentation. This list of yours should take up one or two full pages, and it should be printed on your organization's official stationery. It should be signed by *your* company's VITO. (Here we have yet another example of the *right* way to use your organization's logo and identifying materials, which do indeed play an important role in your sales work.)

Then you say something like this.

You: Seymour, my president has told me to get Ms. Benefito's valued opinion on the questions outlined in this memo. I'm supposed to go over all of this. It would be great if you would come along with me—but if you don't, my marching orders are to get a meeting with Ms. Benefito, ask her these questions, and shake her hand. You know how it is when you get an order from the top, right?

The "if-you-don't-want-to-go-with-me" part is important. Your objective is not necessarily to get Seymour to *arrange* the meeting for you, but to at least *let Seymour know what is going to take place.* In larger companies, it's a good bet that your Seymour has never even met VITO, so asking for help in setting up a meeting is not the way to go. Take the initiative for contacting VITO yourself, but let your contact at the company know exactly what you're doing.

You're probably wondering: What is on that long, official-looking list? *It doesn't matter*—as long as the questions you and your superior select meet five important criteria.

1. There must be a lot of them.
2. The questions must be ones Seymour cannot answer.
3. The questions must cover issues that you can talk about with VITO.
4. The issues you address must reference VITO's annual report or mission statement.
5. The questions must cover issues in which Seymour has no interest whatsoever, and on which Seymour has no opinions whatsoever.

Examples of the types of questions you might decide to include on your list appear below.

- "What are Ms. Benefito's revenue growth plans for (year)?"
- "What are Ms. Benefito's expense reduction plans for (year)?"
- "What are Ms. Benefito's ideas for increasing quality control for (year)?"
- "What are Ms. Benefito's primary strategic goals in expanding into the (Pacific Southwest) market?"
- "How do institutional sales fit into Ms. Benefito's growth plan for (year)?"
- "What dangers does Ms. Benefito foresee in extending financing to health-care organizations considering the transitional phase the nation now finds itself in with regard to payment mechanisms?"
- "How does Ms. Benefito plan to address the growing industry trend of high turnover among upper-level executives?"
- "What marketing initiatives will Ms. Benefito consider during the critical first year of the (King Funds) project?"
- "How does Ms. Benefito plan to attract, develop, and retain talented midlevel employees in (year)?"

- "What expansion of product lines and services to clients does Ms. Benefito anticipate in (year)?"
- "How does Ms. Benefito plan to reduce average cost-of-sale figures in the (Northeast region) in (year)?"
- "What must we do to continue to meet your criteria as a true business partner?"
- "What are Ms. Benefito's plans for (division of the company Seymour has no responsibility for)?"

That last question is a particularly good one to set up. If your Seymour is in engineering, pose a question about accounting. If your Seymour is in accounting, pose a question about marketing.

If you're still uncertain about the kinds of questions you and your superior should put on this list, go back to Chapter 4. You'll find ideas there on things VITOs like to talk about.

"What If Seymour Says I Have to Meet Someone Else First?"

Do it. Work your way up the chain. Present the same list and the same situation to the next person in line. Explain what you've been asked to do by your VITO: get into the president's office, ask a few brief questions, and shake hands. Be firm. Be polite. Be professional. Show your unshakable confidence. You'll build loyalty and start a groundswell. Remember, you're one of the good guys: You're *already* working with this company to solve problems.

"What If Seymour Says It's Impossible for Me to Get a Meeting with VITO under Any Circumstances?"

Call Seymour's bluff. Say, "Seymour, can you please call my boss and tell her I can't go?" Seymour will usually back down.

If Seymour doesn't, there's a good chance you're dealing with a status issue. Ask your sales manager to try to arrange the meeting with VITO. If this effort is successful (and it usually is), your sales manager has an easy job to perform at the end of the meeting: to ask VITO, "Well, Ms. Benefito, I just have one more question—would you like to meet the sales rep who's been parking in your parking lot and drinking out of your water fountain for the last few months?" Usually, VITO will say something like, "Sure, why not. Let's set up a time." You may then call Seymour and say, "Seymour, you're not going to believe this. The meeting went really well, so thanks for helping me prepare my manager and everything, but guess what? VITO wants to meet with me. Do you want to meet with me or shall I go alone?"

This is a nonthreatening scenario for Seymour, and it's an extremely effective tactic for getting you in the door to meet with VITO.

"So What Happens at This Meeting?"

During this meeting, you will simply review your successes with VITO, provide hard information on the benefits you and Seymour have been able to deliver. Your Value Inventory will come in very handy for this purpose. Show off plenty of color pie-charts that show quantifiable, measurable results. Most important, *listen and take notes* as VITO outlines plans for the future in response to your questions. Of course, you shouldn't feel obligated to pepper VITO with every single one of the questions on your list; ask broad questions that encompass all the key points. In the end, the only questions that really matter are the ones you would pose during your initial call to a new VITO.

At the meeting's conclusion, you can adapt two of the techniques we've already discussed: the coffee cup or other small gift with the benefit tag, and the binder for success stories. The difference, for the purpose of this visit, is that with these VITOs, you *already have* successes to attach to these two gifts. Isolate the most impressive success on the tag you attach to the coffee cup. Include two or three informal but compelling success stories in the binder when you give it to VITO. (If, for some strange reason, you are not able to attend this meeting, but your sales manager or some other superior is, they should pass along these gifts for you.)

Pick Ten Customers to Target Right Now

Are you ready for a surprise? The meetings will be fun!

Try it. Stop right now and write it down and put it on your calendar. "I want to meet with the VITO of ABC, Inc., next Monday." Then make it happen!

By the way, if you're working with a contact who's at the Manager level, the same technique applies. Go to your contact and say, "You know what? We've been doing business together for (five years). My president asked me if I'd met with your president eyeball-to-eyeball yet, and I had to say no. Then he asked me to set up a meeting." You may not even have to show these folks a list; they're much less intimidated by VITOs than Seymours are. Managers are more likely to say, "Sure, let's head up to VITO's office right now."

The Three-Legged Stool

Prospects and customers are the reason we show up for work every morning, not to mention the reason your organization exists. Like the old saying goes: "Nothing happens until something is sold." But as important as it is to sell something by persuading prospects to turn into new customers, it's also important to be sure that the solutions you deliver are being used properly and are delivering great hard and soft value and measurable, memorable benefits and results.

Imagine for a moment that VITO is sitting on a three-legged stool. That stool provides good support and a comfortable place for VITO as long as all three legs are there. But suppose one of the legs breaks. Then the whole stool comes crashing to the floor and VITO along with it. VITOs (or anyone else, for that matter) who have the support knocked out from under them are likely never to want one of your stools, or your solutions, again. They'll walk out on you—probably forever.

Your solution and your commitment is in fact supported on three fronts: Trust, Expectations, and Investments. VITOs must trust in your ability and judgement to exceed their expectations. They must get a return plus a margin on the investments they make in your solutions in terms of time, money, and energy. Each of these components of Trust, Expectations, and Investments is crucial to your long-term business relationship. Let's look at them in greater detail.

Trust

When you tell VITO something, is it the truth, the whole truth, and nothing but the truth? Do you keep your word, no matter what? On those rare occasions when a projection or project suddenly looks unrealistic, do you let VITO know ahead of time? Do you always, without fail, determine what is in VITO's best interest, verify with VITO, and then act in accordance with that interest?

Trust is absolutely essential in any meaningful long-term business relationship, whether you're selling computers, designer clothing, cosmetics, chemicals, accounting outsourcing services—anything. What, then, makes trust a reality? For one thing, the authority of your word. If you state something definitively, and then make a habit of coming back and overruling yourself because of some outside force like "the people at headquarters," your trust is going to take a hit, no matter how earnest or innocent your initial statements were.

The basic rule here is: Think before you speak to VITO! Never give any reason for VITO to doubt your word. If you follow this simple rule, you'll never go wrong:

"It's better to say what you know than not know what you're saying!"

If VITO asks something about which you may not yet have all the facts, say so! Keep the trust. Say something like this:

"VITO, this is such an important issue to you that I want to do the neces-sary research before I make any commitment. Let me get the answer from the person who is directly responsible for this area and report back to you no later than Thursday at 3:00 P.M." VITO will love this! Why? Because, that's what VITO wants the members on their own team doing! Of course after you say something like that, what do you do? You guessed it—keep your word!

Expectations

Many salespeople work a lot harder and spend a lot more time in setting up their customer's expectations than they actually spend in fulfilling them. This is a certain formula for a disaster when you're working with VITO, or anyone else for that matter. Whenever you promise a result to VITO, you simply *must* deliver it. As a matter of fact, you simply must do everything necessary to turn it into a reality, and even to exceed it. The best way to do this is to heed my earlier suggestion to create Value Inventories in the form of monthly or quarterly reports delivered in person and on paper to VITO! Without taking this step, you'll leave yourself and your organization open to the pitfall of VITOs developing unrealistic expectations. Salespeople from time to time tend to make unintentional and somewhat vague statements. When this happens with VITOs, they choose to interpret those comments in ways that are convenient to them. By the way, VITOs are not unique in this area. Just about any other person would do the same thing! Although this type of miscommunication isn't exactly dishonest, it can and usually does result in outcomes that are just as catastrophic as situations where we intentionally give erroneous and misleading information. As a result, we may be tempted to tell a white lie or two to "cover up" the initial problem. This type of spiral is usually in a downward direction.

Investments

Here's a news flash: relationships that VITOs associate with financial losses don't fall into the "mutually beneficial" category. VITOs will expect a return on every investment they make, and working with you is no exception. If they don't get a return on the time they spend with you, then what VITO thought was an investment turns into a loss and a liability—and you'll lose VITO as a customer. Period.

You and your organization must prove, not just once, not just twice, not just this quarter but *continually* that a return on investment is taking place. And if VITO is not getting a return on investment, then you have to take personal responsibility for changing what needs to be changed until that does happen.

Investments are realized in two major areas: real, tangible, measurable results that impact VITO's top, middle, and bottom lines; and intangible, hard-to-measure results that do not directly affect VITO's top, middle, and bottom lines. Now, here's both the good and the bad news: Tangible and/or intangible results aren't enough! Your business relationship with VITO must become an appreciating asset. In fact, it must become an annuity that grows without additional investments on VITO's part. When you deliver and sustain this type of investment, you will have VITO's unshakable business loyalty.

A Brief Story for Your Further Edification

A long time ago, before I developed this system, I paid a visit to an account of mine.

This was during my time at Hewlett-Packard. I was doing what a good salesperson was supposed to do. I was getting out there and shaking hands. I was talking to Seymour, reminding him of how wonderful our technology and systems were and how our future systems would be even more powerful.

As I was sitting and chatting with Seymour, I happened to notice a little blue box on his bookshelf. The box had three white letters on the spine: IBM.

I said, "Seymour, what's that up there?"

Seymour laughed and said, "Oh, that's just a demo the production department wants to look at." I smiled and nodded. We continued our conversation.

If I'd known then what I know now, I would have been in a position to contact VITO and demonstrate exactly what my system and company could do, how it could continue to deliver the best results for his organization's specific applications. But I didn't do that. Because I was a "good salesperson" who followed the rules, I knew that Mr. Benefito didn't need to waste his time talking to me. Who was I to talk out of turn, anyway? And why would I want to jeopardize my relationship with Seymour?

During another visit to Seymour's office, I saw three of those little boxes. A few months later, I made my "please-don't-drop-us" presentation to Seymour, when it turned out those little blue boxes had been multiplying at an alarming rate. And just under four months after I had first noticed that first little box on Seymour's bookshelf, I was informed that Mr. Benefito had personally decided to change over to IBM. VITO's company *donated* the system I had sold Seymour to a college in my territory! If I had done my homework as I've suggested with Value Inventories and presenting the VITO binder or coffee cup; if I had gotten and kept VITO involved as I now know how to do, that college would have never gotten the donation!

Chapter 21

Some Common Questions

IN THIS CHAPTER, WE'LL TAKE A LOOK AT SOME OF THE MOST COMMON QUESTIONS that come up during my seminars. (By the way, if you have questions of your own, or any suggestions whatsoever regarding my program, please feel free to contact me. Use the questionnaire that appears in Appendix C, near the end of the book.) Or better yet, participate in my monthly telementoring!

I'm still a little confused about how to categorize some of my contacts. Some people seem to me to be both Managers and Seymours!

With the right-sizing movement in full swing, there is a fascinating phenomenon whereby managers are expected to have a solid command of the technical aspects of the company's needs for products and services, and must at times play the role of Seymours. If you run into a situation like this, just remember the basic principle. Only VITO gets to wear any hat at all in the organization.

It was scary at first, but I tried asking VITO for leads as you suggested. It really worked! The only question I have is this: What do I do with the leads that VITO gives me that seem inappropriate for my business? They must be good for something.

Call them anyway! Sometimes opportunity waits in the strangest places. Remember, lots of VITOs serve as board members of other companies that may need what you have to offer. Never give away or throw away a VITO referral until you yourself have checked it out and exhausted all possibilities.

I'm being stonewalled! What do I do when I've been given a memo informing me that it's official company policy to stay with a certain vendor. The VITO is in the "home office"—in Europe! What do I do?

"Tony, we *have* to buy XYZ—I've got a memo from the head office to work with that vendor only. Look. It's signed by VITO himself." That's the kind of talk I was facing during the dark days when I was competing with "industry standards." I turned any number of those accounts around, and you

218

can too—by tracking down the person with profit-and-loss responsibility for the area you're trying to sell to.

So you can't get VITO to give you an in-person meeting. So what? The vast majority of business today is conducted by phone, fax, or modem anyway. (And I hear that there is actually telephone software available now that provides a real-time translation between callers who don't speak each other's languages.) Obviously, my first preference would be for you to meet with VITOs in person, but when that's impossible, there's no reason for your sales to suffer. A good, solid letter or fax followed up by a phone call can and will work wonders.

Follow VITO across the county, across the state, and across the country if necessary. And don't be intimidated. Stand your ground, make your case, and, when appropriate, ask VITO how much the loyalty is costing.

One important caveat is in order here: If you are trying to do business with VITOs from other cultures, you will have to adapt your techniques to your VITO's background. Obviously, space limitations prohibit me from exploring this complicated topic in detail, but suffice it to say that what is appreciated as an aggressive, no-nonsense style by an American executive may be perceived as incomprehensible rudeness by a VITO of another culture. *Do not* try to use the techniques in this book to sell to a VITO from another culture before discussing the changes you will need to make with an experienced business professional who has worked in that culture.

I still feel a little queasy about calling VITO directly, rather than having someone of comparable stature at my organization initiate the contact. Any thoughts?

We've covered this in detail already, but the issue is worth examining once again—and with a slightly different spin—because *fear* is one of the primary reasons salespeople are slow to implement the ideas between these covers.

Some people listen to what I have to say, think, "Hey, that's a good idea, that might actually work if I ever got up the nerve to try it," then do *absolutely nothing*—because someone, somewhere along the line told them that all business contacts have to be "like to like," with sales reps talking to data processing coordinators, regional vice presidents talking to regional vice presidents, and so on.

Don't let that happen to you.

Think of it this way: If only VITOs could call up other VITOs, nothing would ever happen! Henry Ford would probably never have secured the support he needed to build the Model T automobile. Bill Gates would never have made that fateful deal with IBM that sent his company, Microsoft, into the stratosphere. And, perhaps closest to home as far as this writer is concerned,

I never would have hit my quota at Hewlett-Packard or built a successful sales training organization!

  It does not have to be like to like. You can call anyone you want. It's a free country. (And it's a *really* free country for those who can establish Equal Business Stature with VITO.)

  Again, this is not theory. This is what I put into practice myself, day after day. I have personally contacted Ted Turner and Donald Trump. I've called the presidents of multibillion-dollar companies. I've called public officials, private officials, in-between officials, you name it. The title on my business card is not CEO—it's businessperson! My motto is, if the mayor's making the decision, *I write a letter to the mayor and then follow up with a call.* If "everything's all set" and "the decision's already been made, it just has to be rubber stamped," *I find the person with the rubber stamp.* No kidding. All you have to do to see the wisdom of this approach is to try it a few times.

  That's right, just try it—if only to prove me wrong. If it gives you the willies to say to yourself that this is the way you'll be doing things from now on, then just follow my advice with one hundred new VITO prospects, exactly as I've described it. You'll be so impressed with the results that all the fear will melt away . . . and you'll be surprised you ever hesitated. You won't want to go back. I didn't.

If I hook up with the Chief Financial Officer, does that person count as a VITO?

  Maybe not. Odds are that you're looking at a very high-ranking Manager.

  As a general rule, those who manage financial and accounting functions are not the most important players in the corporate decision-making process. That applies even when the person in question has an upscale title. Of course, there are exceptions, but they tend to be few and far between.

  The CFO may be an important ally in the organization, but chances are he or she is not the VITO to whom you should be targeting your letter and follow-up call. Don't put all your eggs in this person's basket.

  If you're ever in contact with someone you have been led to believe is a VITO, but whom you are unable to classify confidently in your own mind, try this. At the end of your presentation before the group, close your briefcase, look the person you think might be VITO straight in the eye, and say, "VITO, are you prepared to move forward? Are you prepared to begin to use our solution and realize the kinds of benefits we've been talking about?"

  Let's say you get an answer along these lines: "This sounds very interesting, but I need to discuss it with people. Why don't you call me back in thirty days." At that point you can either wait the thirty days, or you can use what I call the "VITO Wannabe Flush."

Here's how it works. You say, "VITO, if you didn't have thirty days—and I know that you do—but if you had to make the decision right now, what would it be?" That takes guts! But it will tell you something very important about the person you're dealing with.

If this person is really a VITO, you will get an answer—something like, "Well, I don't have to, but if I did, I'd have to say that right now I'd stay with the current vendor." Or, "If I had to make up my mind right now, I'd do business with your company, because I honestly like what I've seen so far."

VITOs *will* answer that question for two reasons. Number one, they can. Number two, they won't hedge on a direct challenge like this before members of their own organization.

But if you hear, "I'm not prepared to answer that right now," or any variation on it, guess what? You're talking to a VITO wannabe, not a VITO.

How do you contact VITO if the decision to purchase your product or service is being made by a committee?

Research, persistence, and the ability to pick out the leading member of a group—or the person to whom that group reports. There always is one or the other, and that person is your VITO.

Want to talk about bureaucratic gridlock? My job at Hewlett-Packard was to sell incredibly complicated, incredibly expensive computer systems to colleges and universities! If I'd rolled over every time someone told me that I had to "wait for the committee's decision," I would have been hung out to dry when my sales manager got around to totaling up the results. I called the chairperson of the committee if it seemed appropriate to do so, and if it didn't, I called the dean of the college. Yes, there is a certain amount of judgement involved here, and certainly you are the ultimate authority on your selling environment. But after a while, you will learn to find the opening. The one thing I can guarantee you is that passively waiting for the "board to make its decision" after a single meeting with Seymour is your ticket to mediocrity, disappointing results, and failure.

One word of advice on tracking down VITOs at municipalities or non-profit organizations: find out who signs the checks. Then find out who *that* person works for and approach that person. (If they're one and the same, there's no doubt you're looking at VITO.)

Should you quantify actual or projected savings for a VITO at a small company in the same way you would for a VITO at a large company?

Not exactly. For large companies, use a percentage. For smaller ones, use dollar amounts.

I've said it before, but it's worth repeating here: Don't exaggerate when dealing with a VITO, no matter the size of the company! You'll lose credibility . . . and sales. If you say, "We reduced operating costs at ABC

Company by 3 percent," you'd better be able to prove that you reduced the costs across the board. If what you mean is that you reduced costs by that much in a particular division, operating group, or line-item, say that. Accuracy is the rule of the day.

And don't think that 3 percent savings levels in a division go unnoticed by VITOs. One of my favorite gambits when dealing with VITOs at big organizations is to say something like, "But, of course, that was just a 3 percent decrease. For a large operation like this, 3 percent might not make that much difference." They come right out of the chair.

I felt uncomfortable with the opening sentences you suggested for the first telephone contact with VITO. Are there any variations?

Sure, but they take a little research. Here's one: "Congratulations on being named to the board of (local charity group)," or something along those lines. If you're willing to do the legwork, this kind of opening can go a very long way indeed.

The important thing to bear in mind when talking to VITOs is that they focus on themselves first, on the organization second (although often, the two are fused), and rarely if ever on you. If you can put something together that takes all this into account, you have my blessings if you want to use it as part of your opening statement.

How do you handle unexpected requests for bids?

Usually, I either ignore them or allot a minimal amount of time, work, and effort to them.

Honestly, if you get an unexpected, mailed request for a bid, the odds are that someone other than you has been helping the prospect write the specs. If anything, you may want to use the information to contact VITO directly, but my own experience has been that all you'll be doing is laying the groundwork for the possibility of a future sale. (Of course, there's nothing wrong with that. But there is a question of keeping your expectations realistic.)

Requests for bids are for Seymours, and they are usually sent out after the bulk of someone else's sales work is done. You may have different experiences in your own industry, but my own instinct after a good many years is that this is usually not worth the trouble. I have yet to win a bid that I didn't know about beforehand.

If you're submitting a bid or proposal on a *current* account, one you've spent some time on, one that VITO knows about, then by all means try to get through to VITO and show what you have before you submit it. You'll get a lot further with VITO than you would with Seymour!

What do I do if VITO asks me for the source of my Headline Statement?

No prizes for getting the right answer here. Give the source—and offer to fax it to VITO's office. If you're quoting an annual report, identify it and offer to fax the page. If you're quoting an article, identify it and offer to fax that. If your Benefit Statement quotes someone who gave you information directly, be prepared to provide a telephone number and suggest a time for VITO to call that person.

This question usually comes up when people play fast and loose with the details while developing a Headline Statement. Don't do it. VITO will call you on the carpet every time. And that's not exactly a great way to build Equal Business Stature.

I've tried making the calls the way you describe them. Overall, they went fine, but there sure were a lot of silences. How do I handle those?

Got a silence? Wait it out.

For our purposes, there are only two kinds, and waiting is the right prescription for each. The first is when VITO isn't really paying attention to what you're saying: "No, go ahead Tony, I'm just signing some checks here." I always say, "No, that's okay, I'll wait." And I wait it out. To do anything else is to give up Equal Business Stature at a very early point in the relationship, and you don't want to do that.

The other kind of silence comes when VITO is thinking of how to respond to something you have said or suggested. You *must* wait here, even though it may be uncomfortable to do so, because the conversation and the sales cycle will not progress with a VITO if you talk while your business partner is deciding something. Often we feel an instinct to talk to prove to VITO just how much we know, or to confirm to ourselves that progress really is taking place; usually, we prove only the opposite in each case. Let VITO drive the conversation; no matter how uncomfortable the silences may feel, wait them out.

I tried the "please define price" tactic you suggested, and I bombed. I lost VITO to a firm that was offering a similar system for $10,000 less. Any other ideas on overcoming a price hurdle?

The problem may have been that VITO saw the two systems as identical. Were they really?

In most situations of this kind, the two packages being compared are not the same at all. Your job is to find everything that you offer that the competition does not, and quantify the impact of each one of these to VITO's organization. Perhaps it's training. Perhaps it's follow-up. Perhaps it's higher quality or a lower reject rate. Whatever it is, your job in this situation is to quantify it and present it in terms that VITO can appreciate.

During an initial phone call with a VITO, I asked the big questions I was supposed to—and got shot down on all of them. What do you do in a situation like that?

This one's really pretty simple. Rather than coming up with three more questions about where VITO wants the widget department to go over the next quarter, just ask, "Well, if these are not important to you right now, what *are* you focusing your attention on until the end of the (quarter)?" If you get a positive response, follow VITO's lead. If you don't, and if you feel there's no way for you to do business with this VITO, say thank you and try someone else.

I got through to VITO, made an appointment, had a great visit—and then got stuck with Seymour again, because that's who VITO said I should talk to. The Pigeonhole Recovery Letter might work, but you said that was for a different scenario—when I had not yet met with VITO—and anyway, I'd rather not bring my manager in so often. Any ideas on how I can get out of this?

In addition to the ideas on win broadcast and loss recovery, there are a few additional techniques you can use to get Seymour pulling on the right end of the rope. First, play to existing predispositions. Start the sales cycle from the get-go, just as you would if you had not contacted VITO, and show off all the documentation, all the spec sheets, and all the double-insulated thingamabobs. Win Seymour as an ally. Make it clear that your objective is to turn Seymour into a hero in VITO's eyes.

If you sense that you are being met with resistance at any point in the sales cycle, say something like this: "You know, a couple of weeks ago when I (met/spoke) with VITO, she said that you were really busy, that you had a lot on your plate—but that this was so important that we should get together and spend some time on it." This will usually get things moving again.

More static? During an in-person visit, say, "Seymour, I'm in a funny position here. I promised VITO I would help in (one month/two months/three months, or whatever the time-frame you discussed with VITO was). Could you call VITO right now while I'm here?" If even *this* does not clear your way, either you or your manager should call VITO to bring the roadblock to VITO's attention. You should always *ask* VITO what steps to take next. "VITO, how do you want me to proceed with this?"*

---

* When, after a good first call with VITO, you are sent along to Seymour, I suggest that you avoid, at least initially, mentioning that VITO was the one who suggested you talk to Seymour. Why? You don't yet know how Seymour sees VITO! There may even be resentment on Seymour's part for anything VITO sends along. Mention this endorsement only later on, if at all. Appealing to VITO's suggestion that you talk to Seymour is a tactic to be used when you are looking at a logjam and can see no other way to break it up.

***The VITO I called agreed to meet with me—but when I showed up he
chewed me out about some problem he had with our company five years
ago, before I even got here. How do you respond to something like that?***

If the root causes of the problem VITO has brought to your attention are
still in place, then you can't. Shake hands, say goodbye, and outline the
problem to your sales manager once you make it back to the office. But in the
likelier event that your company has changed things (even if the change is
ever so slight), you can adapt one of the lines we looked at earlier.

You: VITO, I have to ask your advice. If you had this problem in
           your organization, how would you handle it?

This may well bring about a brief respite in the shelling. Of course, if
VITO tells you what is going to be necessary for you to win back the business, you must take it all down on paper and promise to report back on a specific date. If the attack continues, however, you might make one last attempt
to salvage the situation by saying something like this:

You: Well, Mr. Benefito, we didn't do all those things, but we did do
           some of them. The fact is, we have a better president now and
           so I'm back on your doorstep. We are helping some companies
           and I honestly don't know whether or not we can help you, but
           the only way we can go forward is if you tell me the next step
           for us to take.

***I've got a VITO I really want to sell. I followed your advice, sent all the
letters and faxes, did all the follow-up calls—and still can't get through.
What do I do now?***

For particularly tough VITOs, I suggest you get your company to make
the minimal investment required to put together a sharp audiotape, complete
with honest-to-goodness fellow VITOs—or perhaps your own organization's
VITO—praising your problem-solving solutions at the outset. (You may, if
you wish, record these testimonials with a handheld recorder, then have them
edited in. It will add a sense of realism!) In essence, you are assembling an
audio contact letter that VITO can pop into the tape player on the drive home.
By the way, if you keep the basic tracks, you can update this tape for other
VITOs at minimal cost.

The last thing on the tape should be your Action P.S.: "Mr. Benefito, I'm
going to wait three days so you have the chance to listen to this; then I'll be
calling you at 8:00 on Wednesday morning. If I've picked a bad time to call,
please have Leslie call me so we can set up a more convenient one."

Put the tape in a modest, professional-looking package, then follow up.

Chapter 22

Congratulations!

YOU'VE DONE IT! YOU MADE IT TO THE END OF THIS BOOK AND THE BEGINNING of a new (or perhaps renewed) tactical approach to your selling style—and that's a great accomplishment.

If I had one piece of advice to leave you with, it would be that you take what you have learned here and mold it to your own personal selling style. Take my ideas and make them yours. Put them into action—and by the way, do it quickly! Like anything new, it will feel awkward at first, but if you apply an unrelenting sense of self-determination and purpose, you will be able to realize a great edge over your competition. You'll be able to increase your personal income and at the same time experience greater success and satisfaction in your career, which, I can assure you, will carry over into your personal life. So take the tools and tactics you have just read about in this book, muster up all the self-determination you can, and then—do it!

As Dr. Denis Whaitley said in the Foreword: It's a Marathon

I always thought I was a self-determined person. But it wasn't until I celebrated my fiftieth birthday that I really, *really* came to fully understand the meaning of self-determination.

I decided to celebrate this particular birthday by doing something epic: I would run a marathon. But I wouldn't run just any marathon. I decided to run the Pike's Peak Marathon. Now, I've run a few marathons in my day, but this would be something different. You see, the Pike's Peak Marathon is considered to be much more than just a "casual" marathon. In fact, it happens to be the "ultimate running challenge in North America." What makes this run particularly formidable is that it starts at a mere 6,500 feet above sea level and ascends to the summit of Pike's Peak at 14,110 feet. But this is just the halfway point! The race then turns around and finishes at 6,800 feet above sea level. The entire course covers 26.3 miles of cross-country trail—rugged switch-backs of pure, untouched nature.

Of course, I started training several months ahead of time. I ate a total of somewhere around 17 pounds of pasta, ran about 520 miles, and bought about $1,200 worth of Power Bars, chemicals, running shoes, and shorts—all the "stuff" one needs to prepare to run to the top of Pike's Peak. With purpose and resolve, I started for Colorado, arriving four days early to give myself plenty of time to acclimatize to the altitude.

It was a lovely day, and as I checked into the front desk at the hotel, I looked out a huge picture window that provided a beautiful, clear view of an imposing mountain in the distance. "Is that Pike's Peak way up there?" I asked the young man who was checking me in. "Yeah, it sure is," he replied. Then he paused for a moment. "You're not running that marathon, are you?"

"Yes, I sure am," I replied.

His reply took me by surprise: "Man, you're crazy. People die up there!"

For a split second, a shot of self-doubt hit me. What if I wasn't ready? What if I did get in trouble? What if I didn't do enough training?

That night I went out to dinner to carbo-load. I wanted pasta, lots of pasta. And there, sitting next to me, was a fellow runner (his second plate of spaghetti was a dead giveaway). So I initiated a conversation with him, and sure enough, he was running Pike's Peak. This was great—I had a peer, and a little camaraderie. What a way to bolster the spirit! Naturally, we started talking about running, and I learned that my new friend had run five ultramarathons. An ultramarathon is a hundred-mile race—and this guy next to me had run five of them. *And* he was running Pike's Peak on Sunday.

My second hit of self-doubt made me toss and turn all night. *What have I gotten myself into?* seemed to be my lullaby. I thought about people dying from high-altitude edema. I thought about hundred-mile races and marathons to the top of Pike's Peak. I thought about backing out, but I couldn't. My family had already arrived!

Well, thanks to a higher power, it was cloudy on the morning of the race. I couldn't see the peak, otherwise I think I would have bailed out. Before I had time to really understand the full impact of what I had gotten myself into—bang! The starting gun went off and I was running up the trail to the summit of Pike's Peak, back and forth and higher and higher. At 12,500 feet, we ran right through the clouds! The trail got narrow, rocky, and steep. The air was so thin up at that altitude that breathing was difficult, let alone running. And yet—I did it! I reached the top! What a glorious feeling that was— making the summit and turning around, then running back down to finish Pike's Peak Marathon and celebrate my birthday in style.

Yes, I did it—and lived to talk about it! But you know, even with all the training, all the self-determination and sense of purpose, all my resolve, and even with all my friends and family waiting for me at the finish line—even then,

I was paralyzed no less than six times during that race. Yes, six times I stopped short, unable to take another step. Can you imagine what halted me dead in my tracks? Was it cramps, caused by lactic acid building up in my muscles? No, stretching and drinking and eating the right replacement chemicals saved me from that problem. Was it doubt? Well, I have to admit that I did doubt my purpose and self-determination several times, especially when I didn't see anybody else for a while. I didn't know if I was running the right trail or running off the mountain! Sure, I had my doubts and my fears. But that isn't what stopped me cold. Do you want to know what it was?

Pebbles in my shoes!

Imagine that! It was simply little pebbles that had gotten into my shoes, making it impossible to continue. I had to stop and take the pebbles out so I could get back in the race. Think about it. My goal had been to run up a 14,110-foot peak made of solid granite—and tiny pebbles had the power to stop me.

Pebble-Proof Your Future in Sales

How many times in a career or personal endeavor do we set our sights on a big goal and along the way we allow some small, insignificant thing to stand in the way of our making that goal a reality? Obstacles like: "The gatekeeper will reject me . . ." "VITO will be in a meeting, or even worse, in a bad mood . . ." "We've tried to sell this account once before. It didn't work then and it probably won't work now . . ." "I've got too many other things to do . . ." "This looks like too much trouble . . ." "The second quarter is not a good time to try something new . . ." And so on and so on. If you let it, the list will become longer and longer all the time, and the pebbles will find a way to stop you. Well, just remember this: the more obstacles you put in your own path, the farther away the peak of your success will get.

Don't let this happen to you! At the very first sign of an obstruction, stop and remove it, then get right back on your course. Get rid of the pebbles in your shoes *before* they really start to impede your progress, and the road to the top will be free and clear—and when you make it to the peak of your own success, I hope you will in turn help someone else get to theirs.

To greater success!

Tony Parinello

Your Prospecting Ratio

IN THIS PART OF THE BOOK, WE'LL LOOK AT THE FORMULAS YOU WILL NEED TO use to forecast your own sales targets in your daily sales work. Don't leave this work to your sales manager; take control of your own career and monitor your own ratios.

Definitions

A *suspect* is a company representative or decision maker in your product or service market within the territory you've been assigned.

A *prospect* is a suspect you've contacted who has needs that are similar to those you have met successfully in other accounts.

A *hot lead* is a prospect who will give you an equal shot at winning the business, someone you could win within the context of your normal sales cycle. Typically, you have met with this person, looked at he mutual opportunities, and given at least an overview of your products, services, and solutions.

Step One: Targets

Monitor your own sales work for one month (or whatever period is appropriate in your industry) and answer these questions:

If you contacted 100 suspects (via telephone calls, mailings, in-person meetings, or a combination of these), how many prospects would result? Write your answer here: (A)_____

How many of the prospects you identified in (A) would turn into hot leads? Write your answer here: (B)_____

How many of the hot leads you identified in (B) would you turn into actual sales? Write your answer here: (C)_____

Step Two: Ratio

Divide the number on line C by 100. The result is your ratio. Write your answer here: (R)_____

Step Three: Goals
Fill in the blanks.

What is your yearly quota or sales goal, in dollars?
(I) _____

What are your projected sales totals, in dollars, from current customers?
(II) _____

Subtract Item II from Item I to yield the amount of new sales dollars needed this year.

(III) _____

Enter the dollar amount of your average sale.
(IV) _____

Divide Item III by Item IV to yield the number of new sales needed this year.
(V) _____

Step Four: Task
Divide the number in item V by your ratio (line R in Step Two). Write your answer here. _____

This is the number of new suspects you will need to contact in the coming year to reach your yearly target. Now divide that number by 52, unless you plan on taking a week or two of vacation!, and you'll know how many suspects you must contact each week to make your quota.

Note: Aim high! I always shoot for 125 percent of quota if I want to hit 110 percent!

Parinello's Principle: The 75/125 Rule
We've all heard about the Pareto Principle; perhaps you know it by its more commonly used name of the "80/20 Rule." Basically, this rule says that the vast majority of a person's outcomes are brought about by a small fraction of that person's efforts. In other words, most of what people put their time and energy into just doesn't provide any payback. Results like that are quite disappointing, especially since the average person will spend somewhere around 96,000 hours working towards only 20 percent of their outcomes!

With all due respect to Mr. Pareto, I think it's time for another rule, one that favors greater results in shorter amounts of time. I am in favor of the "Parinello Principle"—or, more simply stated, the "75/125 Rule." Parinello's Principle states that 75 percent of your sales activity will yield a 125 percent quota performance. (I bet I've got your full and undivided attention now!) This means, of course, that you'll be focusing only on issues that move each of your sales opportunities forward. To do this, you'll have to become an expert time manager, and you'll have to learn not to depend upon any other person or thing to do this for you. Sure, I know you're probably using some sort of time management system that employs "tagged" records or "wake-up" buzzers to remind you to make the sales call, and maybe even an "activity transaction group" (whatever that is)! But when you come right down to it, the most important element of any "time management system" is you—the time manager!

To become an expert time manger and to make my 75/125 Rule work, you must first know where you're spending your time now. This will require a time log. Make a list that uses time slices of no longer than 30 minutes. (See the sample below.)

Time log:
Ima Success, ABC Office Equipment Company

TIME	TASK
7:00-7:30	Created final pricing and proposal for Baxter Corp
7:30-8:00	Drove to Baxter
8:00-8:30	Made presentation to Baxter committee
8:30-9:00	Returned calls
9:00-9:30	Returned calls
9:30-10:00	Updated sales forecast
10:00-10:30	Updated sales forecast
10:30-11:00	Met with applications specialist for Wiggens deal
11:00-11:30	Worked on preliminary proposal for Wiggens
11:30-1:30	Lunch with Janet Roberts of Roberts and Roberts
1:30-2:00	Called factory to check on pending orders
2:00-2:30	Worked on backlog problem for outstanding orders
2:30-3:00	Made two prospecting calls
3:00-3:30	Drove to the Appleson's to pick-up printer
3:30-4:00	Helped John reprogram fax
4:00-4:30	Checked voice mail and returned calls
4:30-5:00	Drove home

Complete your log every day for a period of at least two weeks, or however long it takes you to perform all the important functions of your job. (You may want to keep a log like this for nonwork related tasks, as well.)

Once your time log is completed, take a close look at it. If events are driving your day, or if your time log shows that most of the events on your calendar are reactive rather than proactive, or if there is no significant conscious time allocation—if any or all of this is the case and you allow this behavior to continue, then you're most likely headed for midrange time management and sales performance or worse!

Use the list below to examine and challenge your entries and your time management "habits":

1. You should always group your sales activities together (cold calling, presentations, follow-up meetings, administrative work, etc.), rather than trying to do a variety of activities at the same time. This will improve your efficiency in these tasks. Taking this method a step further, let's say you're making cold calls all day today. To be more efficient, you should group your prospects into their respective marketplaces (assuming that you call on more than one marketplace). For example: make calls to manufacturers between 8:00 and 9:00, finance people between 9:00 and 10:00, health care VITOs from 11:00 to12:00, and so on. This will make your Opening Statements and conversations that include your VITO call objectives much more effective.

2. Make a serious attempt to minimize administrative paperwork. This means you shouldn't get behind on it in the first place! By the way, this work should be done before or after your selling time.

3. Procure and use as many "productivity boosters" as you can afford and can fit into your level of capability: pagers, cell phones, prospect tracking software, and so on.

4. Attempt to make every lunch a working lunch with prospects and/or customers.

5. Learn to use the word "no" when people ask you to give any of your sales time to activities that do not support your short- and long-term sales and quota goals.

6. Keep a daily "to do" list.

7. Know when your peak energy times are (some people operate best at the beginning of the day, others are afternoon people). Make sure you're performing your most intellectually and emotionally challenging work during these times.

8. Use your drive time productively. Listen to skill-building, motivational, and inspirational tapes.

9. Continually look for ways to improve your time management skills. This includes continued use of some sort of time log so that you don't drift back to your old ways of being a "priority interrupt" time manager.

10. Perhaps most of all, monitor your sales progress. Within this Appendix you'll find a "prospecting ratios" work sheet. Use it. Here's the key: let's say you figure out that your annual cold-calling target has to be 1,645 initial calls in order to hit your quota and income goal. You should monitor this goal *monthly*—not quarterly—since by the time three months go by, you may be too far behind to make a difference!

For a good twenty of my twenty-seven years in sales, I've had the privilege of being in quota clubs, president's clubs, and winner's circles. If I could boil all of the advice for winning down into one simple thought, it would be this:

> *If you want to win all the awards and enjoy the prestige and commission checks that it brings, then begin to do your sales work part-time; start working half-days. That's right just pick twelve hours each and every day and work 'em!*

The Template of Ideal Prospects (TIP) and the Benefit Matrix

A "Tip" You Can Count On!

WHEN COMPLETED, THIS EXERCISE WILL PROVIDE YOU WITH VITAL INFORMATION that will assist you in qualifying new prospects before and during the first sales call. Your Template of Ideal Prospects (TIP) will help you compare your best customers to new prospects—and show you where your best opportunities lie.

To identify your very best existing customer(s), find answers to the key questions in the following categories and record them in the chart provided on page 236.

Company data. In the distribution industry, for example, you might list: number of parts in inventory; seasonal needs; purchasing habits on critical components; shipping unit size; order origin and entry procedures (processed from catalog? counter? telephone?); fleet owned or leased; number of employees; annual revenue; number of salespeople; etc.

Relevant sales parameter data. Determine: specific problems solved through use of your product or service; third-party "value-added" products or services necessary to secure the sale; price sensitivity among key decision makers; your price position among competitors; titles of key contacts.

Tangible and intangible benefits. Highlight the specific, quantifiable benefits this customer is realizing as a result of using your solution and having a business relationship with your company.

That's What Your Happy Customer Looks Like

There will be some exceptions, but generally, prospects with profiles that show extreme differences from those of your best customer(s) should be avoided or placed on the far back burner. While it is not necessary for you to do exhaustive research in preparation for a call on a new prospect, you may do so if you wish. It is essential, though, to have a strong sense of the profile of your *current* satisfied customers, and to be ready to "fill in the blanks" of your templates as you learn more about new opportunities.

Industry _____

1.

Profile: Best Customer: _____	Profile: This Prospect: _____	Match?

2. Notes: _____

3. Benefits: _____

More Tips on Creating Equal Business Stature with VITO

More Tips on Creating Equal Business Stature with VITO

You'll recall from the Network of Influence and Authority that "Directors" carry out the goals, plans, and objectives that VITO creates. Their job is to direct the work force to ensure the timely completion of everything that VITO wants. With this in mind, you would be able to gain a significant edge if you were viewed by VITO as one of VITO's "Directors"—that is, a confidant of sorts.

The very best way for you to capture VITO's confidence and trust is to have a working understanding of the key financial factors that impact VITO's world. Before we go any further, please take note that you should never, repeat *never,* treat VITO as if he or she was a CFO (Chief Financial Officer). VITO's challenges are more global, so VITO's understanding must be more generalized out of necessity—a sort of 30,000-foot view of those key financial factors. Our goal here is not to sound like an MBA but rather to have a grasp on some of the influencing factors in VITO's financial world in order to bring new ideas to the table in a way that VITO can understand (which is the essence of Equal Business Stature).

Let me add here that I am a man without letters (MBA, Ph.D., etc.) so what follows is a collaborative effort between myself and a longtime business partner and respected friend, Mr. Mike Adami, who happens to be a Vice President of Sales for a major U.S. organization and has an MBA from Saint Mary's College.

Profitability Ratios

There are four critical financial factors that VITO is concerned about when it comes to profit. The first and perhaps most important one is *making* a profit. Generally speaking, without a profit, VITO simply is without a job! (The only

exceptions that I can think of here is if VITO is the leader of a nonprofit organization or an employee of the U.S. Government or an elected official.) Let's
take a closer look at the other three:

Return on Sales (ROS): The amount of net income expressed as a percentage of revenue. Many companies and the VITOs that run them refer to
this as the *bottom line,* or the *margin* after all expenses are paid. The Return
on Sales can also be viewed as the profit earned on each dollar of revenue
generated by the company. Think of ROS in this way: If sales revenue
increases faster than expenses, ROS will increase; or if costs are reduced
without negatively affecting revenues, ROS will increase. Here, then, are several tactics that VITO can use to increase the all-important factor of ROS:

- Increase prices
- Control raw materials costs
- More effective and efficient utilization of human and capital
  assets
- Reduce overhead, salaries, and other expenses
- Change the product/service mix
- Cut cycle time

In a practical sense, let's say you sell "outsourcing" services. Ask yourself: "Can my ideas provide greater efficiencies while converting fixed costs
to a variable cost?" Keeping VITO's organization focused on optimization of
core resources will improve their performance from an ROS standpoint. Can
you manage a function more effectively than VITO's organization and do so
while minimizing VITO's financial risk?

Return on Assets (ROA): VITOs have two types of assets: *Capital Assets,*
which are items such as office equipment, fleets of trucks, furniture, facilities,
and "stuff" that was purchased or leased to create whatever it is that VITO
wants to create and bring to the marketplace; and *Human Assets,* which are, of
course, the people that make VITO's organization run. Almost every company
I've ever seen has a combination of capital and human assets. Your ideas and
proven solutions need to bolster VITO's investment in assets, which simply
means: VITO must generate more income/sales/services, etc., from their
existing asset base. Whenever you make VITO's operations (capital or human)
run more effectively or efficiently, you make a lasting impact on VITO's ROA.

Days of Sales Outstanding (DSO): One of VITO's chief concerns is
that VITO, Inc., not tie up all its funds in assets (capital or human) while it
fails to generate sufficient cash flow from operations to meet its financial

obligations to suppliers and take advantage of future growth opportunities. VITO has a strong interest in generating cash, and VITO has only a few areas from which cash can be generated and accumulated:

- A bank in the form of a loan, which creates a short or long term debt
- A venture funding, where VITO gives up a piece of VITO, Inc., in exchange for cash
- A public offering; Giving up equity is the most costly form of accruing cash
- Operations and sales

Let's say for a moment that you're not a banker, venture capitalist, or financial maven who wants to take VITO, Inc., "public." But you do happen to be the person who wants to create and maintain Equal Business Stature, with the ability to deliver a benefit that would improve the front or back end of VITO's receivables cycles. The beauty here is that this is badly needed cash that's tied up in an unproductive hard-value asset called "receivables." By doing this, you are coming forward with ideas that VITO is hoping her team would create, and so have furthered your status as VITO's business equal. You will make the transition from salesperson to businessperson in a heartbeat!

Another way to look at this opportunity would be to look at the cost that VITO is incurring for carrying their receivables. Typically, the cost of carrying receivables is equal to the average receivable balance expressed in dollars, multiplied by the cost of money used to take the place of the receivables while they're being collected. In other words, DSO (Daily Sales Outstanding) is the level of receivables relative to each day's average sales—that is, what VITO must sell every day to offset the backlog in VITO, Inc., receivables. The formula for DSO looks like this:

$$DSO \ = \ \frac{\text{Receivables}}{\text{Average daily sales}}$$

In effect, every day you can improve the collection of VITO's receivables, you help to create incremental cash flow from operations. You can express this in actual sales revenue that your ideas can create for VITO! Here's an example: Let's say that you can reduce VITO's receivables cycle (the time it takes VITO, Inc., to collect from its customers) by seven days. Let's also say that VITO, Inc., has $650,000 in its receivable "bucket" and generates $2,600,000 in sales each year. Your value proposition to VITO looks likes this:

$$\text{DSO} \quad = \quad \frac{\$650,000}{\$7,222} = 90 \text{ days of outstanding receivables}$$

Your solution will improve DSO by seven days; therefore, your solution will create:

$50,554 for VITO (7 X $7,222 = $50,554)

What's interesting to note is that not only will your solution create revenue dollars for VITO, it will also lower expenses (lessening interest payments normally associated with the need for VITO to go to the bank and borrow money). By doing this, you have effectively balanced the equation.

Here, then, are three areas of opportunity that will allow you to create and maintain Equal Business Stature and thus become a "Director" in VITO's eyes. Of course, as you grow and learn more about VITO's world, you can add many other opportunities to add value to VITO and VITO, Inc.

Here's some "homework" for you to do. Find out the meaning and impact of Solvency Ratios such as "leverage ratio," "debt to assets," and "fixed coverage." Then you can dive into Liquidity Ratios like "current ratio" and "quick ratio." Continue to explore ways to make measurable, memorable, and positive impacts, and you'll be well established in VITO's inner circle.

Appendix D:

Talk Back!

I WANT TO HEAR ABOUT WHAT YOU THINK OF THE *SELLING TO VITO* PROGRAM! IF you have comments, questions, or suggestions on how the system can be improved, please take a moment to write them below and send them to the address that appears at the bottom of this page. I will personally answer all this correspondence.

Thanks!

_____

_____

_____

_____

_____

_____

_____

_____

_____

_____

_____

_____

_____

_____

_____

Send to:
Anthony Parinello, *Selling to VITO,* c/o Parinello Inc.
P.O. Box 875
Julian, CA 92036
All letters become the property of Parinello Incorporated.

**Doug Gelatti $180,000, Leslie Jennings $500,000,
Nathan King $1.25 million, Neil Rappaport $8 million.
Lotto winners? No, but they did hit a jack-pot.
They all did it by selling to VITO!**

Tony Parinello gives in-person Keynote speeches, one-day workshop and public seminars. His dynamic, unforgettable style delivers measurable results to sales teams such as:

- Creating more new business! Alumni have set records of up to 25 percent increases in margins while they shorten the length of their entire sales process by as much as 50 percent. Just imagine what this will do for your commission checks!
- Pushing in-process sales through their sales funnel while they free themselves from time consuming decision grid-locks. Alumni report a 60 percent closure rate of previously stalled opportunities that were adding to the cost of sales. Now they're making a contribution to the top line.
- Getting every bit of business from existing accounts. Do you have all the business you deserve from your current accounts or just a thin slice? Alumni report an amazing 120 percent increase in add-on business, and a 44 percent increase in retention and win-backs.

*"This has been the most practical, direct,
solution oriented approach to selling top down
that I've seen in the past twenty-four years!"*

—MARK REISMAN, UNYSIS, WYCKOFF, NJ

"A must for all face-to-face salespeople."

—S. CHRIS ANDES, AT&T, SHARPSBAY, MD

Call: 1-800-777-VITO

Ask the operator for your complimentary
audiotape and Tony's seminar schedule.

or visit our Web site at: www.sellingtovito.com

Turn the page to find out about **Tony Parinello's products!**

YOUR FASTEST WAY TO SUCCESS

The complete *"Selling to VITO"* product line will teach you how to: convert your product knowledge into *VITO*'s knowledge, speak *VITO*'s language, write the one piece of correspondence that gets up to a 40 percent in-person appointment ratio with *VITO,* create the best eight-second telephone opening statement to get *VITO*'s attention, get by receptionist gatekeepers and win the respect of *VITO*'s personal assistant, leave messages that get return calls, and how to leave the ultimate voice mail message for *VITO* that puts the spotlight on you! You'll also learn all the how-to's of answering every single initial objection you may get from *VITO* and ask the three most important questions during your first sales call.

I could go on and on about all the tactics and skill-building information you'll be able to master, but right now it's your turn to take the next step into *VITO*'s office!

CALL 1-800-777-VITO
TO ORDER YOUR PERSONAL SUCCESS KIT.

Here's my unique guarantee:
Order any of my *Selling to VITO* products and receive my prove it to yourself guarantee. Listen, learn and experience my products for 30 days. If you are not absolutely, overwhelmingly and totally convinced that my methods, tactics and ideas will get you appointments at the top where sales cycles are shorter and opportunities are greater, you can send your products back and get a FULL refund. It's that simple.

"Tony's been in the field and his tactics come from practical experience, not from a textbook."

— JACK SLOTOW, OAKBROOK, IL

"After 14 years in sales to Fortune 500 companies with reputations of having the best training programs, I was amazed at the number of powerful, creative new ideas I learned from Tony and his products to excel in my sales career."

— ALICE PRAIS, HIGHWOOD, IL

Index

SELLING TO VITO

the Very Important Top Officer

Selling to VITO—Audio Album

Six audio cassettes, with a workbook and Personal Action Guide on diskette. Listen, learn, and master all the tactics you'll need to get on VITO's calendar right from your car, at home or at work! Your Master Key to the Executive Suite.
Order # 2001

Voice Mail Messages to VITO

Audio cassette with workbook on diskette. Learn the most critical ingredients and the best words and phrases to use and get a call back from VITO. Includes scripts with proven results.
Order # 2101

Contacting VITO Diskette

Examples from the best VITO letters in the world! Letters that have earned millions of dollars in sales commissions! Cut and paste from plenty of samples. This disk also includes the best opening statements that Tony has ever created and is guaranteed to make the best first telephone impression ever!
Order # 2202

Selling to VITO—Computer Version

A unique computer program combining a screen saver with the electronic version of *Selling to VITO*. The entire book is on disk—with powerful search, key words, navigation features and much more! Users need only a PC with Microsoft Windows.
Order # 2201

Appointment Getting Cards

Perfect for every business occasion, including prospecting, follow-up or getting VITO to return your calls. Includes software to enable personalized captions with VITO's name on it! There's not a gatekeeper in the world that will stop this card from going on the top of VITO's in-basket! A perfect way to set yourself above and beyond the competition.
Cards and Envelopes
Order # 1101

Selling to VITO—Video TrainingLibrary

Learn at your own pace in the comfort of your home or office. Revisit any topic for reinforcement and all seven videos include a question and answer session. The Selling to VITO Video Library was specifically produced for one-on-one training and includes career-long telementoring with each set.
Order # 2301

Manager's Facilitator Guide

Created especially for sales managers. If you conduct sales meetings, you'll love how these nine mini-modules facilitate reinforcement of the tactics and tools the salespeople have learned. Guide contains exercises for role-plays of Opening Statements, 1st Call Objectives, and Voice Mail Messages. It's all here, even spread sheets on a computer diskette to measure each member of your sales team's progress. Turn your sales meetings into practical Selling to VITO learning experiences!
Order # 2401

1 - 8 0 0 - 7 7 7 - V I T O   www.sellingtovito.com
Parinello Incorporated

Selling to VITO
Tele-Mentoring Registration Form

Name: _____

Address:_____

_____

City: _____

State: _____   Zip Code: _____

Mail or Fax this form as soon as you have purchased this book.
You will receive your Career-Long Mentoring Card in the mail.

FAX TO: (760) 765-1326

MAIL TO: Parinello Incorporated
P.O. Box 875
Julian, California 92036

About the Author

ANTHONY PARINELLO is one of the most innovative sales trainers in America today. His passion is his sales and public-speaking career. When he's not on the speaking platform, you can find Tony with his wife Nancy trekking in the Himalayas, scuba diving in Palau, on a photographic safari in Africa, or in any number of other exotic locales. Mr. and Mrs. Parinello live in California.